I

AN UNUSUAL LIFE

How To Cope With Difficulties and Come Out on Top

BY
Egon Reich I

EGON REICH PUBLISHING

Costa Mesa California

Books are available in quantity for promotional or premium use. Write to Egon Reich, 2797, Bunting Circle, Costa Mesa CA 92626. For discounts, terms, and general information, telephone (714) 546-2244.

CONTENTS

Chapter 1 . . . and I Found a Way 7

Chapter 2 Uncle Leo to the Rescue! 19

Chapter 3 Thank You, Mr. Van der Walde 27

Chapter 4 Mickey Mouse Wasn't There 41

Chapter 5 The Right Girl 51

Chapter 6 . . . Of Royal Ancestry 67

Chapter 7 The Adventure Begins 85

Chapter 8 I Didn't Lose a Wife, I Gained a Sister! 95

Chapter 9 An Introduction in Sonora 103

Chapter 10 We Found a New Dimension 111

Chapter 11 There's No Reason Why the Farmer
and the Cowman Can't be Friends 127

Chapter 12 400 Miles Long, 100 Miles Wide,
3 Feet Deep - Approx. 137

Chapter 13 . . .and Make the San Fernando Valley My Home 149

Chapter 14 The Pledge of Allegience 163

Chapter 15 A New Enlightenment 179

Chapter 16 The Road to Success 189

Chapter 17 Feeling Our Oat 197

Chapter 18 My Kind of Town, Chicago Is 205

Chapter 19 The Duke of Norfolk Lives in My Castle 213

Chapter 20 Wien, Wien, nur Du Allein 221

Chapter 21 A Killer Stalked 241

Chapter 22 Why Not? 247

Chapter 23 Better Than the Prince 261

Chapter 24 An Exciting Journey to the Land with My Initials 271

Chapter 25 Looking For the Stars 289

Chapter 26 Retirement, with a Look Toward New Achievements . 293

Chapter 27 A Heartwarming Fiftieth Wedding Anniversary 299

Journey Through Life, a Poem 303

This book is dedicated to my beloved wife, Marilyn, without whom it could not have been written, and without whom I would not have achieved the real wealth in my life, the love and beauty we both have always enjoyed!

CHAPTER 1

and . . . I Found a Way

It was December 24, 1933. I was two days away from being ten years old. It was Christmas Eve, the time presents were opened in our home in Vienna, and all over Austria.

The presents for my sister and me were usually necessary clothing items and one or two toys, but this Christmas, there was a large black case under the tree with my name on it from Christkind! (Pronounced "Kriskin d") Christ-kind was the angel who brought presents to us. We had no knowledge of a jolly Santa Clause.

As I opened the case, my eyes opened wide with great wonder, as I saw a real (not a toy) exquisite violin! I immediately felt great love and affection for such a treasure, and remember taking it out of the case, and picking up the bow and drawing it across the strings, listening to an amazingly beautiful tone. As I studied the finely-made case, I looked through an F-shaped cutout section, and down inside the violin, I saw an already yellowed tag with the name Stradivari on it. While that name meant nothing to me at the time, I did know it was the finest violin I had ever seen!

Now my parents were not wealthy. My father was a hard-working tailor in his father's men's apparel store, and my mother owned and operated a laundry. We lived in a modest apartment in quite a nice neighborhood in Vienna. Although our home was not pretentious, my mother kept it so clean you could eat off the floor!

Both of my parents provided a loving and safe home for us, but their combined earnings just covered the rent, clothing, and food on the table. My mother was an excellent cook, and we always had delectable dishes. But with all that, I knew they could not afford such a violin! Of course, at the age of ten, I already knew that Christkind was really my parents, aunts, uncles, grand-parents, etc., so my father told me that the violin was a gift from a departed uncle in Czechoslovakia.

Arrangements were made for me to take weekly violin lessons with a teacher who's studio was in downtown Vienna. I remember the day of my first lesson. My mother and I took the streetcar downtown, and the teacher became quite excited, first about our violin, and then about my immediate aptitude for the instrument! I "took" to the violin like a "duck to water"! I immediately caught on how the position of my fingers created the scale and the notes, and I knew I could learn to play without effort! It was an activity of love. Then, after only two lessons, my parents informed me that the music teacher had died, and we needed the money, so must sell the violin. In retrospect, I now believe that they did not realize the value of the instrument when they gave it to me. Although disappointed, I accepted their decision with understanding, and as things have turned out, I believe I was not meant to be a famous violinist!

Music and songs have always been a great part of my being. Most days after school, I helped my mother in the laundry, sorting the neatly cleaned, ironed and folded shirts, among other things. During these times, my mother and I sang continuously for hours. We sang melodies from operas, light operas, and other Vienna-music type songs. My mother had a beautiful voice, and could harmonize to any song we were singing. I realize now what a talented person she was, in every respect. In everything she did, she excelled, whether it was sewing, cooking, singing, or even the menial task of folding laundered shirts. The shirts looked like masterpieces when displayed in her store window, drawing customers to the laundry. So it is, that at certain times, talented people are not always able to achieve their full potential with regards to recognition by the public.

During the following four years, my life continued in this manner through middle school and highschool. My interests revolved primarily around art and music. My friends were few, but always boys with talent. One young boy played Beethoven on the piano so well, we would go after school to "Wine-Gardens" and when the entertaining-musicians would take a break, he would sit down and play, always to great applause.

These were the days when children in the United States almost all went to the movies on Saturday afternoon. We must have gone occasionally, because I do remember taking my little sister, Lotte (a year-and-a-half younger than I), to a few Shirley Temple movies. I enjoyed them, but do recall being

A handsome twosome. Egon and his little sister, Lotte, at ages 4 and 3.

December 24, 1933. Two days before Egon's 10th birthday.. It was Christmas Eve when gifts are opened in Vienna. Egon had received a real exquisite violin! In fact when he peeked through an F-shaped cutout section, he had seen the name Stradivari inside.

Pictured from left to right Egon's father, his maternal grandmother, his mother, her sister aunt Poldi and Egon. Seated sister Lotte with ever present doll.

December 26, 1933. Egon's tenth birthday party with 3 friends. The tall boy in back is Uncle Josef (4 years older than Egon) and the other boy behind Egon is cousin Gearhardt. Egon's sister, Lotte, is on the left of two of her friends.

Their Christmases were modest, but the spirit of Christmas was in their hearts.

more impressed and excitingly scared when I saw the original "Franken-stein" with Boris Karloff.

Usually, however, on a Saturday afternoon, my sister and I went to an operetta! At the magnificent light-opera houses in Vienna, for the Saturday afternoon performances, they sold tickets for a Schilling which allowed one to stand in the back and watch the performance! We never minded the standing, being so enthralled with the really impressive music and singing, and were grateful to our parents for giving us the two Schillings!

I also enjoyed reading, often late into the night. One evening, my father looked into my room and saw the book, "Robinson Crusoe" in my hands. "I thought you already read that," he said. "About sixteen times!" I replied, "It's my favorite!"

I was a good student in all subjects, but in school, I excelled in art, receiving top honors for my drawings. I must say that I cared nothing about the fighting in school, and though I could defend myself, I abhorred this behavior. Of course, to the "bully" boys, it was always a challenge to get me into a fight.

Now, it so happened that one of my aunts worked in a large stationery store in Vienna, and often brought me gifts of special pens, books, etc. To the boys in school, these items were prized greatly, so I talked to the biggest "bully" in the class. He was also the toughest and could "beat-up" anybody. His name was Oskar, and I made a pact with him that he was to be my "bodyguard", and in payment he would receive some of my treasures, especially the fancy pens.

So it was at an early age, I learned that it is better to negotiate, even manipulate, to improve my situation, rather than fall prey to troublesome conditions. This arrangement proved successful, and I enjoyed school to graduation.

It was on my thirteenth birthday that my parents bought me a new bicycle. It was a "street-racer", beautifully painted silver with black pin-stripes. I quickly learned to ride, and soon became familiar with all the cobblestone highways and byways of Vienna, including the many paths through the Vienna Woods. I even had aspirations of winning the "Tour-de-France", another ambition that did not fit within the realm of time and place. However, I did join a bicycle club, and even though I was their youngest member, I became one of the fastest riders.

An incident that actually influenced my entire life took place during a fifty-mile ride into the countryside with the club. About halfway through the journey, everyone stopped at a roadside inn for a beer. All the rest of the riders that day were adults, but in those days, "guesthouse" proprietors served beer to a thirteen-year-old kid, without a question! Not wanting to look inferior and to prove I was "a man", I soon emptied the large stein that was set in front of me! Feeling a little tipsy, I followed the men back out to the bicycles. They all quickly mounted and rode swiftly away. I had got onto my bicycle alright, but to my chagrin, could not even lift my legs to bend my knees! Shocked and worried, I got off my bike and sat by the side of the road. Fearing that this condition was permanent, I thought to myself, "Well, that's the end of the Tour-de-France race! I, then and there, promised myself that if I could ever ride again, I would never again touch beer nor any alcoholic drink. Of course, I was a very healthy youngster, thanks to my mother's good cooking, love and care, so in no more than about half an hour, I noticed the feeling in my legs returning. With great gratitude and happiness, I got on my bike and rode off, even soon catching up with the others.

Throughout my entire life, however, I took this incident to heart, and have completely abstained from alcoholic drinking. I have seen the many negative effects it has had on so many people, with many becoming addicted. I've seen it create unhappiness and physical agony. I've seen it cause broken homes and children's suffering. Fortunately, my parents did not abuse alcohol, and our relationship was harmonious.

I was now fourteen years of age and graduated from highschool. My parents decided it was time for me to learn a trade. After all, they reasoned, as long as one has a trade, one can always make a living. Occupations such as art or music, during this particular stage of economic existence in Vienna, was an unreasonable and insecure pursuit, especially for the hard-working middle class to even consider. So, I soon found myself registered in a tradeschool for a tailoring course. While I was deft at it, my heart was not into becoming a taylor. I told my parents that I wanted to go to college, and until the next year when I could enter, I would help my mother in the laundry. My understanding parents agreed, and we continued working long hours daily.

Many Sundays in spring and summer, we would fill backpacks with snacks, drinks, swimsuits, sweaters, etc., and walk from Vienna, all the way along the Danube River to a quaint village called Klosterneuburg, which wasapproximately eleven miles from our apartment. We would leave about five in the morning, stop a few times along the way, and take about eight hours to arrive between twelve and one in the afternoon.

My grandmother's brother, Uncle August, had a small plot of land there, which he had made into a lovely little vegetable garden. He had chickens running free, and rabbits in hutches. We sometimes even stopped in a forest on the way and picked wild mushrooms. With my mother's excellent cooking, we always had a magnificent meal. The adults visited, played cards, and my sister and I went romping in nearby fields, or swimming in the Danube.

My sister, Lotte, was very spunky and kept up to me in almost everything! We were excellent swimmers and easily swam across that broad river and back. The swift current always carried us downstream, so we had to walk some distance to get back. One of our biggest thrills was when one of the very large riverboat sidewheelers came along, creating huge waves! Riding those rolling waves was the ultimate in river-swimming!

As evening came, we packed-up and walked actually still a few miles to where we could get on a streetcar and ride the rest of the way back into Vienna. As of this writing, I am now seventy-eight years of age, and find myself feeling astonished at how all of us, my mother, my father, my sister, and I, each with a large "Rucksack" on our backs, accomplished this trip almost every fair-weather Sunday, without giving the effort it took a second thought!

Another occasional summer-Sunday adventure was in an uncle's 1930 Chevrolet truck. Benches had been built to sit on in the open back, and we would take trips to the Austrian Alps. Of course, the truck did not travel very fast, and on more than one hill, we would all get out to push it over the last incline! There was no traffic to speak of, except sometimes a farmer with a horse-drawn, or even an ox-drawn cart.

For my sister and me, these trips were the most exciting and beautiful adventures! To really understand this, perhaps one has to have seen the Austrian countryside with the mountains, green pastures, charming chalets decked-out with flowers in windowboxes and along balconies. There were mountain-houses with "masterpiece" paintings of scenery on the outside walls. There were small patches of forests filled with perfect "Christmas Trees". There were lakes tucked deeply between high mountains, and surrounded by charming villages of quaint homes, guesthouses, and decorative churches, all presented with a quiet beauty one could see and feel like a breath of the exhilaratingly fresh air!

The city of Vienna had a different kind of beauty which still today remains the same! The many historic buildings represent a mixture of Roman, Greek, and Turkish influences, together with that uniquely Viennese touch of charm, as well as impressions of opulence from the Royal Emperors, all providing Vienna with an atmosphere of grace and beauty beyond compare!

The city first began in the early eleven-hundreds as a fort with a church in the middle, and with the streets and a high wall all in a circular pattern around the church. Today the main streets in Vienna are still the Ring and "The Guertel", so even as the city grew large, they continued the circular pattern of the streets. This causes most cross-streets to form a wagon-wheel-spokes pattern, so it is wise to study a map of the city if you plan to try to find your own way around.

Through the centuries, each generation of builders has featured their own style and fashion. Vienna has always been a melting pot of many cultures, providing great art and fabulous music from Strauss, Shubert, Beethoven, Mozart, and many, many others. There are several art museums, with the Museum of Fine Art being one of the most magnificent buildings ever built, with marble pillars and floors, high Baroque ceilings, a great work of art in itself, and containing one of the largest and finest collections of old masters anywhere in the world! From mural-sized Bruegels to fifteen-foot high Rubens, each exhibition salon you walk through becomes more and more overwhelming!

The Roman Catholic Church always was, and still is the prevalent religion, and whom we have to thank for many spectacularly beautiful churches built throughout the entire country of Austria. St. Stephen's Cathedral (or "Stephensdom") in the center of Vienna took several hundred years to complete. It is a glory of medieval architecture, breathtaking like a jewel, and with the tallest steeple in the world! The cathedral with surrounding cobblestone streets is now a shopping promenade. There you will also find the celebrated "Demel's Pastry Shop", for centuries the Emperors' personal bakers, creating the original famed "Viennese Pastries".

Viennese cuisine and its music, as well as its home-grown wine from its vineyards surrounding Wienerwald villages, always gave the whole area a special feeling found nowhere else quite the same!

However, from the middle 1930s, Austria was almost constantly in political upheavals. Various rulers who gained power by overthrowing the previous regime, claimed to have the answers for an Austrian economic revival. More and more Socialistic laws were passed, accomplishing nothing, and becoming a burden on the economy and on freedom. One such

Chancellor was named Dollfuss, only to be overthrown by another named Schussnick.

Then there was Hitler gaining popularity in Germany, and promising great wealth and a fine life for all! Of course to accomplish this, it would be necessary to conquer other nations who were opposing this great new plan of ultimate living! Hitler began developing a powerful army, and being a great orator, as well as very forceful, he convinced or frightened the people into following, for fear of being annihilated! Their slogan, "Guns or Butter!" became a big propaganda scheme!

Unfortunately, after the First World War (1914-1918) most of the world was tired of fighting, and also because of various peace treaties, the various countries did not think of arming themselves as a priority. Therefore, Hitler's Nazi (National Socialistic Party) was the only one making a huge army a priority, so they soon achieved armed superiority in Central Europe.

So it was that in 1936-37 Hitler's powerful army invaded and conquered Austria, without a shot being fired. It is a strange phenomenon how people react after being conquered, partially or mostly out of fear, they gathered to cheer their conquerors! Hoards of Nazi soldiers (called SA-Men or SS-Men) stormed through the city. Hitler, himself, with several sentries paraded through the streets in open cars, Swastika flags waving, followed by tanks and trucks with heavy artillery, never before seen by most of the Viennese populace!

One of Hitler's mad theories was that Jewish people were responsible for all the poverty and misery in Europe! Having a Jewish father, I know the Jewish people to be honest, very hard-working, and perhaps with above-average intelligence, which is why many have achieved leading positions in trade and commerce. In reality, it was only the suppressive systems of socialistic governments and their oppressive laws which were keeping the poor from being able to improve their lives!

I've always thought it inconceivably strange that with the United States already sitting there with the average working family owning a house and a car, that most governments in Europe were not really trying the free enterprise system! Instead, Hitler found many followers for his "quick-fix" credo, "Kill the Jews and the Capitalists and everyone else will be rich!" Unbelievable!

Meanwhile, either by subversion or by force, many of the people of Austria, were following this madness, and the destruction of Jewish merchants and totally innocent people was carried out. A hatred of Jews was so infused into the masses that many stood by to see Jewish people beaten and arrested for no crime at all! People in Europe were always heavy beer and wine drinkers, and I do believe that alcohol at least somewhat restricts or destroys human reasoning, allowing a person to be more easily coerced into believing fanatic, illogical theories. I also believe it keeps people from progressing to higher standards.

These were extremely uncertain times, and although my mother and father kept working as usual, there was an air of fear surrounding us as we heard about more and more friends and neighbors of Jewish heritage being taken from their homes, and in cattle trains, shipped to concentration camps. Many tried to escape, especially those who had friends or relatives in other countries. My sister and I, being half-Jewish, were not as persecuted; however, we were told we could not attend institutions of higher-learning, such as the university I was registered to attend. We were only allowed to hold menial jobs.

For several years, we had been living in a nice, middle-class apartment. The building surrounded a large courtyard with grass and big trees, and we had a large balcony with an awning and many potted plants. One morning in June of 1938, two Nazi SS-Men forced entry into our home, and arrested my father. They then ordered my mother to move out within two days, and she was told that with my sister and me, we would have to live in a newly assigned Jewish sector, called 2 Bezirk. Apartments there were already overcrowded, but people were willing to share their apartments with others who were being persecuted. We moved in with a very friendly older couple who made us feel at home. The distance from 2 Bezirk to my mother's laundry was much farther than from our other apartment, which was within walking distance. My mother now had to spend extra time and streetcar-money just to go to and from work every day. My sister was still in school, and she transferred to another school nearby.

I was fourteen, and could not help having thoughts of escaping the country. Even though I loved Vienna, and could still ride my bicycle daily throughout all the impressive, historical streets, as well as the enchanting Vienna Woods, somehow leaving Austria became an urgency for me! But how? I knew no-one outside of Austria who could help, nor did my mother!

Then about the middle of the summer of 1938, someone told me about an organization in downtown Vienna, called The Society of Friends. They were supposed to be arranging for certain persecuted children to go to England, where they could continue their education. I really never knew what the conditions were to qualify; however, I found out where they were, rode my bicycle to their offices, walked in and introduced myself, stating the urgency of my plight! They did tell me that they were compiling a list of youngsters who would be sent to England as students. I made it my daily routine to ride my bicycle to their offices, stop in with a friendly, "Hello!", and, "Don't forget me on your list!"

For some reason, the people did not seem to mind my daily visits, and always gave me a friendly greeting in return! The summer passed, and then September when I would have gone to the University, but instead continued helping my mother with her work in the laundry.

We struggled through, and I never told my mother about my daily visits to the offices of The Society of Friends because I did not want her to be needlessly concerned. She had worries enough about my father who was being released from a concentration camp, but with the demand that he leave Austria immediately. He escaped with some friends to France where they joined the French Army to help fight the Nazis; however, France was also conquered by the Nazis, and my father was again arrested. This time, he was sent to the death camp of Auschwitz where he met a torturous death at the age of forty-two.

I grieve terribly for my father, an honest, hard-working man, devoted to his family, and an asset to humanity. I often to this day think many loving thoughts about him. Perhaps if there is a Heaven, somehow, he knows my thoughts.

By the middle of November, I really did not have much hope of being part of the group of students being sent to England, when a letter arrived at our apartment. It stated that I was to be ready with my Passport, at midnight on December tenth, to leave on a train in Vienna, bound for a Channel crossing to England. As my mother read this, I could see shock and surprise in her face! Of course, I was jumping for joy, and quickly told her of my daily visits to the Society of Friends offices in Vienna! Although I was only fourteen years of age, my mother realized this might be my only chance to escape the Nazi insanities.

The following days were a whirl of activity, trying to obtain my Passport. It was not an easy task, and time was short. The Passport offices were over-crowded with people leaving the country, and the Nazis made everything more difficult than was necessary! Their SS-Men and SA-Men were everywhere, harassing the immigrants. I remember one of them asking me where I was going, and when I said it was England, he replied, "But, that's

Egon's wonderful father Oscar Reich, just before his abduction by the NAZI'S.

Egon's father, bottom right in the French Army, doing his part to fight the NAZI'S.

NAZI brigade marching through the streets of Vienna circa 1937.

Seicherl im Dritten Reich   (© Kmoch/Reich)

A political cartoon published in Vienna's daily newspapers as it appeared prior to Hitler's hoards marching into Austria. The little dorky guy "Seicherl" was a very popular cartoon character, who with his smart talking dog "Struppi", appeared in daily fun anecdotes.

where all the Jews are going.". I gave no answer, of course, but just thought, "What an idiot!".

Finally, within only a day or two of departure, my treasured Passport was in my hands, and so about ten in the evening on December tenth, my mother, my sister and I left for the Central Train Station in Vienna. I had one suitcase with a few shirts, underclothes, socks, and so forth, but I knew a whole new world was opening up for me, and I was exuberant!

My darling little sister, Lotte, twelve years old, had to stay behind, and I often think of one small episode that happened. On the way to the train station, we passed a Hot Dog Stand. My mother knew I liked Hot Dogs, but only had enough money for one, so she bought it for me as a "going-away present". Lotte immediately said, "It's not fair! Not only does he get to go away, but he gets a Hot Dog too!" It's always amazing to me how different standards make people appreciate small things in life, and which can actually help keep people from becoming spoiled and demanding, or from taking things for granted!

Anyway, I hugged and kissed my mother and sister, and boarded the train at exactly midnight.

CHAPTER 2

Uncle Leo to the Rescue!

The train very quickly chugged on its way, and I found myself in a passenger car, filled with boys about my age or a little older. As we all settled back in our seats, the train, now moving at a good clip, advanced toward Rotterdam in Holland. I guess we fell asleep for awhile, as boys that age are able to do, and I remember us all being in good spirits!

No-one had more than one or two small pieces of luggage, and very little money. We were all given sufficient nourishment, and felt thankful to our benefactors. Arriving in Rotterdam mid-morning the next day, I remember a roll-call being taken, then being guided onto a ship for the Channel crossing. The sea was calm, and everyone seemed to be enjoying the trip!

We landed on the South Coast of England, and were transported to a large camp which was prepared to receive the thousand or so young people. There were small huts made of wood and corrugated metal. Each accommodated twelve boys, and had two bathrooms with tubs and showers, and hot and cold water. We were given comfortable blankets, other bedding, and good food to eat. It was getting late in the evening, that first night, and it was quite cold, although the huts were some-what heated. I decided to take a long bath in a tub of hot water, and so enjoyed a comfortable first night in my new country!

In the morning, we arose to a hot breakfast in the "Mess Hall", and were told we would be organized into groups according to religion and background. It seemed that everyone in England, families, Churches, and other organizations were willing to take-in these young people who wanted to escape the Nazis. The British government subsidized the entire operation, even giving a small com-pensation to those giving homes to the young "Germans".

Because I was raised as a Catholic, I was one of twelve boys assigned to live in a large house owned by a Priest. It was at 54 Wellington Road, in the town of Bournemouth. There were many rooms, and usually, the Priest lived there with only his sister and her husband, who did the chores and took care of the property. The Priest's name was Father Monaghan, and he presided over a large Catholic Church in Bournemouth. The house had nice grounds, and was actually quite luxurious. The first few days, we got acquainted with each other. The boys were all from Germany or Austria, and conversed in the German language, but we were all anxious to learn English, and did so rapidly. I had to adjust to some of the British food, such as sweet potatoes and chutney, and kippers for breakfast seemed a bit strange. Because of the war, there was food rationing, and some things were rather sparse. Sometimes we were even a little hungry, but we did not starve.

There were daily English lessons, and we took long walks together around the town and into the peaceful countryside. It was summer, and we all were anxious to find jobs. I wished I could earn even a little money, just to buy more to eat.

I especially missed my mother's good meals, and was in continuous correspondence with her. She still worked daily in the laundry, and somehow she got enough money together to send me my bicycle! This gave me the opportunity, although it paid very little, to get a job on a farm ten miles away. Riding my bicycle that far was tiring to begin with, and not having been raised doing farmwork, I found I was not able to do the amount of work an adult, experienced farm laborer could do.

On one occasion, I was asked to cut Kale for cowfeed. Each stem of that Kale was over seven feet high with huge leaves! I was shown two hills full, and told to cut three truckloads in one day! The tool they gave me was a hand-sickle. I worked as hard and fast as I could, but after a few hours, they saw I was not fast enough, so they assigned me to take care of a group of large pigs.

Nice going, until one pig got out of its pen, and it took four men to get it back in! That night, I was feeling very homesick and wrote to my mother that I wanted to return to Vienna! She apparently was in touch with my father who at that time was still in France. He wrote me a very nice, but concerned, letter, encouraging me to remain in England. This gave me the strength to remain, and not give-in to the terrible alone-feelings.

Having my bicycle helped a lot. On weekends, I rode twenty-five miles from Bournemouth to Shaftsbury where my Uncle Emil and his wife, Aunt

Mitzi, lived. Emil was one of my father's brothers, and they always welcomed me with open arms, and served a very good meal! They were; however, not able to afford to have me live with them.

At this time, the war in England was at its worst. Many plans were curtailed, and even the University schooling for the German boys was delayed. Throughout all of England, there was only a very subdued Christmas! It was an especially difficult time for the group of homesick boys in the Priest's house. There was a small, decorated tree, but no gifts were exchanged. I read my father's letter over and over, trying to find the courage to conquer my loneliness.

Feeling the same as I did, there was one exceptionally nice boy, also named Egon (Pfleger) which was quite unusual because it was not a common name in Vienna, or anywhere for that matter. We were about the same age and became good friends. He was a very handsome young fellow, and very intelligent, and I often thought, here is someone who will be greatly successful in life! However, while I remained in England, even before this first Holiday Season, Egon Pfleger had returned to Vienna.

Throughout the war, we lost track of each other, but I was glad to discover after meeting him again many years later, in Vienna, that he had become a successful Doctor of Optometry, and he had a wonderful family. During my many later visits to Europe, I always enjoyed visiting with him, and reminiscing about days gone by.

But back to that first lonely winter; the days passed, and soon it was early springtime. I also had another uncle, Uncle Leo, who lived in Liverpool, and one day I asked the Priest's permission to ride my bicycle there, which would take two days. The weather had turned quite nice, and I was allowed to go.

When I arrived at my Uncle Leo's house, I spent two days there, telling him many reasons why I was not happy where I was living. I enjoyed my visit, and looked forward to my ride back to Bournemouth. About halfway back, I found myself in a small town. It was nearing nightfall, and I found a park with a bench. It seemed like a good place to sleep awhile, and then get an early start. I stretched out on the bench with my arm around my bicycle, and after a full day's ride, fell soundly asleep.

I awoke to a bright sunny day, and found myself looking up at the pleasant face of a Bobby (local policeman). He smiled and asked where I was going. I told him, and explained that I did not have the money for room rent for the night, but I had slept comfortably, and appreciated the use of the park bench.

He asked if I had anything to eat for breakfast, and when I said no, he invited me to his flat around the corner. His wife made me biscuits, eggs and kippers, and I told them how much I appreciated such a good meal and thanked them very much! Well charged-up, it only seemed like a short ride, and I was back in Bournemouth.

Every Sunday, all of the boys were expected to take part in the Mass at Father Monaghan's church, and I had always attended. Now, this one bright and sunny Sunday, I thought how I would like to take my bicycle and ride down to the pier by the sea. I was certain no-one would ever miss me.

When I arrived back at the house, several hours later, Father Monaghan, a small, sprightly, gray-haired, older man was waiting for me with angry and questioning eyes, and said, 'I did not see you in church today!'. "No," I answered, "I am sorry, but it was such a beautiful morning, I wanted to look at the ocean.". He told me to go to my room, and I went straight there.

Just seconds later, he came into my room with a walking-stick in his hand, and ordered me to hold out my hands. As I did, he swung the cane hard onto my open hands which immediately started swelling. I turned away from him and felt the cane hit my back and my shoulder.

Besides swollen hands for a couple of days, I had no serious injuries. After thinking it over; however, I decided I did not want to continue living there under such conditions. I wrote a letter to Uncle Leo in Liverpool, telling him about the incident, and that I desperately wanted to leave there.

Only about a week or so later, one day about mid-morning, we were sitting and studying English, when one of the boys looking out the front window remarked, "I wonder who this is!' He had seen a chauffeur-driven black Bentley four-door sedan stop in front of the house, and a tall, impressive-looking gentleman coming toward the door.

The doorbell rang, and when the Priest's sister opened the door, there stood my Uncle Leo, government-papers in hand, which gave him permission to take me with him, right then and there! Uncle Leo was the husband of one of my mother's sisters, and he definitely had a no-nonsense manner about him! In any event, our care-givers acted very friendly, and helped me gather up my belongings.

We thanked Father Monaghan and his sister, and were on our way! I found myself sitting comfortably in the back seat of the big Bentley, beside Uncle Leo who explained where we were going.

It so happened that he knew Lady Conan Doyle, the widow of Sir Arthur

Egon's Aunt Frieda (one of his mother's sisters) and her husband Uncle Leo, who rescued Egon.

The Priest's house in Bournmouth. Photos taken years later on a trip to England.

The house was being renovated.

Egon, age 14 on the bicycle his mother sent to him at the Priest's house in England.

Conan Doyle of Sherlock Holmes fame. She lived in the manor-house on a large estate, and being a kind and generous lady, when she was told my story, offered to take me in. The Conan Doyle mansion was about an hour's drive away, on the outskirts of a quaint, lovely village called Crowborough, in Sussex. When we arrived, "Her Ladyship" came to greet us. She was originally from Scotland, and was still very nice-looking, and seemed very bright! She and my uncle spoke briefly, and then her chauffeur drove Uncle Leo to the train station to return to Liverpool.

So here I was in this beautiful house! There was a butler and there were two or three other house-servants, but Lady Conan Doyle, herself, showed me around! It was an extraordinary place, and I became more and more amazed as we toured through a formal sittingroom, a very-large diningroom, a billiard room, a green room, a blue room, a Safari Room, and a small "office" with a large desk and bookshelves up to the ceiling, where Sir Arthur did his writing.

Best of all, was the large library with walls full of shelves displaying all of the Sir Arthur Conan Doyle's writings of Sherlock Holmes, and many other stories and subjects, including his later interest in reincarnation. There was also a multitude of volumes by other famous and fabulous authors. Needless to say, I spent many hours during the ensuing months in this marvelous room, getting acquainted with the English language and scenarios from around the British Empire, in fact the entire world!

Every room was filled with fabulous artifacts, paintings, china, and during Sir Arthur's time, African Safari hunting was in vogue! His Safari Room contained lion skins, the head of a zebra, an elephant foot and tusks, ornate shields, and ominous-looking spears! The world in the 1800s and the early 1900s seemed smaller and more mysterious than our time now with jet planes, satellites, and even space travel!

Her Ladyship (My uncle had told me to call her, "Your Ladyship".) then showed me to my room, an upstairs guest bedroom with a comfortable bed, a dresser with a large mirror, two chairs and a closet. A bath with a shower was in the hallway. I felt like I had been transported into a regal realm, and spent much of the first days there studying the large paintings and various works of art, and even just the atmosphere of those fabulous rooms!

I was paid an "allowance" and was given certain responsibilities, such as riding into town with the chauffeur, and helping with the shopping in some of the local stores, which I very much enjoyed doing!

It was the summer of 1939 and I was planning to enroll for the fall semester in an art school or college for further education. I bought some art-instruction books, was spending quite a lot of time working with their lessons, and giving serious consideration to pursuing a career in art.

I was fully enjoying life at the mansion! Being an impressionable young boy, I remember deciding that all my shirts must be silk, and with no expenses to pay out of my allowance, I soon saved enough to even buy a camel's hair coat! I also opened a savings account in the amount of one pound at Lloyd's Bank in the little town of Crowborough. Besides the square brick bank building, Crowborough consisted of nice homes, two churches, and a few restaurants, shops and markets. All were exceptionally well-kept and in British style. Many were built with stones and over one hundred years old. It was a very charming place!

As time went on, my life was wonderful, but the war was becoming more intense. There were soldiers everywhere, along every road, in every village, and an atmosphere of nervousness became intense! There was talk of the British government's intent to confine all German and Austrian people in England because there might be some who would side with the Nazis, should there actually be a German invasion. I would soon be sixteen, and was afraid this declaration could include young men my age.

I often rode my bicycle into downtown Crowborough, and on this fateful day in the fall of 1939, I was just cruising through there as usual, when I saw a long line of men in front of a building. I saw one man who looked quite young, perhaps in his early twenties, and went up to him, asking what was happening.

He told me he was very sad because he had just recently got married, and he was one of the Germans required to register and be confined in a relocation camp. He had no idea where they were going to be sent. I was convinced that when I turned sixteen in just a month or so, that I would also be taken anyway, so I told him that if he would pay me a pound and give me the candy bar he was holding in his hand, I would go in his place. He also promised to take my bicycle to Lady Conan Doyle, and to tell her that I was summoned to register, which everyone was expecting anyway. I guess when one is that young, all things seem possible, so I simply took his place in line!

CHAPTER 3

Thank You, Mr. Van der Walde

As my turn came at the door of the building, there stood a stout Army Sergeant with a large pad in his hands, calling the name of the man I was replacing. I told him that there had been a mistake, and the name should have been Egon Reich. For some unknown reason, he not only believed me, but he crossed out the other name and put my name on his list!

The next few hours are somewhat vague, but I remember all of us being put into buses, and transported about two hours away to a large, empty building. It was made of brick and had a high, factory-type ceiling with steel beams, and high windows. There were rows and rows of bunk beds, all with mattresses, pillows, and blankets, and we were served an adequate meal.

It was apparently a central gathering place, because there were many hundreds of people already there. Most were refugees from Nazi oppression. It seemed like quite a dismal place, and no-one knew where we were going, or how long we would be staying in this factory. As a healthy fifteen-year-old boy, I was not too worried about the conditions, but some of the elderly persons, or those who had been separated from their families, and some who were ill, were quite distraught.

But the Nazis were creating Hell over London with continuous bombing, and all the British people were suffering. By comparison with those in Nazi Concentration Camps, we were very well off!

During the days we were detained in that factory, I found that among the many people there were artists, musicians, and many well-educated professional persons. It seemed strange to see all these people imprisoned for being German when almost all were in England to escape the Nazis, but it was wartime, and many things seem to happen that are certainly not normal

After just a few days in the factory, a list of names was called to line-up for transfer, and my name was among them. After a short bus trip, we arrived at the Port in Liverpool, and I was among those taken onto a freighter called the "Ettrick", and it was after dark when the ship pulled out to sea. We were still not told where we were going, and many of us were put in the hold of the ship where there was a section secured with heavy metal fencing for Nazi-uniformed prisoners of war. The trip lasted ten days, and every day, a few of us at a time, were given a guarded walk on deck, and we could see that we were part of a large convoy of freighters heading for somewhere!

We were told that the convoy was taking a northerly route to avoid German submarines; however, one submarine did find our convoy and the freighter right in front of ours was torpedoed. After a huge explosion, it sunk like a rock with all on board lost! I thanked God I was not on that ship!

After two or three days, the ocean got rough, and I began feeling seasick. Unfortunately, this lasted the rest of the trip, but as soon as we docked, and my feet were on solid ground, I was fine!

Of course, my first thought was, "Where are we?" I saw motorcycle police on the dock. It was a bright, sunny day, and it seemed like things were well organized. I had already begun noticing a feeling of elation, when a voice came over a loudspeaker saying, "You are now in Canada!" Then I really felt excited because I now felt I had actually got far, far away from the Nazi hoards, and was in a country of opportunity and freedom!

Another thought that came immediately to mind, was that if they ever tried to send me back by ship, I would "jump ship" and swim to shore!

We were transported by bus to a camp near Sherbrook, Quebec. There were several large, barracks-type buildings, each with about one-hundred metal bunk-beds with metal springs, a mattress, blankets, and a pillow. The beds were in rows, and each building had several bathrooms.

There was a "Mess Hall" building, and several Austrian Cooks had been chosen from among the refugees. They prepared really good Austrian food which tasted just like my mother always made. There was a large recreation room with a stage, and a crafts room with equipment for woodworking, and also painting, and other hobbies. We could also requisition books, magazines, and other items, which we usually received. It was a great relief to find we were definitely not treated like the enemy, and it seemed every effort was being made to make our living as comfortable as possible. Soon, however, I began to worry about our being held for the duration of the war, and how long that might be!

I decided I would have to find some activity of interest, and I was intrigued by several artists who were doing excellent artwork. One very good young artist in particular, told me he had been a very successful commercial artist in Germany. They were called "Gebrauchsgraphikers", and he said he was well paid, and that commercial artists in America made good money too. I showed him some pencil drawings I had done, and he was quite impressed. He was willing to instruct me in learning illustrating and commercial art. One of the basic and most important factors, he said, was for me to do as much drawing as possible. He said to draw what I saw, whether from photographs or real life. I was able to obtain art paper, artist's watercolors, brushes, pencils, and everything else I needed. I also studied techniques from magazine illustrations, and began doing a lot of drawing daily. After about two years, I was almost eighteen, and was now quite proficient at my craft.

Because there were no girls for company, I began drawing "pin-up" girls! Some of the soldiers who were our guards, and whose camp was next to ours, saw my drawings, and asked me to draw some for them. My drawings of girls became so popular with the soldiers, even with some officers, that I was given a private room with an art table, and any and all art materials I wanted. I was able to spend all day every day practicing and practicing with no distrac-tions, until I really became accomplished in commercial illustration techniques.

As months passed by, and then years, the most frustrating feeling was from not knowing how much longer internment would last. Many would have loved to join the British Army but were not accepted. We had full access to National news, and eagerly hoped Hitler would be defeated. On December 7, 1941, it was announced that an important message was being broadcast by the United States' President, Franklin Delano Roosevelt. Everyone stopped what they were doing and listened as Roosevelt's shocking words came booming out over the loudspeakers, about how the United States had been attacked by Japan, and how this day would go down in infamy! He then stated that the United States was hereby declaring war, and would be victorious, and his famous line about the only thing we have to fear is fear itself!

We were now all hopeful that the war would be brought to a speedy and victorious conclusion! However, as history records, the conflict lasted for several more arduous years.

Finally, in 1943, the war was turning against Hitler, and gradually some of the refugees were being released. To be released at this time, in Canada, one had to know someone who would guarantee your subsistence. Now there were Canadian merchants who became aware of this situation, and of skilled refugees who were willing to work at a reasonable rate, just to gain their freedom. One such manufacturer came to our camp, and inquired if anyone was experienced in tailoring, and would work for $5.00 per week, a very low pay, even then.

There was another condition that was required for release under this merchant-plan, and that was that the work had to be necessary to the war effort. This particular merchant manufactured army shirts. Now I had not stayed in tailoring school long enough to ever even use a commercial sewing machine, but I applied, and within one week of my application, I was hired! I was given "Temporary Landing Papers", and I had a few dollars I had earned in Camp, and was off by bus to Montreal!

I was now twenty years old, and had grown out of all of my clothes, so I had almost nothing in my small suitcase. However, nothing deterred me! I was young, strong, healthy, and had a very positive attitude! Also, I had a good sized portfolio of my artwork!

So it was when I arrived in Montreal, my first order of activity was to find lodging! I looked in the local paper and found a room for rent, near the shirt factory where I was supposed to work. The main problem was that the rent was $10.00 per week, and I was to earn $5.00. Well, I just thought, I will have to find work I can do in the evenings. After getting settled in a very nice, comfortable room, I went for a walk and was amazed at what I felt, seeing people walking freely, going wherever they wanted to go! There were streetcars and cars moving with complete freedom! I even felt surprise as I watched streetlights go from green to orange to red, and back to green! I felt like I was in wonderland! The feeling of just being able to go out, anywhere you want to go, was indescribable! I thought about browsing through a store, buying an ice cream cone, and as I looked at all the people, I hoped they were enjoying their freedom, and I felt that they seemed to.

It took me several days to get adjusted to this wonderful feeling of freedom! Actually, today at almost eighty years of age, I still appreciate freedom! Anyway, back then, I felt very strong and felt like nothing could deter me from success in whatever I would undertake! I had faith and was willing to work hard, and everything, even some things the average person would consider a matter of course seemed wonderful, fun, and exciting to me!

With my positive attitude, I had absolutely no fear, because hurdles and difficulties were just there to be overcome and mostly resolved. So it came to be that actually to this day, I enjoy solving problems which it seems everyone experiences on various occasions. Decisions often need to be made which could either resolve a problem, or if made wrongly, multiply it. For this reason, I have always felt it is of the utmost importance to keep my mind as clear and active as possible. Alcohol and drugs constrict mental clarity, and wrong decisions can result in more confusion and unhappiness! To me, to be free also meant being able to think freely, and so I was ready to "take on" this wonderful world with so many wonderful people!

My first "order of the day" was to find extra evening work, to earn enough to pay for my room rent, and sufficient nourishment! So during my lunch break from the shirt factory, I paid a visit to the art department of the major Montreal newspaper. They were running daily short stories in a section of their paper, and were using eye-catching illustrations. After presenting my portfolio of the artwork I had done in Camp, they seemed to be very impressed, and immediately gave me several stories to illustrate. So every night I rushed straight home from the factory and worked until late or into the morning hours to finish the illustrations. In a few days, on my lunch-hour, I delivered them, was paid $40, and felt very rich!

Meanwhile, I was having a problem at the shirt factory, simply because I did not even know how to thread a sewing machine! There were several nice young girls, all making their machines run like lightening, and producing many shirts! Watching them, I tried to follow their movements, but their actions were so swift, it was hopeless! As soon as I looked back at my machine, they were already sewing another part of the shirt! I kept trying, and actually had one shirt about half-finished, when the factory-owner realized I was not going to be fast enough.

Because he was a nice fellow, and I was working for so little, he said he could use me in the cutting room. I don't remember doing very much there, but there was an enormous table with several men doing the cutting, and I guess I must have been of some use to them or I would have been fired.

Meanwhile, I got more artwork from the newspaper, and also from a department store, which made enough for me to live on, but I was working day and night. I was not unhappy, nor did I feel sorry for myself, but rather felt the right answer would somehow present itself. So one day at the newspaper, someone mentioned that a nearby art studio was looking for an artist. Well, my problem was that the condition under which I was released from the Camp, was that I must remain employed by the Army Shirt company for the remainder of the war.

Nevertheless, I stopped by the art studio with my portfolio. When I presented my work to their art director, he wanted to hire me on the spot, and at $75.00 a week! I explained my predicament to him, including the fact that I was not doing well at the shirt factory. Now the art studio was doing war posters, so I suggested to the art director that he write a letter to the Immigration Department, and perhaps they would allow me to change positions. In a few minutes, he handed me a very well-written letter.

The next day, I decided to show my art samples to the owner of the shirt company; also to tell him of the work I had been doing nights, and of the position I had just been offered. He was very impressed with my art-work, and he also wrote a letter for 'Immigration' declaring me to be of good character, and wished me luck in my career as an artist. I thanked him and left his factory.

Now the only hurdle was how the Immigration Department would re-act to my somewhat unorthodox situation! At that time near the end of the war, there was not much Immigration activity in the city of Montreal, and the Director of The Immigration Department personally took charge of unusual cases. I telephoned for an appointment, and was given a time for an actual Hearing in just a few days. On the day of the Hearing, I dressed my best, took along some of my art samples and my two letters, and arrived on time at the Canadian Immigration Department. I was cordially led to the Office of the Director. He looked at my letters and my artwork, and for awhile he seemed to be deep in thought. He said that the problem was that according to the law, I was supposed to have a sponsor to guarantee my financial support.

Suddenly, there was a knock on the door, and a nice looking elderly man with a cane entered the room, and the Director greeted him very cor-dially. The gentleman asked the Director who I was, and the Director told him that my name was Egon Reich, but then turned to me and asked if I would mind waiting in the waiting room for a few minutes. As I sat alone outside the office, my mind was open to whatever my fate would be, and just felt happy that I had been given an interview.

In about half an hour, the Director and the elderly gentleman came out through the waiting room, said goodbye to each other, and I was asked to please return to the Director's office. He already had some papers ready for me to sign, and said, "These are your permanent entry papers to Canada."

He then explained, "The gentleman who had stopped in, a Mr. Van der Walde, has signed as your guarantor, and you are now free to pursue your art career."

To this day, I do not know why Mr. Van der Walde, obviously a man of respect and influence, stopped by to see the Director right at that time. I do know I'll never forget his name and what he did for me, a boy he only knew through two letters and some drawings!

It was September 1943, and I never felt happier! I was completely free to build my own future! I worked hard and kept learning, and soon took a job with a much larger studio, and with an increase in earnings. There were several good artists working there, and I made longtime friends with some of them. Besides work, there were many opportunities for fun! My idea of fun was seeing the countryside, and pursuing certain sports.

Visiting a gym one day, I saw some people hitting an odd little thing with feathers all around it. I asked one of the players, "What is the name of this game?"

He replied, "'Badminton', and this funny feathered thing is called a 'Bird' or 'Shuttlecock', and when played correctly, really is a game of great skill!" Well, it looked simple to me, so I went out and acquired the outfit and equipment for the sport, white shorts and shirt, tennis shoes, a Badminton racquet, and a tube of the best shuttlecocks.

In my first game, I was astonished that the experienced player I was playing with, hardly let me gain a point! Being at the peak of my youth and health, I was determined to become skillful at the game, and began practicing daily! As I got better and better, I realized that the more skillful the player becomes, the more difficult and strenuous the game becomes. It is a very unique sport, and it became a part of my life. I actually became one of the best players in the country.

At one time, I had an offer to become part of the Ice Capades show, playing "Badminton on Ice" but I did not want to travel, and basically, there was no money in a Badminton career! So I just enjoyed playing some evenings, which was a great exercise for keeping in shape!

In the winter, skiing was especially popular. There was lots of snow, and only a couple of hours drive from Montreal were the Laurentian Mountains where there were several elegant ski resorts and wonderful ski-runs!

During 1943 and 1944, automobiles were not being produced, and even used cars were very hard to find! There was no building of homes or businesses either, and office space was scarce. After some searching, I found a small corner in the offices of a merchant whose family manufactured men's ties. I placed an art table in my corner-studio, and worked on extra artwork at night.

The owner of the offices was a friendly man who admired my artwork, and one day remarked that he had an extra car, a 1930 Chrysler convertible coupe, that he would like to sell for $350.00. It was yellow, a nice sporty-looking car with a long hood, real wire wheels, two leather seats, and a fold-up "rumble seat" in the back. I had never owned a car before, nor had I ever driven one. He assured me that driving was easy, so I bought the car, which made me one of the few artists at that time in Montreal, who owned a car of any kind! It had a clutch and a gearshift, which indoctrinated me into car-driving the hard way! During these early learning experiences, I felt many uncertainties but within a few days, was driving well, and the car became another toy of joy!

By comparison, todays' requirements for obtaining a driver's license make getting one in those days seem funny! After filing-out a form consisting of nothing much but, "Name, Address, and Age," there was only one question to answer, "Have you ever driven a car before?" If the answer was, "Yes," as in my case, you were issued a driver's license. No "Rules of the Road" written test! No physical driving test! Maybe many people would like to still get a driver's license in this easy manner today, but I'm really glad its not the case!

Having a car, even a 1944 model, which in those days was referred to as a jalopy, I nevertheless became very popular with fellows and girls alike. I was especially pleased about the girls part! It was wintertime, and several friends and I would pack-up our skis and squeeze into my car, even the rumble-seat, and head for the Laurentian Mountains. As one got near the mountains, the roads were not the way they are today! The snow was deep on the road, and even though there were only a few cars driving with chains, they created deep, icy ruts that made the road unpredictable and dangerous!

I recall one episode which turned out somewhat eventful. I played Badminton with a friend who was an all-around athlete, and we enjoyed playing together because we presented a challenge to one another. One night, about midnight, when we stopped playing Badminton, he suggested we jump in my car, drive all night, and go skiing bright and early in the morning!

We had done this once before, and I remember taking the ski lift to the top of a hill, then just sitting down against a large tree trunk, falling asleep for a couple of hours, then awakening feeling fine and skiing the rest of the day. Of course I had warm enough clothing to not be in danger of hypothermia.

On this one occasion, however, as we set out after midnight and drove toward the Laurentians, the roads became particularly rough with deep ruts and fairly deep holes in the icy snow. We were anxious to get there, so I was driving at a good clip when we hit a big hole with a loud boom and a bang, and as the car bounced out of the hole, I had to look <u>up</u> to see my friend sitting beside me! His side of the car was about a foot higher than my side! I stopped and got out, and saw that the body of the car was resting seriously crooked on the wheel-base! Now I knew very little about cars. It was a dark night, and there was not a soul in sight, so the only sensible thing to do was to turn around and drive slowly back into town! It was Sunday, and we both felt sleepy, so he went home, and I went to my place for a good snooze!

Early the following morning, I wobbled the car to a repair shop. A "leaf spring" had broken off its hinge, and pushed the whole side of the body sky-ward! They repaired the spring and the car was back to normal, but my friend who was with me that night and I had many a good laugh about how funny the car looked in that shape!

I fully enjoyed my life in Montreal! One time I went out to the northern woods of Quebec, where thick forest surrounds a lake, and there are just a few private cabins along the shore. I was trying to visit a girlfriend who gave me directions how to find her and her parents' cabin there. She said to ride the train to a stop at a small village, and then walk west to a certain crossing where you turn north. When you come to a big rock, she continued explaining, you go around it and keep going north about another quarter mile, and you'll come to the cabin in the trees on your left.

Well, I started out late from Montreal because I had to finish some artwork. When I arrived at the named village, it was dark and slightly drizzling. It was summer so I just had on a jacket, and my complete luggage for two days in the woods was a toothbrush and swimtrunks. I tried to follow the directions, but when I came to the same "big rock" for the third time, I decided I was walking in circles! It was now midnight, the woods were very dark, and I felt sleepy.

There was a large bush by a tree, and I decided to sleep beneath it for awhile. I stretched out, taking off my jacket and pulling it over my head to ward off mosquitos, and slept like a log!

I was awakened by a slapping sound on the water of the lake, and was surprised how close I had come to it in the dark! It was just daybreak, but through the haze and giant trees, I could see the edge of a dam being built by a busy beaver clapping its tail on the water. I could even see a man in a rowboat with his fishing rod ready for an early trout! I stood up and gazed in amaze-ment at the beauty that surrounded me! The woods were so very quiet! No traffic noise! No sounds of any kind except the occasional clap-clap of the beaver's tail, and a few birds were just beginning to chirp a hello to their new day! In this silent environment, the birdsongs sounded splen-didly precise!

I just stood and gazed around for quite awhile, watching the haze rise, and the fisherman casting his line, and was glad I had not found the cabin the night before. Then, in the daylight, I started walking along the shore of the lake and very soon found the cabin. My girlfriend made a hearty break-fast for the two of us, and I told her I felt like swimming a few strokes in that amazingly clear lake. She said to go ahead without her, that she had some things to do, and we'd go for a hike later. It was sunny and warm, and when I dove in, the water was fresh and invigorating. I kept swimming, and suddenly found myself on the opposite shore, about a mile away. I was an excellent swimmer, and because I didn't try to break any speed records, did not even feel tired.

The thought never entered my mind that I was alone and far away from help if I got hurt or needed something. I just jumped in the lake and swam back to the cabin. We spent a very pleasant afternoon walking along the mountain paths and enjoying the great outdoors.

One day during a discussion with a fellow artist, I mentioned that I never got tired swimming, and wondered if I could swim across the St. Laurence River at a point where it was five miles wide. He said that he bet I could not do it, so we decided on a gentleman's bet of one-dollar, and made plans for him to accompany me in a rowboat in case I needed assis-tance.

The day arrived, and he shoved-off from a small dock where we had rented a rowboat, and I jumped into the great, always cold St. Laurence River! I started with leisurely strokes and was enjoying the swim when we both realized that the very swift current was carrying us rapidly downstream! However, I soon reached the opposite shore without even feeling tired, but we decided to both row back, because of the current, and it was getting late in the day.

Those months in Montreal were wonderful! Of course with all of life, sometimes one has to cope with unexpected mishaps, sometimes caused by poor judgment or carelessness. One such incident occurred when I invited a girl to go golfing. She had never played golf before, and I decided to be an eager teacher, even though I was far from being an expert myself!

At tee-off, I stood behind her, showing her how to hold a rather large driver-golf-club. With the club positioned in her hands, I moved to the side, told her to keep her eyes on the ball and to swing as hard as she could. I saw her swing the club, miss the ball, then heard a loud "pop" as the large head of the golf club struck my left jaw! It hit with such force, I did two somersaults backwards, my whole face full of blood!

My first impulse was to run to "First Aid" in the clubhouse, but as I passed a mirror, I saw my entire face was crooked with teeth sticking out the side! "Hospital Emergency" time, I thought, and the girl and I jumped into a waiting taxi! Hospital X-Rays showed a splintered left jaw, and my whole face out of alignment! I was immediately taken to surgery for reconstruction of my jaw and face. Because of the force of the impact, the nerves were so damaged, I was awake without pain throughout the entire two-hour long operation. My teeth were wired in position, and held together with strong rubber bands, so eating solid foods was impossible..

Soups, milk, and even very-soft cooked eggs, however, could be drawn-in through a small opening just under my front upper teeth. During the two-and-a-half months I spent in the hospital, I got along well with the friendly nurses. They let me go into the kitchen and make my own concoctions of mashed vegetables, eggs, milk, and soft cereals, so I never went hungry!

Also, because I didn't want to lose any artwork, I set-up shop by my hospital bed. With a small art table and a box-full of paints and brushes, I continued my business!

The hospital doctor told me to rinse my mouth every hour with hydrogen peroxide mouthwash, which I did, and they were amazed that I developed no infections and healed well and quickly. Besides a small scar on my lower left cheek, I was as good as new!

Happy to be back at the art studio, I continued doing various art projects. As a commercial artist, one does not have the liberty to choose what one wants to draw or paint. However, you are often given an assignment to create whatever is necessary to display or help-sell a client's product, or convey his message, hopefully with a unique attention-getting design. So there are advantages to being a commercial artist, because of these challenges. Of course there are advantages to creating fine-art paintings, if you have the time to wait until you sell one. Sometimes at night I would stay and do some oils on canvas, sitting in the corner I still rented from the tie merchant. His name was Mr. Watson, and when I was there evnings, he had time to stop and talk to me. He was very impressed with my advertising art, and one day mentioned that I should be working with Cockfield-Brown, Canada's largest advertising agency. I enthusiastically said I would certainly like to, whereupon Mr. Watson said that Mr. Brown was a very good friend of his, and that he would talk to him about me. I really did not think too much more about it, but just a few days later, Mr. Watson came by and said Mr. Brown wanted to meet with me and see some of my work, and I was to call him for an appointment.

I could hardly believe my good fortune, especially as I was most cordially received by Mr. Brown, and he was seriously enthusiastic about my advertising artwork. Right then and there he offered me the position of Creative Director. All advertising layouts, all artwork, even overall campaigns would be under my supervision and require my approval. I would have a private office and a secretary.

My basic salary was to be $400.00 per week, and for any layouts, designs or illustrations that I produced, I was to bill the agency 15% of the price being charged the client. This was 1945, a time when $50.00 a week was an acceptable salary. I had not yet turned twenty-two, and could hardly believe all this was happening!

I was shown to a very nice office with a view of the park in Central Montreal, and was introduced to my secretary. She was a nineteen-year-old blond, very attractive, and had been with the agency long enough to have complete responsibility for the time-schedules of all ads going through.

As it happened, I was a good designer, but also had developed an ability to put myself in the client's position, to ascertain what the client wanted or needed to best sell his product. It was also important to keep in mind whom the advertising message was being created for - manufacturer, wholesaler, retailer, or the general public. I found my new position made use of more of these abilities I had acquired, so I got along exceptionally well, and thoroughly enjoyed every day's challenges!

My income was never less than $800.00 to $1,000.00 a week. I saved some, and gave money to several charities. One weekend, I took six friends on a plane trip to Niagara Falls, and spent quite a lot on such small but fun adventures!

Now, in hindsight, I can see that at age twenty-two, when one makes quite a bit of money that easily, the tendency is to believe it will always be that way! A good attitude, but better if more savings had been included!

I dressed well every day, somewhat artistically with the newest fashions, and enjoyed a congenial relationship with the account executives and writers. Often writing advertisements, even themes for whole campaigns myself, I felt I had reached a pinnacle in my life.

I don't know why, but something within me kept reaching for something further.

CHAPTER 4

Mickey Mouse Wasn't There

There was another artist who had become a good friend of mine, and who kept talking about the glamour of Hollywood and the sunny weather in Southern California! He and another artist got jobs with Walt Disney, moved to Hollywood, and wrote back letters, glowing with pictures of glamour and opulence!

After working at Cockfield-Brown for almost three years, and probably because of my friends' California-propaganda, I felt I must try to make-it in Hollywood. "Certainly they were waiting with open arms for talents such as mine!"

I had been seriously saving my money for awhile, when it so happened that three friends bought a new car to drive to California, and were looking for a fourth to share expenses on the trip. I gave a month's notice to Cockfield-Brown, sold my car, and packed my bags! My art portfolio was now filled with illustrations and complete layouts for very impressive National and Inter-National accounts!

And so the four of us left for what we had all been told by friends and relatives living there that it was the "Land of Milk and Honey", of free orange juice in every store, and where there was really a "chicken in every pot and a car in every garage"!

It was mid-summer of 1946, and the drive to California was exciting, along the famous highway, "Route 66". We traveled through many interesting, natural sights in Oklahoma, New Mexico, Arizona, and Nevada. Route 66 was the highway appealing to the driving tourist. There were many cafes and gas stations, and each had some special display of a local historical or natural marvel! There was no shortage of dinosaurs and other phenomenon inspired by very impressive fossils, etc. It seemed that the entire length of

Route 66 had developed a special character of fun and interest, and I enjoyed every minute of it. The song, "Get Your Kicks on Route 66" is well-titled!

One particularly unusual experience occurred when we stopped for the night at a motel on the shore of Lake Meade near Las Vegas in Nevada. It was almost midnight, and as we got out of the car I noticed a slight but very hot wind hitting me. On the sandy beach of the lake, a small diving-dock extended out into the water, which gave me the idea of putting on my swimtrunks and going in.

After that dry, almost oppressive heat, the clear water of that large lake felt cool and refreshing! I pushed myself out onto the wooden dock, and noticed that before I could dive in again, I was completely dry, so hot was that mild wind! It was an interesting experience I had never encountered before!

After a good night's sleep, we were on our way. We did drive through Las Vegas, but only stopped for a great buffet lunch, because we were then so close to Los Angeles, my three companions were anxious to meet with their relatives there.

When we arrived in Hollywood, they let me and my suitcases off at a Greyhound Bus Depot. I knew I wanted to go to "the beach" because I had visions of palm trees right in the sand and perhaps cottages where one could enjoy the tropical atmosphere for awhile!

So I asked the ticket agent for passage "to the beach". He asked, "Long Beach?" Of course, I did not know, so I said, "Fine!" I remember thinking it was a longer drive to "the beach" than I had thought it would be, but the bus finally drove along where I could see the sea and the sand, so I got off, and walked to an actually very nice beachfront hotel.

It was a pleasantly hot day, and what I wanted now was to go swimming in the ocean, play around that dazzling-looking amusement-pier I could see from my hotel window, and generally get acquainted with my very different-feeling new surroundings!

I had saved a few thousand dollars, and was not even slightly worried that with my portfolio and my background, I wouldn't soon be earning every bit as much as I had at Cockfield-Brown. My plan was that as soon as my money began running low, I would see the agencies or perhaps the Disney or Warner Bros. studios, and my career would be on its way!

Meanwhile, I began spending my days lying on the sun, swimming in the ocean, meeting and talking with interesting people on the beach. At night I usually went to the extensive amusement-pier with its spectacular roller coaster, games, and many stimulating diversions.

One day it was slightly overcast, and the sea seemed a bit rough. I alsonoticed there really weren't any people in the water, and this did seem strange, but not knowing about the ocean and it's dangers, I decided the higher waves might be fun to ride to shore. So I swam out and caught a good-sized wave, but as it was carrying me in, another wave hit right on top of me, sending me to the sandy bottom! Then before I could surface, another wave dragged me down again, and I was running out of air! I remember thinking with determination, "I'm not going to die here!", and with all my strength, fought my way to the surface and back to shore. Later I learned about words like "undertow" and other hazards of the "deep" and have great respect for the ocean!

The days soon began seeming all too much the same, and I was getting bored with this type of existence. I also did not realize how fast I was spending my money!

So suddenly came ~ The Rude Awakening! ~ One morning, I counted the last of my money and was shocked to see only $11.00 left! Of course, I realized I had waited a little too long, so I had better get to Hollywood and start my career! I rode the bus, and checked my suitcases into a locker in the Hollywood depot.

My first local-busses destination was the Disney Studios in Glendale. There was a closed gate with a guard who asked who I wanted to see. I thought I might as well go right to the top, so I said, "Mr. Walt Disney." "For what purpose?" the guard asked, politely. I showed him some of the work in my portfolio, and although he seemed impressed, he apologetically informed me that Mr. Disney was between pictures and had just laid-off six hundred men, mostly artists!

Not to be deterred, I headed for Warner Bros. Cartoon Studios. There I did get to talk with one of the art directors, but he told petty much the same story! The artists were hired for one picture, and between pictures, sought work through other channels.

From a telephone booth, I called major advertising agencies like J. Walter Thompson, Young and Rubicam, and several others I knew about from Montreal. They all claimed that their artwork came from their main offices in New York. Besides that, I was told that artists seemed to be flocking to Los Angeles where hardly any artwork was to be had, and two major art schools were turning-out artists by the droves!

Seeing Warner Bros. Cartoon Studios had brought me back to Holly-wood, and as I walked away from their offices, I noticed several very large, empty buildings which at one time had been movie studios. Most, or all major film studios had moved out of the middle of Hollywood. MGM moved to Culver City, Warner Bros. general studios to Burbank, and because this was before television production, these large buildings remained empty at that time.

However, walking down a street along these buildings, I saw an open door at the side, and a small sign with just the name, "Badminton", printed on it. Being a very good Badminton player, this of course intrigued me. As I went through that small door, I saw a new world of Badminton open-up inside! There were sixteen gorgeous Badminton courts, with the best hardwood gym floors and preferred deflected lighting! I was absolutely amazed!

I walked over to a large counter near the door and met the owner. He told me that no expense had been spared in converting this studio-building into the ultimate Badminton gym! To be played well, the game requires thirty-foot ceilings, and because the original building had that and more, it was an ideal basic location. The best news was that it was open to the public for a nominal hourly fee!

I then met a young man who was the manager, and asked if I could rally with him for awhile. He loaned me tennis shoes and a racquet, and when he saw that I was good at the sport, became very friendly, and we both enjoyed a few games.

It was mid-afternoon and the place was empty except for a couple playing on one of the courts. As early evening arrived, more people began wandering in, so the manager had to go back to work. I sat down on a bench to contemplate my next move. By this time, my total money left was $5.00 and change.

Just then, a young man walked in alone. Usually people come in in pairs or groups of four, because you can't play Badminton by yourself. Anyway, this fellow asked the manager if there was someone who could play a game with him, and the manager told him he might want to ask me, and said that I was a good player. Because I had no other plans yet, I agreed to play some games with him.

He was a fair player, not as good as the manager, but we both enjoyed the workout! As we sat down for a "breather", we started talking, and I told him of my predicament! He immediately said that he only lived a couple of blocks from there, and that there was a couch on his veranda where I could sleep for the night or two. "This was great," I thought, and as I thanked him, also remarked that I had to get some kind of a job very quickly!

He replied that he knew of no job openings in my trade, but that right down the street, "Good Humor" ice cream was advertising for help. I figured, "any port in a storm", and after sleeping fairly comfortably on the veranda couch, the next morning I walked straight to the "Good Humor" ice cream plant. They were hiring people to push little three-wheeled carts, and if memory serves me right, if you sold the entire contents of the little freezer-wagon, you cleared eight dollars.

I started out, and being a fast-walker, covered a large area and returned early in the afternoon, however ended up with only two dollars, because I found I had eaten six dollars' worth of my profits in ice cream sandwiches! I continued this job for two or three more days, always selling all my goods. Then as I was coming in the next morning, I noticed some motorized-scooter-type ice cream carts. I asked the manager about them and was told that they were only for salespeople who had been with the company for a year or more. My answer to that was, "But I am your <u>best</u> salesman!" I had seen that the other cart-sellers were all elderly men, and was certain they were not as dynamic as I, and that I could out-sell any of them.

"If you want me on your team, give me the motor, and I'll sell twice as much!" I added, and to my surprise, he said to go ahead, and took me over to one that was all gassed-up.

Wow! I hopped onto that motor-scooter, stopped by the house where I was staying and picked up my art portfolio, and with it still being very early morning, headed straight toward Santa Monica, which I now knew to be the beach only about ten miles from Hollywood.

It was summer, and when I got there, lots of people were already on the beach. I parked at the edge of the beach, filled a sack with ice cream bars and sandwiches, and ran from one blanket to another, selling them all! After repeating this performance several times, I was shouted-at by legitimate vendors in little stands nearby, "You can't sell ice cream like that!"

Too late! I was already sold out, and hopped back on my scooter with plans to spend the day trying to find any sort of art studios or agencies who might possibly use me as an artist! Not finding any art employment that day or the next, I did keep selling-out the ice cream at one beach or another. The third day out, on my way back along Santa Monica Boulevard in Hollywood, I passed a two-story light-gray building with large letters on it, "Amos Carr Studios". I had heard of them because they were known for their excellent publicity photos of many major movie stars. Then I noticed that on the entrance door was also a sign saying "Aristo-Art Studio", and I thought that it could not hurt to stop and talk.

The art studio was on the second floor, and I met a very nice, middle-aged, good-looking man. I introduced myself and he said his name was Grant. Most of the artwork he did was for the photography studio, airbrush and other kinds of retouching. I showed him my artwork and he was greatly impressed, especially with the diversified experiences it showed! He said he wished I could work with him, but he did not have enough work for two artists.

I suggested that perhaps my being there would generate more business. We talked some more, and I told him my story of success in Canada, and being unaware of the tight art-market in Los Angeles. He finally agreed to try to work something out with me, and he solved my temporarily out-of-funds problem by agreeing to advance me a dollar a day. That was enough in those days to buy a can of sardines, cream cheese and crackers. Fortunately, this meager, but not too bad diet only lasted a few days before we did get more work, and more money was coming into the studio.

Grant also had an extra room in the studio, and he brought a mattress, blanket and pillow from his house. There was a bathroom in the hall and a shower downstairs. My immediate problems were solved!

When I took the scooter back to the "Good Humor" manager, of course I had sold everything, but was afraid he would be annoyed when I told him I was quitting. Instead, he was very friendly and wished me good luck. I think he realized his job was not my idea of a career!

During the first few days with Grant, things were becoming enjoyable, and he and I developed a good rapport. Several of his manufacturer clients, who used his services primarily for the airbrushing of product photographs, were shown my art samples, and began using our more complete art service. We also tried to keep our prices reasonable. I became very busy doing designs, layouts and illustrations for many of Grant's old clients, and as word spread of our service, many new clients as well.

I might mention that from the beginning, part of my agreement with Grant was that I would charge for all the artwork I did, but that 25% would go to the studio, which I thought was very fair. I even re-designed the studio's trademark, so it would have a more professional look to it.

It was not long before I had many of my own clients, mostly manufacturers of some sort or another, and I was soon making more money than

Grant. But Grant and I worked well together, and I greatly appreciated his generosity in taking me into his studio in the beginning! Even though I was making enough money, I saw no reason to rent a room or apartment, because I was very comfortable sleeping on my mattress, and another advantage was that the studio was close to the Badminton Courts. As I became a better and better player, I became more enthusiastic about the game. I kept playing more accomplished players, and I usually won.

As time went on, I had such a large volume of work, with one major account in particular, that I decided opening my own studio would be advantageous. I would still be able to give assignments to Grant, assuring him of a full work-schedule.

When I discussed the idea with Grant, he encouraged me to "move ahead" as he put it. Grant was one of the nicest, finest persons I have ever met! In a building about a block-and-a-half from Amos Carr's there were several studios occupied by cartoon animators, and I arranged to occupy one of their empty offices for only $5.00 a week. I had already bought a very good art table and a storage chest for art supplies, paper, etc.

The day before I was moving, one of Amos Carr's top photographers called me and said, "Egon, I want to take a portrait of you." He also mentioned that they knew I had generated some photography business for them during my stay in the building, so I put on my tie and jacket, and went down to his studio where he was arranging the lights. He made silly, funny remarks as he kept snapping my picture, which resulted in my smiles and expressions looking very natural in the photographs! His lighting was extremely professional, making me look like a movie actor!. He made a large print for me, and when I wanted to pay him, he refused, saying it was my "going-away present"! What wonderfully nice people I've had the good fortune to meet in my life! To this day, that is the best picture I've ever had taken!

The next day, I moved my art table and equipment, and Grant helped me notify all of my clients of my new address and telephone number. I still did not see any reason for renting separate living quarters. There were several bathrooms in the building, and I showered every night at the Badminton Gym, still just a few blocks away. I was in top condition and could sleep anywhere, so I bought an army cot which I could fold-up and store in the corner of my studio. Now an army cot consists of two six-and-a-half-foot-long wooden poles with a piece of green canvas between them, about twenty-four inches wide. It has criss-cross legs on each end supporting the whole thing. Being physically fit, I actually found it comfortable!

What I really liked was being able to get right up and start work. There was a "lunchroom" in the studio with a refrigerator where I kept milk and snack items from the Hollywood Ranch Market nearby. They had a hot-food counter right along the sidewalk, and their barbecued chicken legs were a main part of my daily lunch.

Most days, having begun my day early, I would stop working around noon or one, and stop for a quick hot lunch at the Ranch Market. I would then go straight to the Badminton Courts and play until late, sometimes until midnight when they closed.

Often when they closed the Courts, the owner and the manager would go to a restaurant in the neighborhood where they served extra-large dinner plates filled with a feast! Sometimes I went along with them, and I remember the roast turkey platter, piled high with all the amenities, and how I used to amaze my two companions when I always ate every last morsel!

Sometimes, instead of going to play Badminton, I would go to a night-club to hear the band and the singers. Famous stars appeared in person at the better clubs in those days. I still had a great love for music, and often practiced my voice at night in the studio when everyone had gone home! I had a powerful tenor voice, easily reaching high-C without forcing, and without slipping into falsetto.

I sometimes thought of singing as a career, but felt that it would have to wait for sometime in the future. As I look back, I now know that the future never comes if you don't make it the present!

I really enjoyed working in my own studio! Assignments continued to come in steadily, and most afternoons and evenings, I played Badminton. I did not want to obligate time to play in tournaments, but when I played the tournament winners, I usually won.

One time, I played a man who was performing "Trick Badminton on Ice" in the Ice Capades Show, and he wanted me to join him. I tuned this down, because I did not feel like traveling all over the country. I still wanted to build my career in Hollywood.

Playing Badminton daily, and being at a prime age of twenty-four, I got so good that one day I played one of the top players in the country and won fifteen-to-two, and knew I would not have had to give him those two points.

After that game, I began to take stock of my situation! I began to realize that to keep playing this well, I would have to continue with Badminton daily, and there was no money in it! I suddenly felt I had been letting major free-enterprise opportunities pass me by!

Furthermore, Badminton had not proven to be a social place to meet girlfriends! The only girls playing arrived with a partner! I had just finished a large art assignment, and decided it was time to change my whole lifestyle! I even had a strong desire to get married and raise a family!

CHAPTER 5

The Right Girl

It was November of 1948, and I realized that in one month I would be twenty-five years old, and did not yet have a steady girlfriend! I even remember wondering why God had not yet sent me the "right girl"! But then I immediately thought of the saying about God helping those who help themselves, and a plan began forming in my mind.

Somehow, I strongly felt that my first move must be toward my lifestyle. I believed at that time that I should have a regular, eight-hour-a-day job as a foundation for marriage. For some reason I also felt that a department store art department would be the most stable, and one of the largest finer department stores with several locations around Southern California was The Broadway. Their advertising department was in their store in downtown Los Angeles, and for some reason, I felt determined to get a job at that Broadway store!

I had done some department store art in the past and was familiar with their needs. That very day, I dressed well, arranged my portfolio with appropriate samples of my work, and took a streetcar from Hollywood to downtown Los Angeles. There was a streetcar stop just a half-block from The Broadway, and I was very soon upstairs in the art department, meeting the art director. My art samples as usual received positive accolades, but he commented that while he would usually welcome a person with my abilities, at the moment, there were absolutely no openings! He even explained that their current staff of artists often found themselves waiting for assignments.

Somehow, I found myself saying that I <u>needed</u> to work at The Broadway! (I don't know what made me say that!) Then further, I said I would be willing to clean up papers, sweep the floors, fill-in with art during a sale when part-timers were usually needed, anything!

I guess he thought if I would work cheap enough, it might not hurt to try my ideas, so he offered me $50.00 a week. It was not a very good salary for an artist, but many department store positions paid even less at that time, so I accepted. Actually I never swept the floor, but was immediately given a furniture assignment. My first drawings were so enthusiastically received, I enjoyed a heavy workload of drawing furniture and appliances.

A few days passed, and there kept awakening in me the strong desire to meet "the right girl" to marry and raise a family! I felt I was still "young and handsome", and with many attractive young girls working at The Broadway, I thought I would look around the store. I decided I would start with the best looking girl and ask her for a date. I decided to start with the main floor, and as I got off the elevator, right there in the book department, I saw a miracle! The most beautiful girl I had ever seen!

Usually I'm very talkative, but found myself a little nervous about approaching such a stunning girl! She was in a "bookclub" booth, and there was an aisle-display of calendar books nearby. I walked over, pretending to look at the calendars, trying to get up the nerve to talk to her, when she asked me if I was interested in the calendars. Her beautiful smile seemed friendly, so I walked over to her counter, and I said "Not really, but I am interested in you!"

She asked me my name, and I picked up a paper and pencil from her booth-counter, and wrote, Egon Reich. She looked at the paper, and I liked the way she pronounced my name. She Americanized the "E" of Egon, but as she later told me, newscasters during the war used to say "The Third Reich (Rike)" which was how she said it, and it sounded normal, and we've pronounced it that way all of our lives together.

I told her that I was an artist working in the advertising department of The Broadway, and then I said I would like to draw her picture (Oh, Oh, I thought! Old pick-up line! Wrong approach!).

But to my astonishment, she smiled that radiant smile, said her name was Marilyn, and that she would like to see my drawings! I suddenly felt totally at ease. In fact I had never felt as compatible with anyone before. Even though we had just met and only spoken a few words, there was a magnetism between us!

I told her that I had a studio in Hollywood which was part of a group of artists, but we could go there if she wanted to see my artwork. The next day was Saturday, and I must have mentioned that I did not have a car, because

Egon was looking for the best looking girl at the Broadway Department Store, where he worked, and found the best looking girl in the Universe.
Judge for yourself!

Marilyn as camera girl in a night club at Catalina Island, the summer she turned 21.

Egon, age 14 in his Passport Photo.

Marilyn, at age 14, photographed at a trade show photo machine.

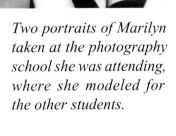

Two portraits of Marilyn taken at the photography school she was attending, where she modeled for the other students.

we arranged to meet at a bus stop at Hollywood and Cahuenga, where a small, local bus came directly there from where she lived in Beverly Hills.

I remember sort-of floating back to the art department, like I couldn't feel my feet touching the ground! The rest of the day, and part of the night, I kept thinking what I would say, and how I would say it! I kept praying that she would feel about me as I already felt about her!

That exciting Saturday morning arrived as a sunny day, and the world was beautiful! The bus stop was near my studio, and we had arranged to meet at twelve noon. I got there about ten minutes early, and when the bus arrived, I carefully observed everyone getting off, but there was no mistake! Marilyn was not on the bus, and somehow we had neglected to exchange telephone numbers!

I was able to find out that that Beverly Hills bus ran once every hour, but I was afraid to leave, in case she might take another bus line, and not find me there! Well she wasn't on the next bus either, but at two o'clock, my heart jumped as I saw the most beautiful girl in the world walking toward me!

She said she was so glad I had waited, that when she was delayed, she realized she had not given me her telephone number, and frantically tried to think of some way to reach me, but couldn't!

Anyway, we "talked a blue streak" as we walked to my studio, and I found out she was a year-and-a-half younger than I, and had never been married either! She was a photographer and photo-colorist. She was also a professional makeup artist, and had most recently been working at the first color-film portrait studio in Beverly Hills. Because color film was really not perfected yet, the studio closed, and Marilyn found herself "between jobs" when she met a lady from Doubleday Publishers in New York. Doubleday needed someone for their Book-club booth in the Los Angeles Broadway Department Store, and Marilyn was talked into managing it temporarily.

When we got to the studio, we started looking at my art samples. Marilyn had studied art, and she really appreciated my work! As we sat in the studio going over various Canadian illustrations, she kept asking me questions until I had told her almost the entire story of my life! How easy she was to talk with, and she was obviously as intelligent as she was beautiful!

Time passed quickly, and I asked Marilyn if she would like to go to dinner at Tom Breneman's. It was one of the better restaurants in the area, but because I wasn't thinking too clearly right then, I forgot to call for reservations. Well, I quickly told the Maitre d' that this was a special night in my life, bribed him of course, and we were immediately shown to a lovely table by a balcony railing. It gave an inviting, distinctive impression.

Marilyn was impressed how I handled the situation, but I wanted to have our first dinner together where there were white tablecloths, elegant silver, nice china and glasses, all the amenities for romantic ambience! When we were seated, a steward handed me the wine list. I still did not ever drink alcohol, so I passed the list to Marilyn, saying to her that she was welcome to select something if she wished. Marilyn graciously declined also, and I felt secretly elated! As we waited for dinner, to be served, a young lady with a camera came by and asked if we would like to have our picture taken. We both immediately said, "Yes!". I moved my chair over beside Marilyn's, put my arm around her, and a smile came very easily.

As we finished dinner, the girl brought the photograph in a nice souvenir folder, and I saw that Marilyn was not only good to look at, but very photogenic. She had blinked her eyes slightly from the camera flash, but she still looked gorgeous! (I thought the slight closing of her eyes looked sexy!)

During dinner, Marilyn told me about her many interests, including acting-groups, and that she kept taking various night-courses, all of great interest to me. We even discussed writing and illustrating books together, and I felt I didn't want the evening to end!

When we left the restaurant, we walked along Hollywood Boulevard, which in those days was still very nice and elegant. It was a comfortably warm night, and we walked along on a cloud of Heaven! It was still early evening, and I said that I thought it would be nice to take a bus to the beach, and go for a walk in the sand. Marilyn suggested that we go to her home and borrow her father's car.

Really? "Great!" I said, and we took the bus to Beverly Hills. She and her father had a house a block north of Wilshire, near Robertson Boulevard. It was a one story, Mediterranean style with a large, covered courtyard entry, on a very pretty tree-lined street, Clifton Way.

There I met Marilyn's amazing, wonderful father, a tall, handsome man in his early sixties. He looked strong, with straight, manly features and beautifully intelligent, piercing blue eyes. His mannerisms suggested kindness, understanding and gentleness, love and caring! I was extremely impressed with him at first meeting.

Marilyn asked him if we could borrow his car to drive to the beach, and I'm sure he trusted his daughter's judgment implicitly, because he said, "Yes,"

Egon and Marilyn enjoyed dinner on their first date at elegant Tom Brennamen's Restaurant, in Hollywood.

Two poster-frames filled with a small sampling of Egon's commercial illustrations through the many years.

and handed us the keys! I was amazed, and thought how lucky I was to have met such wonderful people!

We leisurely drove along Wilshire to the beach, never at a loss for words, and enjoying each other's company immensely! We parked on a semi-secluded cliff overlooking the ocean, and I finally got to kiss Marilyn! We both enjoyed our closeness, and I knew I wanted to ask Marilyn to marry me!

Well, it was never my nature to just "blurt things out"! No, my proposal was long-winded, but Marilyn did not seem to mind! I first reiterated that I loved her, and that no-one else could ever love her as much as I, and that I knew I was the best husband for her, and finally asked if she would please marry me!

Marilyn did not keep me in suspense, but immediately said, "Yes." It was at a later date that she told me that by that time, she "knew" I was "the one" she had been waiting for! For at least two years, she had been telling family and friends that she would never marry anyone except "a real artist", and for several reasons, she was absolutely determined that she would only marry a man who did not drink. In 1933, when Marilyn was eight, right on the front page of the Los Angeles Times Newspaper were headlines stating that it had been scientifically proven that the 'lightheaded' feeling, even just from beer or wine, was caused by millions of brain-cells being destroyed! It also stated that it had been proven that brain-cells are selective, so theoretically, one sip of wine could destroy the very brain-cell one might need someday to accomplish something one wanted to do! Marilyn told her mother, right then and there, that "drinking" would have no part in her life, and even all through her teenage years, remained firmly resolved!

Of course, "everyone" kept telling her that there was "no such thing" as "an artist who did not drink", so she had resigned herself to an interesting, "single" life, when suddenly, there I was! She said that as impressed as she was with my artwork, and the fact that my dark hair and blue eyes were the "look" she liked best in a man, she did not really dare hope until I handed her the wine list at dinner! She said that that was the moment when her head really started spinning, and she "knew" I was her future husband!

Marilyn's mother had passed away several years before, so Marilyn said she had no-one to help her plan a wedding, but because she "knew" I was the right husband for her, she said, "Why wait? Let's get married right away!"

Well, that was my way of doing things, so I said, "Let's get married tomorrow!" On the way home, we got a little more realistic, and started making plans for a wedding the next Saturday! Remember, this was still Saturday, and our first date!

The drive home seemed to take about two minutes. It was then about ten-thirty at night, but Marilyn's father was still up. When we walked in, she announced to him that I was the man she had been waiting for, and that we were going to get married in one week. He did seem surprised at first, but almost immediately shook my hand, and said something about taking good care of her. I assured him that I would with all my heart forever!

We talked awhile longer, and Marilyn wanted to telephone her sister who lived in Northern California, early in the morning, and she wanted me there when she called. So because of unreliable bus schedules at night and Sunday mornings, she made-up the big, feather-down davenport in the livingroom, into a bed for me to spend the night. We both did not want to occupy the same bedroom before our marriage, and I was very happy just to be near Marilyn, and I slept very comfortably on the big sofa.

In the morning, "Dad" made us a hot breakfast. It was Sunday and Marilyn had been helping with the nursery-school at Westwood Community Methodist Church, so she called and told them to 'sign us up' for the "Merry-Weds" church-group instead! We almost immediately began talking about Marilyn's sister, Phyllis, who lived in Stockton, California. She was married, had three children, and a lovely house. Marilyn also talked about the minister of Central Methodist Church in Stockton. He was such an amazing speaker, that not only was his large church filled every Sunday, but as many as two-hundred people stood and sat in cars listening to his sermons over loudspeakers in front of the church. She felt that we would have a well-spoken service if we could have Dr. Melvin Wheatley perform the ceremony.

We called Phyllis early, and asked her if she would help us arrange the wedding at Central Methodist, on this coming Saturday, at five in the afternoon, and if we could have a small reception at her home afterwards, because Marilyn and her father knew some of her sister's family and friends up there.

Phyllis excitedly agreed to everything, and said she thought it might be early enough to reach Dr. Wheatley before his services started, and she would call back. We went ahead with our plans, wording a wedding "Announcement" and a separate "Reception" card on which the date was the following Saturday after the wedding, at our house in Beverly Hills. That way, we could send just the Announcement to family and friends all over the world, and enclose the card for the reception at our house, for the local addresses. I knew a printer who would print them the next morning, so if we addressed the local ones Monday night, that was almost two weeks before the reception, which wasn't bad protocol at all! About an hour later, Phyllis called back and had everything arranged!

Dr. Wheatley had said that he could perfom the ceremony at five in the church's chapel, and that there was going to be a big wedding there at eight that night, and we would have the benefit of their church flowers, so all we would need would be the bride's bouquet. Marilyn told her that she only wanted a white roses corsage which she would carry with a small golden purse for the wedding, and then wear at the reception. Phyllis then suggested that her wedding gift to us be the flowers and a nice three-tier wedding cake for her reception, and we happily said, "Thank you!".

It was still early enough in the morning that we decided to drive to Glendale for me to meet Marilyn's maternal grandmother and grandfather, and an Uncle Marlin and Aunt Madge DeSilva, who lived there across the street.

Marilyn's Grandma Sexton was a petite and sprightly lady in her middle seventies. She was very lovely with white-white hair, very friendly, and one could not help but like her immediately! She was completely devoted to her Seventh Day Adventist Church, and lived the closest to the Ten Commandments of anyone I have ever met.

Marilyn said her grandmother was from Germany, so I spoke a little German with her, and was very happy when she openly expressed approval of me as the husband of her cherished granddaughter. We made plans to take her and Grandpa Sexton along in our car for the wedding in Stockton.

Grandma made us an early Sunday dinner of one of her specialties, the most delicious chicken with light and fluffy dumplings! Apple pie topped off the sumptuous meal, and afterwards we took a short walk across the street to Aunt Madge and Uncle Marlin's house. Aunt Madge loved Marilyn (as did everyone else!) and I found her to be one of the nicest persons one could ever meet, and she seemed to like me! We couldn't stay long, but before we left, she invited us to their Thanksgiving dinner, which was that coming Thursday. We accepted with many thanks!

Marilyn and I were both back at work at The Broadway on Monday, and enjoyed being close to each other! During lunchtime and after work, we made more plans and shopped for our wedding! We enjoyed looking for rings, both wanting basic gold bands! Marilyn knew a jeweler across the street from the Broadway. He was a funny sort of jolly man who was very congratulatory, and said he would give us the lowest price on our rings! The Broadway had some (very thin!) for $9.00 each, which we mentioned, so he showed us a (much thicker!) pair which he said we could have for $8.00! Of course in 1948 things cost so little compared to now, but even then, those were worth far more than he charged us! He even mentioned that the difference in value was his wedding present to us! Again we were delighted to be saying a sincere "Thank You" to someone!

My printer-friend actually had the Announcements ready Monday night at six, and Marilyn's dad picked us up at work so we could drive to get them. Marilyn said that we could never forget our anniversary because it's the Saturday after Thanksgiving! We addressed most of them that night as planned!

Looking back, it's still so amazing how everything seemed to be going along so perfectly! I had a dark blue suit, and Marilyn wanted to find a dress she could use for more than just the ceremony. She tried the Bridal Department, and did find a little white hat there. (Marilyn says it was made of Soutache-Braid, with pearls around the curved edges.) She already had a gold-chain necklace, gold crocheted open-finger gloves. as well as the little golden purse she planned to carry with a white rose. Then also right in The Broadway, she found a pale pink knitted dress, which made her look like an angel! Or maybe more like strawberry shortcake with whipped cream, in other words, delicious, scrumptious, adorable, huggable, lovable, kissable, and on and on! I kept thinking that of all the millions of men in the world, here I was, the one, the only one to win the "ultimate" lottery, worth far more than dollars!

We both counted the days in anticipation of the coming Saturday, and being together, they passed quickly and happily! On Thursday, Thanksgiving provided a nice interlude in our anxious anticipation! Around their large diningroom table, we joined Uncle Marlin, Aunt Madge, and their four children, as well as Grandma and Grandpa Sexton for a grand turkey dinner!

I met their three girls, "B", Marsha, and Odette, and their son, Lane.

I was drawn to Lane, who was a very courteous, bright, good-looking, active ten-year-old, whom I felt would grow up to be an outstanding person! Now, some fifty years later, time has proven me right! Lane had an impressive career, and served in some important government positions. He has a gorgeous, wonderful wife, three fine grown children, and is now semi-retired. It is always a pleasure to talk with him, and reminisce about the days gone by!

Finally, the big day arrived - Saturday, November 27, 1948! We arose early, fixed a nice breakfast, and the three of us drove to Glendale to pick up Grandma and Grandpa. To save time on the 400-mile drive to Stockton, Grandma had packed a lunch for us, and had brought some apples and other snacks. Not having the freeways we have today, meant that the trip took about eight hours, so her snacks really helped pass the time!

Driving the old highways. though slower, presented spectacular scenery! Through the mountains, over the Ridge Route, down into miles and miles of flat farm valley through Bakersfield, the weather was California gentle in late autumn. With rolling hills in the distance, the sun sent gentle rays, and painted shapely shadows between them.

Between Bakersfield and Fresno, we could see expansive farmhouses, barns, and outbuildings, for both vegetable farms and cotton plantations, as far as the eye could see! It was fascinating to see the cotton trucks, sometimes lined-up for a mile where they were picking, and to think that some of those truckloads could be for distribution all over the world!

One also saw canning factories and even grain elevators, and I found I felt very elated, seeing so much farming industry, all operating so cleanly and efficiently. We saw freight trains transporting earth's bounty throughout the country!

There is a saying, "Youth is wasted on the young." Somehow, I cannot feel it was being wasted on us! Marilyn and I were young and felt as good as any healthy young couple could possibly feel, and we both appreciated every minute of the day and were exhilaratingly happy!

Dad's car, a 1936 Dodge sedan, drove along faithfully. Of course, he had owned it since it was new and had always taken excellent care of it. At four in the afternoon, we arrived, and the drive had seemed short and lovely! We had driven straight to the home of Marilyn's sister, Phyllis, and her husband, Raleigh Chalmer Wallace, and their three children, two girls, Dana and Susan, and the three-month-old baby boy, Bruce.

There was much excitement, and we rushed to change clothes and hurry to the church! Marilyn told me later that while she was dressing, Phyllis came in and said I was so handsome, and Marilyn said she thought so too, but just wait until she could tell her all the reasons she "knew" I was the man "for whom she had ben waiting!"

The wedding rings were in my pocket, and as we drove to the church to

♪ The Bells are Ringing ♪ ♪

And we could hear the heavenly
sound all around us Riding on a
cloud from LA to Stockton, where
Marilyn's sister Phyllis had arranged
for their marriage at Central
Methodist Church and a lovely
reception at her home on that
wonderful day
November 27, 1948.

Egon and Marilyn's first Christmas together at their home in Beverly Hills. The closeness and spirit of their wedding just a month before was still with them, and still to this day in 2002

Marilyn's lovely sister Phyllis, married a handsome Marine, Raleigh Wallace. They lived in Raleigh's home town, Stockton California, had three children and a nice house near University of the Pacific.

Getting domesticated! This only shows one way they cooked together.

exchange our vows, a feeling of excited anticipation came over me, and a commitment to embrace this new life before me with all my love and being!

The church was filled with flowers as promised! On the alter, along the pews bordering the aisle, all filling the air with a fresh floral scent!

As I stood at the alter, and Marilyn's father walked her down the aisle, I was experiencing a love greater than one can describe. There was a Holiness about the joining in matrimony, and a strong feeling of love to our union. I still give thanks that we were married in that church by the minister Marilyn admired for his inspiring sermons.

I remember reflecting back to when I wondered why God had not sent me the "right girl", and realized that God works for you, but he needs you as his partner!

Back at Phyllis' house, guests were arriving. Stockton was Raleigh's home and his family came, as well as some of their friends and neighbors Marilyn knew. We received gifts of cards with money, and a few silver and porcelain "treasures" for our home, all thoughtfully small enough to take in the car going home.

The three-tier wedding cake had an ornament-top with two satin "wedding bells". It was on a table with a lovely crystal punch-bowl (non-alcoholic punch, of course!), and for me to just meet everyone took quite awhile! Besides giving us the cake and the gorgeous white roses corsage, being a good planner, Phyllis had also made reservations for us at a famous "honeymoon hotel", The Madonna Inn, near San Francisco, almost a two hour drive away. It was already into the night, and we needed to start early to make it back on Sunday.

Phyllis had arranged beds in her house for Dad, Grandma, and Grandpa, so we could use the car. Marilyn took off her little hat, transferred her corsage to the shoulder of a white coat, and we drove off amid showers of rice, and many good wishes being called our way!

Frankly, as we started off down the dark highway, we were both so sleepy we could hardly keep our eyes open! Suddenly there, off to our right was a really gorgeous large hotel-motel. We hardly had to discuss it at all, but drove right in. They had a very nice room available, so we had at least four hours longer together that night, than if we had gone to San Francisco!

Lacy hearts and cherubs were not needed to make our honeymoon night a memorable one. We awoke in each other's arms to a glorious sunny day! Showered and dressed, we enjoyed a quick breakfast in a coffee shop, and were soon back at Phyllis' house. Dad was happy to see us so early, and they all agreed that it had got too late the night before to drive so far!

It was hard to leave Phyllis and Raleigh, without staying and getting better acquainted after all they had done for us, but they promised to come down to us for a visit soon. We thanked them so much for how perfectly and wonderfully they had planned and arranged everything for us!

Of course, there was no time for a longer honeymoon, because Marilyn and I had to be back at work Monday morning at The Broadway! But somehow, feeling slighted because of not going away somewhere on a honeymoon never entered our minds! We had so many plans, so much to do and accomplish together, and we would be seeing each other and having lunch together daily at work! Both of us being very active and creative people, we found ourselves constantly discussing many projects we wanted to undertake!

CHAPTER 6

... Of Royal Ancestry

On our eight-hour drive home, Marilyn and Grandma Sexton started telling me about their royal ancestry. I guess the days before our wedding were so involved with work and planning, we didn't get around to this most fascinating subject!

"Sexton" was Grandma's married name from her second husband, Archie. Her maiden name was Elizabeth Roggasch, and she was born in Germany in 1878 as a member of the Royal Family. When Elizabeth's mother, who was Kaiser Wilhelm's sister, was young, she had married a man who was not of royal birth, and was chastised by most of the Royal Family. However, her brother visited her often, even giving her money to immigrate to America. At that time, Elizabeth's mother and father had seven children, including a small baby, and they reluctantly agreed to leave three-year old Elizabeth behind with Kaiser Wilhelm as a companion for his daughter, just until they could get settled.

There was a German settlement near Lincoln, Nebraska, and they homesteaded a large farm. When Elizabeth was ten, they insisted she be sent to them, so she was duly outfitted, and royally put aboard a great old ship sailing from Hamburg to New York. Elizabeth was heartbroken. She loved her life of wearing white lace dresses, private tutoring in the mornings and playing around the park-like grounds of the palace every afternoon!

She hated the trip and the ship, and was quite a "handful" for the Captain who had been given charge of her! As we drove, Grandma told us of one incident near the end of the ocean voyage. They were finally nearing the shoreline, and great herds of Sea Lions or "Sea Dogs" as the sailors called them, began following the ship. The captain came forward along the main deck, wondering why he had not been hearing Elizabeth's constant chatter as she thought of one query after another to ask the busy seamen. The corner of his eye caught her skirt billowing out in the wind, as she hugged the massive bowsprit, where she had shimmied out for a better look at the "sea-dogs" and to also see the "beautiful lady" carved onto the bow of the ship.

Slipping up silently behind her, the captain got a good grip on her full skirt with one hand before scooping up her little body with his strong arm around her waistline, standing her safely on the deck, and then giving her his best tongue-lashing of the entire voyage!

When she landed, her parents met her, and by train they continued to their final destination. Her brothers and sisters were strangers to her, but she was so tired, the first night she slept soundly in her new bed. However, when she awoke, the place seemed foreign to her because all she had known was the royal palace in Germany, and this was a farm! She saw the barn and pigs and cows and roosters, even cats and dogs. While to some, this environment would be beautiful and interesting, to little Elizabeth everything was depressing. With the mentality of a ten-year-old not being able to comprehend worldly circumstances, she spent a few days crying. Never quite happy in this environment, Elizabeth nevertheless consoled herself by finding new friends in school, and making the best of her situation.

Royal family history recalls that Kaiser Frederich, second to the last emperor of Germany, was very ill at a time when German royalty in general was facing an uncertain future. One day he called all of his close family to come to him, and gave each of them a fortune in jewels and other valuables, and he died shortly thereafter.

One of his favorite nephews had been given a large bag of jewels. He was able to change about half of them immediately into money, and left for America, assuming the name August Rex. He chose "Rex" because it meant "King" or "Royal" in English. Before leaving the Continent, he went to visit a friend in Lenk, Poland. His friend helped him make arrangements with the Nuns in a Cloister there, to keep a box for him, safely in the catacombs beneath their sanctuary until he could return from America and retrieve it. The box contained the bag with what was still a fortune in jewels.

August Rex had the largest farm in the same German community where Elizabeth's family had settled. He had never married because he did not wish to wed outside of the royal family. From her time of arrival, he had been noticing Elizabeth. She had several older sisters, but when Elizabeth turned sixteen, she was petite with blonde smoothly-curling hair, still had

August Rex

Marilyn's grandfather at the time he married Elizabeth (shown below on right). He was the nephew of Kaiser Frederick, one of the great Emperors of Germany, who's lineage reaches from a long line of royal families. Hence the name Rex.

Elizabeth with her mother, Augusta Roggasch, sister of Kaiser William, the last German Emperor.

Daughter of Elizabeth Rex, Emma Maria Hildegard Rex, Marilyn's mother.

the royal mannerisms learned in Germany, and Rex decided she would be suitable!

He was then sixty years old, but a very handsome man, and when he approached Elizabeth's mother and father with the proposal that Elizabeth and he be married, they were highly in favor of the arrangement! Poor Elizabeth again cried and cried, saying she did not want to marry an old man! Her parents finally persuaded her to accept this handsome, wealthy, man of royalty, and their wedding was a grand affaire for that small farm town.

Rex worshipped Elizabeth, treating her like a little princess! Servants "did everything", he showered her with gifts, and tried to make her life as nearly as he could to being back in "her palace" in Germany!

It was three years before their first child was born, a beautiful, blond baby girl! Elizabeth's mother chose the royal names, Augusta Eugenia Armgarde Rex, using the feminine version of August's name.

Two years later, in March of 1900, Marilyn's mother was born, and Elizabeth chose the names, Emma Maria Hildegarde Rex. The new baby had the dark hair and blue eyes of the German royal families, and bore a strong resemblance to her father!

When Armgarde was five, Elizabeth decided she was too small to go to school alone, so they waited two years until Hildegarde was old enough and the girls started school together. They were bright students, and besides being well-taught in the academics, enjoyed singing and many other activities.

Unfortunately, August Rex passed away in 1905, at the age of seventy four, and Elizabeth was left to raise her two little girls by herself. She almost immediately had several offers of marriage, but had also heard stories about "stepfathers" and "step-daughters", and made a vow to God and herself that she would not marry again until her girls were grown. She remained true to her convictions, and religiously raised the girls always and foremost with good principles, having joined the Seventh Day Adventist Church which had become the largest denomination in their community.

One summer when Hildegarde was only ten, a "Music Man" with a band came into town. They were holding "tryouts", so the town could establish a band of it's own, and Hildegarde loved to sing, so she talked her mother into taking her. After hearing her sing, the "Music Man" came over to Hildegarde's mother and said he realized he would have to wait a few years, but that he had just found the one girl he wanted to marry!

Both Armgarde and Hildegarde graduated from highschool with hon-

In her later years, Elizabeth Rex married Archibald Sexton.

She will always be known to the Reich family as their darling Grandma Sexton.

The small spinning wheel was one her mother used to spin wool, on her farm in Nebraska.

Young Edward W. Mitton, Marilyn's father, a handsome man of many talents.

Hildegard Rex, Marilyn's mother, here shown in her dress design studio.

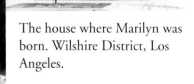

Edward and Hildegard on their honeymoon at Big Bear California.

The house where Marilyn was born. Wilshire District, Los Angeles.

ors. Armgarde married a local boy and remained in Nebraska.. Hildegarde had grown tall and beautiful with long, dark hair, still resembling the royal side of her family. She graduated from Omaha State University as a Dress Designer and took a position as Designer with M. E. Smith, a Couture Fashion Company in that city. Her talents were soon noted, and a story about her was printed with her picture in the Sunday Rotogravure section of Omaha's largest newspaper.

This led to her going to New York to design for Vogue Patterns. After two years, she had ambitions of having her own fashion design studio. She had been living in a very fine women's hotel, and when she first arrived, had met a lovely mother and daughter from Boston. They were there temporarily, settling the father's estate, and planning to move to the Los Angeles area and build a house near the sea. They kept writing letters to her and sending pictures of the two-story white colonial they had finished building in Culver City. Back then, they were at the edge of miles of bean fields, with ocean breezes rustling through the leaves of a row of huge Eucalyptus trees which lined their driveway. They kept saying that Hildegarde was welcome to stay in their guestroom until she could get settled in California!

Meanwhile, Elizabeth, Hildegarde's mother, did get married again to a fine man, Archie Sexton. They had a son they named Dayle. Armgarde lived nearby with her husband, Dayle Hewett, and their son, Donald, and daughter, Lorraine, all nicely settled.

So Hildegarde took a two-week vacation to visit California, and immediately fell in love with the atmosphere at her friends' house! She went back to New York, to resign her position. and she moved to Los Angeles as soon as she could arrange everything.

She did stay with her friends again, so she could become acquainted with the various parts of the city. She still sang beautifully, and asked her friends where she could buy some sheet music. They told her of a large piano store in Westwood, and as she walked in the door, a very handsome man came over to her and asked if she had lived in a certain small town in Nebraska when she was ten years old. Suddenly, she remembered him too, and right then and there, he proposed, and they were married three months later! He owned the piano store, so he could arrange to be away, and they enjoyed a beautiful two-week honeymoon at Big Bear Lake in the nearby mountains.

His name was Edward William Mitton. His grandfather was from France where Mitton was pronounced "Mee-tow". Edward was an English teacher in the days when he spent his summer vacations helping small towns establish community marching bands, and giving band concerts. He learned to play many of the instruments and serenaded Hildegarde while strumming a lute. He also wrote beautiful love-poems to her, and was a fine, gentle, and giving man.

Edward and Hildegarde had two little girls. They named their first Marilyn, and almost four years later, their second, Phyllis Adelle. They bought their first home on Eighth Street in the Wilshire District adjacent to Hollywood.

Edward did very well in the piano and musical instrument business. He became "business-friends" with many celebrities including Jimmy Durante. Hildegarde was extremely successful with her own line of "Hildegarde Rex" designer dresses being sold exclusively in the Couture Salon at Sacks Fifth Avenue on Wilshire Boulevard. The wife of a movie producer once 'discovered' her fashions, and when she took her next annual trip to Paris came back 'empty-handed', saying she was completely 'spoiled' by "Hildegarde Rex" designs!

Marilyn, a beautiful little girl, unfortunately contracted childhood-rheumatoid arthritis, which caused some destruction of cartilage in her knees and one ankle. However Marilyn's mother met a famous nutritionist, Adelle Davis, with who's help in nutritional therapy, Marilyn was able to enjoy a normal life with no recurrence of any inflammatory condition of any kind. We continue to be most thankful for all the help and information Adelle Davis gave, not only to us but to the whole world! Her books were translated into several languages and sold over fourteen million copies!

As Marilyn grew up, her father had chosen books for the ultimate home-library, and she was an excellent student. One day when she was ten, her fourth-grade teacher walked home with her, and had her mother take some of Marilyn's crayon-drawings from class, and tack them up on a diningroom wall. Then the teacher showed them that when you walked from one side of the room to the other, paths, eyes, and other objects in Marilyn's drawings 'followed you'. She claimed that such 'talent' was rare at such an early age, and put a statement in Marilyn's school records which gave her an art class every year for the rest of her school-life.

She also enjoyed languages, and had many of her poems published in her junior-high-school "weekly newspaper", including a Christmas one that was a full-column long. Once for her eighth-grade French class homework, she wrote a little poem, searching her French dictionary for rhyming words!

The assignment had been to write a 'paragraph' in French, so at school the next day, each student, in turn, stood and read their writing. When it was Marilyn's turn, she read her poem, and the teacher couldn't believe that after only a few French lessons, Marilyn at thirteen years of age, could write such a good little French poem. Marilyn had indeed composed it , and I think it's a enchanting little poem to have been written by a person of any age, so here it is . . . (The English translation loses some of the original charm. Those who are able to understand the French version, I'm sure will find a greater appreciation for this amusing little poem.)

MON AMI
Il n'a pas un grand maison;
Il ne pas beaucoup de monnai;
Mais il est toujours un bon ami,
En l'hiver et en l'ete.

Il n'a pas jolie costumes;
Mais si je ne suis pas bon chaque fois,
Ou si je suis mechant.
Il est toujours avec moi!

Pour un ami,
J'ai choisu bien.
Pour mon ami,
Est un chien.

MY FRIEND
His only house is small and funny!
He has absolutely no money!
But he is always a friend to treasure,
In winter, in summer, for time without measure!

He does not wear clothes from a fashion-plate!
But when I'm upset, or full of hate,
Or when I'm very, very, sad,
Just being with him can make me glad!

I have chosen well,
For this friend of mine
Is my big shaggy dog
So loyal and fine!

Marilyn also loved Theater Arts, from directing and acting-in "back-yard plays" as a youngster, to taking Public Speaking and Drama at John Burroughs Junior Highschool. She was selected for the "Makeup" committee, and took her first classes as a "Makeup Artist" at the Max Factor building on Highland in Hollywood. The peak of her "acting career" was still in her junior highschool, playing the lead in the senior class play!

Several years later she joined two "reading" clubs. They met evenings, one in Beverly Hills, and one in a business building's conference room on Wilshire. When Marilyn joined the Wilshire one, they were looking for a new director, and soon obtained Chandler Stanley, head of the Drama Department of UCLA at the time. At his first meeting, he asked what each person considered the greatest play ever written. He said his was Riders to the Sea, by J. M. Synge, which Marilyn was very familiar with, thanks to her dad's extensive home-library. Marilyn spoke-up and said she had read it through aloud many times, because a dialect was written-in so well, all you had to do was read and you really sounded like a Celtic fisherman, which was fascinating! This turned out to be a good part of the reason Chandler felt it was such great writing!

Marilyn described the format of Chandler's meetings, "The members read; Chandler critiqued. It was a rather serious group, no applause allowed, and no general discussion, just Chandler's very firm, expert comments after each reading. The members were mostly working people who enjoyed theater as a hobby. Most had studied, and were accomplished readers.

Marilyn went on to describe one night when she was handed a script in which a young girl was crying over a lost boyfriend. She did it with slight sarcasm, but found as she read, she could make little catching-sounds in her throat that sounded like small sobs. When she finished the reading, there was a long silence, and she was afraid she was going to get one of Chandler's famous almost-cruel remarks. The silence continued until suddenly, Chandler himself began to slowly applaud! That "brought down the house", and the other members clapped, even whistled, and Marilyn said she just sat there blushing. Nothing like that had ever happened before!

But back to the schoolgirl, Marilyn, as we were talking on the ride home from our wedding. For highschool. she went to Marlborough. Her mother and dad had sold the lovely Eighth Street house and bought a magnificent Tudor on Plymouth near Rossmore, about four blocks from the school. Marlborough was and still is one of the finest girls' schools in Los Angeles, and students who did not maintain "straight-A" grades were not allowed to remain in the school.

Marilyn enjoyed the many social activities, and especially the much higher caliber of teaching than found in public schools. Professor Bowerman, her "English Lit'" teacher, was a lady absolutely dedicated to making 'writers' of all her students. Although later in life Marilyn took "Creative Writing" courses, she claims it was the rules 'drilled into her' by Professor Bowerman that come to mind whenever she has to stop and think about the correct way something should be written. As you will see later in this story, among many other important writing assignments for our own accounts, for four years Marilyn wrote advertising copy for (the then named) Cole and Weber, a major International advertising agency in which I was a staff artist.

Also at Marlborough, again most certainly thanks to that fourth-grade teacher, Marilyn was given two back-to-back art classes daily, and the art teacher, Marie Roget, had taught at the most famous art school in the world, "The Paris Academy"! She had escaped to America when the Nazis invaded France, and blessed Marlborough with her amazing talents and knowledge. Marilyn loved learning all the Paris Academy rules about eye-path and compositional-lines, way beyond simple 'composition' taught in public school. There were daily "Life" classes, with strict adherence to 'contouring' required. Although Professor Roget was a petite young woman, and Marilyn was five-foot-ten. she used to call Marilyn 'her little Michaelangelo'!

When Marilyn was in her senior year, and registered to attend UCLA as an English major, unexpectedly a most tragic event occurred. Perhaps due to stress brought on by her intense devotion to her work and art, and always having been somewhat fragile, Marilyn's beloved mother (Hildegarde) suddenly passed away in March that year. She had lived to see Phyllis play the piano solo (De Bussey's Clair de Lune) at her graduation from John Burroughs Junior Highschool, as a mid-term in January. Phyllis wanted to go on to public highschool with her friends.

Their beautiful home in the Wilshire district reflected so much of Marilyn's mother's character in the decor and even in the house itself. It kept rekindling memories, and their intense sorrow over her passing so young, until they all agreed to sell the house. They immediately bought a smaller house just north of Wilshire, near Robertson, in Beverly Hills. World War II was causing a severe housing shortage in all of Southern California, and rental-tenants could not be evicted.

Marilyn and Dad knew the Beverly Hills house had a tenant when they bought it, but did not know they could not evict him. The tenant turned out to be a very nice fellow, Harry Barrett. He had been one of the original "Rhythm Boys" with Bing Crosby, and he assured us he would move as soon as he could find another suitable house.

In the meantime, Dad had sold Plymouth Street, and we had to move! As was his nature, he found the fun way out, and because it was now summertime, he bought a beachhouse! It was vacant, with five small bedrooms, several baths, and a sturdy stairway on one side to large sundeck on the roof! It was up a small hill, one block from a broad white sand beach in Playa del Rey (now Marina del Rey). Venice Boulevard ended there, and a bus ran to Los Angeles, making any connection one could need. In fact, Phyllis was in the district for Venice Highschool, and immediately started arranging for a transfer to University High in Westwood, all of which worked out well.

Still because of the war, they rented two of the bedrooms to defense-factory girls, very nice ones from Goshen, Indiana. Marilyn had had a basic cooking course in seventh grade, so she juggled red tokens, experimented with horsemeat, and had dinner ready every day when the girls got home from work. They helped with the dishes, and always gave her cooking suggestions, until she became an excellent cook!

There were always servicemen down at the beach, and Phyllis met a Marine from the El Toro Air Base. He owned a moving van company, called Pleasant Way, and was the Mayflower franchise in his hometown of Stockton, California. He was head of Base Transportation at El Toro, and would soon have served his time and be going home. It was about Thanksgiving time when the Beverly Hills house became available to move into.

Phyllis and Raleigh got married. Dad sold the beachhouse, and gave the profit to Phyllis to buy her and Raleigh's first house in Stockton. Living in Beverly Hills, Marilyn found an active social life. She went to plays at the Biltmore Theater, Operas, Concerts, and even USO Dances at the Beverly Wilshire Hotel. She would take a bus to San Francisco to see a Helen Hayes play. At that point in time, Helen Hayes was not scheduled for Los Angeles.

After a few months, Marilyn decided to register for a Commercial Art class at "LA Tec" (Los Angeles Technical Institute, in those days called Frank Wiggins). She was in their registration offices, being told her application was being put on a waiting list, when a photography student walked in, saw Marilyn, and asked her to model for their portrait class. She had not had a formal portrait taken in her Marlborough graduation dress, which was a long white chiffon, so she asked if that would be appropriate. He asked her to go to meet the teacher, which they did, and arranged a day and time for the sitting. She immediately noticed some of the impressive equipment, backgrounds and props owned by that great school.

The day of the sitting, she was shown around the studios some more, and she was hooked! She went that same day to the offices and found that she could start with the summer semester, and that being a three-semester course, she would be finished a year from June. From the first day, Marilyn absolutely loved photography! She had to take the Wilshire bus to the end of the line, then two red cars to reach the school every day, and never missed one day of class, the whole time!

It was the April before she would finish, when she was called into the offices and offered a job. The war had just ended, and Catalina Island, after being a Naval Base for years, was having a grand opening for the public! The great white steamship would be running twice daily, plus water taxi services would be in full swing, and they needed a "Camera Girl" for two dinner-dancing-clubs, the Brazil Club and the Chi-Chi. One requirement was that the girl they would hire had to be twenty-one, and Marilyn's twenty-first birthday was just one month away, which they said was close enough!

But what about two more months of study? Kenneth McCombs, the Photography Instructor, was quite famous with several published hardcover books. One was called Illustrative Photography, and the others had similar titles, and he was a wonderful person too! He said those last two months would be mostly review, and in a few days, sat Marilyn down in a private office with the printed Final Examination Papers, which she passed with only one error (in chemicals!), but 99% was a very passing grade! And she was off to Catalina for the summer!

Marilyn rented a room in the home of a local family. After dark every night, the father would go out in a little rowboat and pull-up his lobster pots. His wife had the water boiling when he came home, and we had all the sweetest fresh lobster we could eat, in the 'fridge all the time!

Marilyn always loved talking with people, which was part of her job, so she was ecstatic. Most nights, she worked until two in the morning, when most of the young club-workers went to a deli and had a huge pastrami and Swiss cheese sandwich and glass of milk. Marilyn would still not drink alcohol, not even beer.

Soon business was so good on the island that summer, that they hired another girl from the school, named "Rusty". She was Mormon, so she and Marilyn got along fine! She shared the room Marilyn was renting.

Marilyn's dad had brought her bicycle over to her, and every morning at eight, she would roll out of bed, take a large blanket, a book she would be reading, a box of writing paper with a pen, and go down to the beach, where she would sleep two or three more hours, then write letters or read until noon.

By then, Rusty, or other girls who worked on the island, would have come to the beach, and would use her blanket and watch her things. She usually had a hamburger and a milkshake for lunch, then rode her bicycle up the hill and through a gorgeous bird park which is no longer there. She loved coasting her bicycle fast down the hill, then daily stopped for a round of nine-hole (or Pitch 'n' Put) golf. She got good enough that on one of two holes, she always made a 'hole in one'!

There were many highlights to the summer. She and Rusty went out on commercial "Tuna Boats", helped sail a seventy-foot sloop, went dancing at "The Casino" where Leighton Noble's orchestra played all summer long! It sounded like every girl's dream of a twenty-first summer!

Marilyn stayed after "the season" until the weather began getting cold and blustery, and she finally moved back into the Beverly Hills house with her dad, just before Thanksgiving. Her sister in Stockton had just had her first baby, a little girl, and Marilyn went up for a visit. There was an extra bedroom in Phyllis' house, so Marilyn thought she might like to stay awhile. She went to the largest portrait studio in Stockton to see about a job, and as Christmas was approaching, they needed photo-colorists. She worked one day in the coloring room, in the basement of the studio. When she came to work the next morning, she saw an art table setup right in the middle of the large window of the studio, right on the sidewalk of a main downtown street. She was told to do her photo coloring, sitting in the window. Well, little did they know, Marilyn was a showman too! She would place four eight-by-ten portraits on the center of the table with push-pins, then take the curls of hair, and pieces of fabric she was to match, show them to her 'audience' with flair, and pin each by it's appropriate photograph. She then very quickly colored all four faces, shadows, cheeks, and eyes, then pro-

Marilyn attending a photography class at a trade school in Los Angeles, with a much respected teacher Mr. McCombs.

Marilyn was chosen to work as a camera girl in a night club on Catalina Island.

Top photo: Marilyn as camera girl at 21, taken by a night club patron. Bottom photo: Marilyn enjoying a daily sun bath and friends at a Catalina Beach.

Marilyn's father Edward Mitton, displaying the Pectoral Fins of a Flying Fish.

ceeded to match individual needs, one picture at a time, and would finish all four in less than an hour. Right up to Christmas Eve day, she always had a large crowd watching in front of her window. After Christmas, the owner 'gave' her his "Baby Studio" to operate. It was well equipped with a portrait setup, and upstairs a darkroom and production room. Marilyn was the photographer, did the developing, printing, and selling.

She enjoyed it for awhile, but was being paid a straight salary, which was far less than she could earn as a colorist, and besides was missing her life in Los Angeles. When she first returned home to Beverly Hills, she took a few orders for painting "Ivory Miniatures" for a portrait studio in San Francisco. When Marilyn first received the request, she went to Huntington Library to study the techniques in their antique originals. She soon found she could finish five in about two or three hours. In those days, a secretary earned one dollar an hour, forty dollars in a whole week. The photography studio charged two-hundred dollars for each miniature, and only paid Marilyn twenty, but she established a minimum order of five and made one hundred dollars only working half-a-day!

While Marilyn was in the photography school, she took the coloring courses and negative retouching in 'adult nightschool' at Hollywood Highschool. When she finished those courses, she kept taking more, such as fabric painting, metal tooling, lapidary, and two whole semesters of "Home Decorating" which turned out to be both interior and exterior (actual landscaping!). She particularly delighted in the course because it turned all the compositional rules of art into three-dimension! A room's main-grouping was like a painting's center-of-interest, with sub-groupings pulling your eye comfortably around the room, like compositional lines!

One day Marilyn met a man and his wife whom she said had a charming decorator studio on La Cienega, called "The Clock". It was only a few blocks away from her house in Beverly Hills, and they hired her on a job-basis to accompany them to houses they were redecorating. It was a time when most movie people around Hollywood were converting from "Art-Deco" (Twenties-Modern) actually all the way to "American Country". The couple also had an interest in a "Honey-Maple" furniture factory, as well as a home-remodeling company, specializing in bay windows and general facades.

When there was an appointment at a home, the couple would pick up Marilyn at her house, in a station wagon filled with fabric and wallpaper samples, and she would bring a large sketch-pad, pencils and crayon-chunks..

The wife was very good at selecting impressive wallpaper and other embellishments, and the husband did the arrangement suggestions. Marilyn sat and sketched, supposedly following the man's ideas, and soon handed him a quick, colored sketch of the room with her own arrangements, mostly quite different from his! Invariably, the man would smile, and hand her sketch to the client, saying, "Yes! See, this is what I meant!" Marilyn of course 'caught on' to the money-aspect, and made as many changes as possible, from large plate glass windows into bay windows, adding beams to ceilings, and much, much more, so the couple adored her.

One Sunday afternoon, Marilyn was attending a benefit party, and met a lady from New York, who worked for Doubleday Book Publishers. Among other things, she had come to California to find a replacement manager for their book club 'booth' in the Broadway Department Store in downtown Los Angeles. They sat and talked and talked! The outcome was that Marilyn would manage the booth until they could find a permanent person.

The store also had one salesclerk assigned to the 'booth' which was right by the elevators, on the main floor, at the edge of the book department. The store clerk was a girl from Wales who had married an American soldier during the war, and Marilyn liked her a lot, and was fully enjoying being back in a 'talking to people all day' situation!

Marilyn was not allowed to sell book-department books, but if she saw customers near her booth who seemed to need a salesclerk, she would ask if she could call someone to help them. This is why, when she saw me looking at the calendars on a table near her booth, she asked if I were interested in them, not if she could help me! Here, I had thought she was just being creative in her talking! Actually, she was, but in a different way than I had thought!

CHAPTER 7

The Adventure Begins . . .

As one goes through life, most of the time, the course of one's fate is determined by the occurrences we experience, as well as by necessities which are needed for the pursuit of happiness! Part of it is always hard work and concentration on making correct decisions which will be beneficial to the family and provide a measure of security. Marilyn and I both wanted several children. We felt we had the morals and dedication to bring children into this world who would be an asset to human society.

The first Sunday after our wedding, we had a reception at the house in Beverly Hills. Marilyn had ordered two large white sheetcakes marked into squares with a pair of white sugar wedding bells on top of every piece! She and her dad had a gorgeous big, old diningroom table which pulled-out to eight feet, and she used a white damask tablecloth. We had a white floral centerpiece, with the sheetcakes on each end of the table, and platters and platters of crusts-cut-off triangle sandwiches. I remember the sandwiches quite clearly, because Marilyn and I spent all day Saturday making them!. Family and friends made up a large group of guests, and a girlfriend of Marilyn's remarked that she had never been to a lovelier party!

Marilyn slept in the master bedroom in their house, because it was large enough for twin beds, and she sometimes had a girlfriend spend the night. We spent the first two weeks in one of the twin beds, until we had a free weekend to go out and buy a double bed. We also bought two long, low double chests to balance the room, and fitted my art table in nicely by a large front window.

Besides my job, I always looked for extra work (artwork and printing-production-art) that I could do evenings. One such assignment was to produce a Nurses' Annual Yearbook. I indoctrinated Marilyn into the world of art for commercial production and printing. She spread-out the Year-book pages on the big diningroom table, and quickly learned how to do the page-designs and pasteups. I was immediately impressed with her deft, artistic hand-movements as she expertly completed each production-board.

Marilyn had a four-by-five Speed Graphic camera with sheet-film, and we went together to take photographs in and around the hospital. She also set up a 'studio' right in our livingroom, and took all of the portraits of the graduating nurses. Those were still the days of black-and-white photography, and Marilyn did negative retouching on all of them, so they looked 'big-studio' professional!

There were also some written pages that needed editing, and Marilyn even turned out to be an excellent writer! She claimed to be equally impressed with my extensive English vocabulary, and 'way with words' I had developed as Creative Director at the advertising agency in Canada, Cockfield-Brown.

That very first project we did together showed us what a great team we made! We were both unbelievably excited over this discovery, and always felt elated when we worked on other commercial jobs together in the evenings.

Our blissful life together brought us daily joy, and we were exceedingly happy when we discovered Marilyn was expecting our first child! The baby was due in December 1949. Marilyn immediately went to the library and looked-up every book about babies! She found that a popular book at the time was one of the first 'natural childbirth' books by a doctor in England, Grantly Dick Reed. She faithfully followed his diet and exercises. and besides, we were told by our doctor that Marilyn had broad bone-structure and was 'built' to have babies! So as expected, even with the first baby, Marilyn had a quick, almost painless delivery, and it was a beautiful baby girl we named Heidi.

Marilyn quit her job so she could stay home and nurse, and be with Heidi who grew into an active, happy baby. Heidi at an early age showed high intelligence, an amazing understanding of compassion, and definitely had great physical coordination.

I took a different job with a major printing company in Los Angeles, to make more money. They had a large art department with twelve or fourteen staff artists. We did a lot of color illustrations, many for orange crate end-labels which were very popular in the forties. Many are today's collectors' items, and whenever we see a 'show' of them, I invariably see some I'm quite

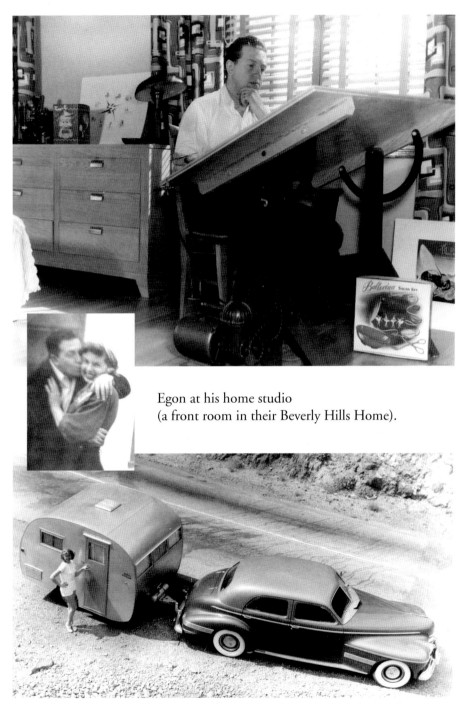

Egon at his home studio
(a front room in their Beverly Hills Home).

Marilyn and Egon's "Love Bug" Trailer and snazzy car. They took
many weekend, or just Sunday trips, enjoying the fabulous
California scenery.

certain are my illustrations.

My earnings were not really high, so living with Marilyn's dear father in his house really helped. He was still in the musical instrument business, doing well, and even gave us money from time to time. He went on week-long fishing trips, and even joined his sister, one time in Arizona for several months on what I seem to remember was a business venture of some sort, so we felt like we were alone in our own house most of time.

I was very healthy and energetic, and kept managing to earn additional income. I knew real estate could provide big profits. and was always search-ing for opportunities, when one day an advertisement caught my eye. It consisted of three houses for sale in the Hollywood hills above Sunset Bou-levard. The immediate area was very exclusive, and I always thought high property values would bring the highest profits.

I did not have enough money ahead for a down payment on those three houses, however I went to meet the owner. He turned out to be a very pleasant older man who wanted to divest himself of the responsibilities of his rental properties. We made an arrangement, on a contract basis, that part of my payments to him would apply toward a down payment. All three houses were new and empty, and the anticipated rental income would only cover the financial obligation for a few years, but I had the right to sell at any time and gain from the appreciated value. It seemed that that should more than cover any efforts the property had cost me.

Unfortunately, these homes were a bit too high calibre for the general Hollywood area at that time, and even though I advertised in the Holly-wood Reporter and other publications read by movie stars, I soon realized I could not keep them rented at the amount our contract would require. The owner could afford to take less rent, and very amiably cancelled our agree-ment. In fact we had become friends, and he mentioned that among his other holdings was a large home in the Wilshire district. It was a Mediterra-nean mansion with all hardwood floors, a twenty-by-forty-foot livingroom with ten-foot ceilings, a diningroom so big that Marilyn's mother's gor-geous Kimball pump-organ fit into the bay-window at one end! It had two very large bedrooms, one with a balcony overlooking the front gardens. It had a master bedroom the size of the livingroom, with a fireplace at one end, and a conservatory looking out on the back gardens. That was so large it became our second daughter's nursery, and there was also a dressing room that Marilyn used for her sewing room, with walls full of drawers to orga-nize things! Every bedroom had its own bath, completely custom with imported Italian tile!

I offered the same contract arrangement, except I would be living in the big house, and he accepted! Marilyn and I both enjoyed elegant surroundings. Well, it turned out that the Beverly Hills house rented for enough to cover <u>both</u> house payments, and of course Dad moved with us, into the nice front bedroom with the balcony.

We had lots of fun redecorating that house! Marilyn put the rug, she had grown up on, in the middle of the livingroom. It is a ten-foot by twenty-foot Karastan in blue and rose soft colors, and she arranged the sofa and two large chairs, plus several tables and 'occasional' chairs, all into the main grouping. She created an 'entry hall' at the end where the front door opened and the stairs came down. The other end had a smaller Oriental rug in front of the fireplace, and there was a grand piano by it, in the front corner between two windows.

The facade of the fireplace and an oval above each window had bas-relief flowers and birds, all just painted beige when we moved in. We had the walls painted a very pale 'dusty-rose' with 'eggshell' white woodwork, and the draperies dyed a Burgundy-rose. Marilyn and I then took artist's oils and tinted the flowers and birds. She did the fireplace, while I stood on a ladder and matched her colors over the windows. It was so beautiful, I felt like I was back in one of the palaces in Vienna.

Things moved along nicely, and I continued to do illustrations for the Los Angeles printing company. I had purchased a good-looking Oldsmobile and a cute little house trailer. We took many weekend, or just Sunday, trips. Southern California is such a wondrous place! There are mountains and lakes; beautiful ocean beaches , coves and harbors; the vast desert-lands'; hills amass with yellow poppies in the springtime; and all with a mild and sunny climate year-round!

Those who live here are bestowed with these blessings! Open your eyes, your ears and your heart! Life is a window through which you can experience this beauty! There are false prophets, such as alcohol and drugs, whose aim is to shut your window of life, so keep your window open, for life is relatively short!

Soon we were made aware of another blessing. A new baby was on the way! An adorable baby girl with blond curly hair arrived January 26, 1951, and we named her Rebecca (Becky). As previously mentioned, Marilyn's mother had become friends with the notable nutritionist, Adelle Davis, whose books on medical nutrition had already sold many millions of copies. Marilyn had continued our friendship with her, and we often visited her in her home in Palos Verdes, just south of Los Angeles by the sea. Adelle was just finishing a 'baby book', she called "Let's Have Healthy Children". Adelle asked me to do some sketches of babies and children for the book, which I was most happy to do for her.

Just before Becky was born, Adelle sent Marilyn a typewritten manuscript of the book, which Marilyn eagerly read. There was an interesting idea in it, that even though nursing, from the very first day, the baby could be given one bottle for the six o'clock in the evening feeding. This accomplished actually three wonderful things. It got the baby used to a bottle, so a 'baby-sitter' could feed the baby. Then secondly, perhaps partly because the yogurt made the formula thicker, after only a very tiny burp, babies never seemed to have any colic!

Also a bottle could contain more nutrients than just mother's milk, so the baby would sleep longer in the night until the next feeding. I remember when we came home with twelve-hour-old baby Becky, I kept telephoning our doctor to make sure Marilyn's concoctions were safe! At six the first night Marilyn put a pinch of Brewers Yeast and a spoonful of yogurt into a bottle of partly her breast milk, and partly the choice Certified raw cow's milk we used to be able to get in those days. Each night Marilyn increased the yeast and yogurt, and by six days of age Becky was sleeping through the night to six in the morning!

(Our next two babies followed exactly the same pattern, and as they now are approaching their fifties in age, they are all athletic, even doing triathalons!) Again, I must say how grateful we all are to Adelle Davis. She had seven doctorates in fields of medical research, was a fully credentialed "Pre-Med" professor, and was undoubtedly the most knowledgeable nutritionist who ever lived.

Baby Heidi was fourteen months old when Becky was born, and Heidi immediately began talking and talking to her! Even though some of it sounded like gibberish to us, the most amazing thing happened. At six months, you could carry on a conversation with Becky! She understood anything you asked, and would answer "Es" or "No", and it was always the appropriate answer! By ten months, Becky was saying whole sentences, like, "Es go bye-bye now!"

At Eastertime, when Heidi was about a year-and-a-half, we discovered an amazing thing about her! We already knew she was careful with her dolls and other toys, so we brought home a little yellow baby duckling from a pet

The birth of Egon and Marilyn's first Angel Heidi.

...and their second Angel Becky, already on the way.

Sunday morning, time to go to church.

A fancy house deserves a fancy car. Heidi and Becky agree.

Christmas at their elegant home in the exclusive Wilshire district of LA.

shop. Out in the yard, we put the duck down in front of Heidi, and it ran right over to her. She squatted down and made motions with her hand like she was petting it, but kept her hand about half-an-inch above the duck's head and back! She obviously knew she could hurt that little duck by touching it! I've read many times since that that kind of sensitivity is unheard of in that young a child!.

That little duckling followed Heidi around outside, always only inches away from the heels of her shoes. When Heidi stopped, the duckling stopped, and when Heidi started walking again, the duckling kept right up with her, the same little distance behind her. We have a home movie of this performance, and it is the cutest thing to see how that duckling must have thought Heidi was it's mother!

We had named the duckling Leslie when she was too small to know her gender, and she grew into a beautiful white female. At night, she would jump into a box in the kitchen, and not move until we let her out in the morning.

While at first, she definitely thought Heidi was her mother, as she grew, the role reversed and Leslie thought she was Heidi's mother. If Heidi was in the yard, and would do something like trying to open the gate, Leslie would quack loudly so Marilyn would come and check on them! One day, Dad asked if we would like to give Leslie to a good home. It seemed that he had met some people who had a duck farm. Their ducks were laying too many eggs and they were looking for large female ducks to sit and hatch eggs that were pushed from the nests. We let him take Leslie out to try it, and she became the perfect mother to many little ducklings, and had a long and happy life!

A couple of years flew by, and Heidi and Becky had grown into two little dolls. We lived about three blocks from the big Wilshire Methodist Church, and every Sunday, the four of us walked to the eleven o'clock services. About this time, Marilyn started a morning schedule which she continued for around the next fifteen years or so. She loved a nice breakfast table. Dinner, too, of course, but breakfast was her favorite! She awoke (without an alarm clock) every day at four in the morning, sewed for an hour, and then started breakfast by cutting a fresh orange for each person, served in glass stem-dishes with a small cocktail-fork standing in each. (To this day, when grandchildren spend the night, she still follows this ritual.)

Breakfast also consisted of two eggs per person. Besides her many inventive omelettes and 'shirred' eggs, she even has a way of 'forcing' two eggs into one piece of "French Toast", and so on through a multitude of recipes!

She was constantly reading 'baby books' which all stressed the importance of a steady daily routine in children's lives. As our children grew older, she used to say she "stopped her life" every day at four o'clock to start dinner. The children picked fresh garden flowers for the table every day, and besides the regular five o'clock dinner hour, at exactly seven o'clock, it was bath time. Toothbrushing was done to colorful little plastic egg timers, all followed by story-time and singing-time with lights-out every night at eight.

CHAPTER 8

I Didn't Lose a Wife, I Gained a Sister

When Marilyn and I had been married about five years, my sister had married and had two children. They lived in an apartment in Vienna, and even though it was small, my mother lived with them. We talked several times by telephone, and knew my mother wanted to come here and live with us, and we wanted her too! She had applied for a United States immigration quota number when we first got married, but it seemed like it would be many years before we could bring her here on that basis.

Because I always believed in trying 'other' ways, I telephoned Immigration and asked if there was something I could do to expedite her coming here. Their first question was what was <u>my</u> citizenship status?

I simply stated that I was from Canada, but was now married, had two children and good employment. The next question was, "Do you have a Green Card?" I answered that I had a Social Security Card and a Driver's License, but that I had never heard of a Green Card!

He explained that a Green Card was like a permanent visa, and that I must immediately come to their offices to apply for a status showing why I should not be deported! My heart sank with fears of being sent back to Canada or even to Austria! I had no desire to end-up in either place, probably without ever being able to return to what I now fully considered my 'homeland' - Los Angeles, California, U.S.A.!

Marilyn was completely calm, sweet, and assured me we would all stay together wherever they might send me! I realized more than ever that Marilyn was not only beautiful and highly intelligent, but completely loving. I knew I was lucky and blessed, and ready to 'take on' whatever needed doing. I made an appointment, and we all went together to Immigration. After many 'forms', character references and 'searches', proof of birth and marriage, and so forth, an impressive, two-inch-thick file showed an impeccably clean record, with no hint of any criminal activity ever! The outcome of it all, was that I had to make a 'legal' entry into the United States. Canada agreed to accept me as a legal resident, so I could 'enter' from there, and we only had to fly to Vancouver, Canada. My legal entry would be at Bellingham, Washington.

We were elated and planned a pleasant trip. It was spring of 1953, and Marilyn was pregnant with Karen. Heidi and Becky wore little tailored coats in navy and red, and a stewardess pinned a 'wings' pin on each of them. I think Becky still has her pin and remembers how proud she was!

We stayed at a large hotel, and everyone was impressed with our well-behaved little girls. We believe that the good nutrition had a great deal to do with it, but while Marilyn has a very calm nature, time-schedules and rules were always followed 'to the letter'.

If we had an art or printing job where Marilyn was involved, we always hired a baby-sitter, but one day something came up and we took 'the babies' along to some offices. The reception room had a lady behind a counter and a leather sofa for people to wait. Marilyn talked to the receptionist for a moment, and left the girls each with a blank-paper-tablet and a new box of small colored pencils. We were in a closed-door office for well over an hour, and when we came out, the receptionist said she had never seen anything like it! Those two tiny girls had sat still, talking and drawing on their papers the whole time! We were proud of course, but not surprised!

At the hotel in Vancouver, we ate in a very fine dining room. Our girls had fine table manners, and the waiter always brought them a small scoop of ice cream for dessert, along with a demi-tasse spoon. The girls loved the small spoons, and felt very special.

Vancouver is a beautiful city, and we had a high room with a spectacular view. There are many big trees among the buildings, and a small rain-forest right in the middle of the city! When you walk along the paths through it, it feels like a children's story forest! Of course, the luscious green of the trees and plantlife are from the considerable amount of rain in the area. Looking out over one of the buildings, we saw a large sign on the roof, foretelling the weather. Several times we saw the sign reading, "Sunny Today", when it would start to rain, and some men would come running, and quickly change the sign to "Rain"! We all laughed and said it was nice they were letting us know! I guess that weather forecasting wasn't then what it is now, with all the new technology, and satellites cruising around our planet! Usually the

Heidi and Becky showing their special wings they got from United Airlines, as Egon and Marilyn were getting ready to fly to Vancuver Canada for Egon's legal entry into the U.S.

Egon and Marilyn stayed at the fancy Vancouver Hotel. The girls were adorable.

In the afternoon we took a stroll though the close by beautiful Vancouver forest park.

rain was short-lived, and they changed the sign back to "Sunny"!

Marilyn, the girls, and I went for walks every day along the beautiful forest path, where we saw all kinds of big trees, ferns, squirrels, and many birds chirping about! Actually, it was sunny most of the three days we were there. Marilyn dressed the girls beautifully with pretty dresses, coats, hats, and little white gloves. Even for such a few days, and the fact we were forced to take it, it was one of the nicest vacations ever! We arrived home, and I was proudly in possession of a "Green Card", thinking, "Nothing can stop me now!"

I was happy in my job, but always working evenings to make extra money, so I really listened when a salesman came into our art department at the printing company. He was bragging to someone that he had made ten thousand dollars in less than six months. By this time, a good salary was a hundred dollars a week. Here was a salesman with no art talent making that kind of money! I immediately thought that I must be in the wrong end of the business! I had complete knowledge of printing and production, and between my artwork, Marilyn's photography, and both of our writing abilities, we started "Reich Advertising".

I had long been aware that many advertisers, especially smaller manufacturers did not consider art to be important, and actually expected it to be part of their printing orders - free! So I developed a plan whereby I would show them they would be getting expert artwork free, and even pay less than they had been for their printing!

Approaching several small and medium sized manufacturers, I found that everyone needed some advertising, even just packaging, brochures, or catalogs. We attained certain accounts by clever ideas, but more often total cost became the issue, and my free artwork aspect seemed to be my best selling-point!

I became very inventive, buying my own paper, stripping-up my own lithography films, even purchasing my own offset printing plates. I developed good customers, and we definitely began making more money!

In the meantime, Marilyn's dad, my beloved father-in-law, was also keeping busy, and at sixty-five he was strong and healthy, and as handsome as ever! Perhaps by coincidence, there was news at that time of a new immigration law that was passed to help to bring home soldiers from World War II who were still living overseas. These were servicemen who had married 'over there' and their wives were still waiting for their quota numbers!

The new law simply read that any spouse of a United States Citizen was eligible for an immediate permanent visa. Of course, Marilyn and I instantly had the same idea, and almost in unison said, "Let's send Dad to Vienna to marry Mama (my mother) so she can come here now!"

I remember approaching the subject with Dad the next morning at the breakfast table. True to his congenial nature, he immediately agreed to do it, providing it met with Mama's approval. Of course Dad (Edward) and Mama (Greta) had both been seeing pictures of each other for five years, and knew a great deal about each other from our letters. We immediately telephoned Mama, who spoke no English, and I asked, "Liebe Mama, würdest du Marilyn's Vater heiraten, so das Du sofort nach America kommen kannst." A definite, "Ja!" was her answer! It so happened that we had just recently sold the Beverly Hills house which gave us the five thousand dollars needed for their trip.

Dad, being as great as he always was, right away started studying German. I got such a kick out of him when he would start a normal conversation with me in German! It took a few weeks to obtain Dad's passport because he had never needed a birth certificate before, and he found out that the City Hall in the small Nebraska town where he was born had burned down. He had to complete a document, and obtain several signatures of people who knew of his birth. Everything was finally accomplished, and off he flew to Vienna!

We later heard that Mama was waiting for him with my sister, her sister, and her mother, and when Dad got off the plane, he smiled and said, "Grüss Got meine liebe Frau!" (Greetings, my dear wife!) Besides a very quick 'phone call that he had arrived safely, we heard nothing for three days, when a telegram arrived, saying. "Having big wedding! Staying married!"

Well, eventually we heard all the details! There was great excitement in Vienna! My mother's sister, cousins, aunts and friends came from all over to help with preparations for the wedding! They had all seen pictures of Marilyn's handsome father, and were calling him "The Knight in Shining Armor" My mother was only fifty-two, and still quite pretty with her natural light red hair. Shortly thereafter we received a letter from Mama, saying that she and everybody adored Edward! Dad also added a few words in German which translated into, "I love my dear future wife!"

During those years, the Russians were still occupying part of Vienna, and government functions were in somewhat of a turmoil, so it took several weeks to obtain the marriage license. While they waited, Mama showed Dad around Vienna, and because he always enjoyed fishing, they spent

Flying O'er the Alps

Pageantry of The Clouds

WORDS and MUSIC by EDWARD WILLIAM MITTON

COPYRIGHT CLASS E. #51945

Cover photo of song, written by Marilyn's father on his way to Vienna to marry Egon's mother. (Story on page 99).

Mama and dad as they arrived in the U.S.

afternoons sitting on a shore of the Danube River. Even after the wedding, there was more waiting time for my mother to obtain a new passport and visa.

Vienna was divided into an American section and a Russian section. Luckily my family lived in the American section, and no-one was allowed without proper papers to enter the Russian zone. During one of his long walks, which Dad always enjoyed, he unknowingly strayed into Russian territory and of course did not have a correct entry visa. He was actually detained for a short time, but probably because of his pleasant and congenial manner, they released him to return to (relative) freedom.

The day finally arrived when Mama and Dad were ready to return home! Their flight home was quite an experience. There weren't any jet planes like today, which could fly at very high altitudes, so at certain times on the trip, they experienced strong turbulence, especially over the Austrian and Swiss Alps.

At one time, they flew right into a black thunderstorm, and Dad said later that he really wondered if they would make it. But soon the sky cleared and the sun shining on the snow-capped mountains below inspired Dad to write and compose a love song to my mother. It is called "Flying Over the Alps" and when they arrived home, he had it published for a keepsake Mama always treasured.

Our two little girls, very-pregnant Marilyn, and I, all anxiously awaited their arrival at Los Angeles International Airport. It was the ultimate height of excitement, especially for me to see my dear mother again, after not having seen her for fifteen years! Especially because those years were the ones when I matured from a young boy to almost a middle-aged man!

We were all exuberant, and so glad Mama and Dad were back on 'terra firma' in the good ol' U.S.A.! Mama spoke of the trip. Never having flown before, she loved how beautiful the clouds were with the sun's bright rays making bright colors on the tops of them! We had a nice car, a Cadillac sedan, in which we all fitted comfortably for the ride home.

After a short time of getting settled, Mama was rapidly learning English, especially from her two little granddaughters, because with them, she was not shy about trying words she 'thought' she knew. I had told her almost immediately that I wanted to only speak English, and she wanted to be able to talk with Marilyn, neighbors, clerks in stores, and everyone of course! Within only two weeks, she could actually converse in English! She was using some 'baby-talk', like 'eggs' were 'eggies', but of course, that came from learning from little Heidi and Becky!

It was a lovely summer, and our new baby was not due until the end of August, so we decided to take a trip and visit Marilyn's sister, Phyllis, and introduce her to her new stepmother, and to her 'new' step-sister and 'new' step-brother! What a jolly mix-up! Yes, by Marilyn's dad marrying my mother, we were not only husband and wife, we were also brother and sister! We loved the idea of this even closer relationship!

CHAPTER 9

An Introduction in Sonora

By this time, Marilyn's sister, Phyllis and her husband, Raleigh, had sold his moving-van business, and were living on a large beautiful property near the town of Sonora in the mountains above Yosemite Valley in Northern California. The area is on Sutter Creek, in picturesque "Forty-Niners' Gold Rush" country. Nearby is also the historic town of Columbia, which is a State park , and all of the old wooden buildings are beautifully preserved, including an authentic melodrama theater. Gold-panning is still done in Sutter Creek, and a real stagecoach and horses give children and adults a thrill-ride down the center of the main street during the summer season.

There are quaint souvenir and antique shops, a 'candy kitchen', a sandwich shop with a soda fountain serving 'Sarsaparilla', all along the old streets bordered by big shade trees. There is even a small museum with both 'gold-rush days' memorabilia and local Indian relics and artifacts.

Down the mountain a ways, is Jamestown. It's small and very attractive with most of the buildings light blue with white trim and lots of red brick-work. It's a fully functioning town, like Sonora, with shops, a grocery store, restaurants, a hotel, and even the local offices of the Sacramento Bee newspaper. It's main attraction is a pretty park with a very large white gazebo for band concerts and weddings.

There is even a beautiful antiquated train with a steam engine which takes tourists through the magnificent mountains and golden countryside. They offer a daytrip with luncheon served in the old (but updated) dining car, and during the trip they keep pointing out various historical points of interest.

～　　　～　　　～　　　～　　　～

Although we were anxious for Marilyn's sister to meet Mama, we decided that on the way there, we should drive through the magnificent Yosemite Valley State Park. We started early and by lunchtime were having a picnic on a bank of the crystal clear Merced River. Marilyn, Heidi and Becky went wading. There was a big rock in the water for the little girls to climb on, and kept busy taking home-movies of everyone.

There were rental cabins right in the middle of the Valley, with spectacular views of famous picture-perfect natural wonders like "Half-Dome" and "Bridal Veil Falls"! There were giant trees, and amazing sheer cliffs resting right on the Valley floor!

We obtained two cabins, one for Mama and Dad, and one for us and the girls. The girls loved the squirrels and birds who were so tame they seemed to be playing games with them! Yosemite Lodge, very large and rustic looking, was nearby, and we enjoyed our meals there. Spending the night in the cabins, however, seemed a little closer to nature, and nature in Yosemite is beautiful indeed!

As we settled in our cabins for the night, I thought I'd be a little adventuresome, and see what it was like out there after dark. I pulled on boots and a jacket, and as I ventured out, found the air crisp and fresh, and a full moon lighting up the Valley with a gentle subtle bluish glow. It was so quiet. Just an occasional gentle breeze whispering through the leaves of the great old trees.

Faintly, just a short distance away, I heard a different sort of rustling sound, and followed it until I began seeing small shadowy creatures moving around a neat row of rubbish cans by a small concrete facility building. I quietly moved closer and closer when suddenly I came upon four of the biggest raccoons I'd ever seen! These smart animals carefully removed the tight-fitting lids of the cans, and helped themselves to various morsels inside! They were so healthy-looking, and though big, they were so cute, I felt a great urge to pet them! They showed no sign of fear as I approached, nor did they show any aggression, so it was very hard for me not to reach out and try to stroke their little heads. Maybe they would not have minded if I had, but my better judgment won out, and after watching these amazing creatures for a few minutes, I retreated back to our cabin for a pleasant and good night's sleep.

We tried to see all the important sights of that amazing Valley, and in the afternoon, I found myself in a grassy meadow feeding some bread to a buck deer. He was young and not very big yet, but already had his "five-

These drawing depict typical old buildings of Sonora and Columbia California's gold rush days. Phyllis, Marilyn's sister who lives in Sonora, is a fine artist who did these charming drawing which are reprinted with her permission.

Egon and Marilyn's visit to Sonora with Mama and Dad, pictured on left, are Phyllis and Marilyn with their children left to right Becky, Heidi and Phyllis's children, Bruce, Susie and Dana. Phyllis later in life had another girl she named Margo Ann, all beautiful children.

Bridalvail Falls (Yosemite National Park in California) near Sonora appropriately depicted here in honer of the newly wedded couple.

point" antlers. As he ate the bread from my right hand, I tried to gently touch his neck with my left. He suddenly made a very slight downward movement with his head and one of his antlers just touched my arm. It hurt enough for me to pull my arm back quickly, and I realized that if he had put just a little more force behind the move, I would probably have had my arm in a cast for a few weeks!. So went our contact with the Animal Kingdom in Yosemite, and as we left the Valley, we felt a strong affection for all the natural beauty we had seen.

Phyllis and Raleigh joyously greeted us, and served us a nice lunch. Mama was very happy to meet her newfound daughter! With Mama's English still being limited, I translated much of that first conversation. Dad told all about his travels to Vienna, how he and 'Greta" immediately fell in love. He told about their very festive wedding with many friends and relatives providing good wishes and their Blessings! Phyllis showed much affection for Mama, and was exuberant that her father had found and was enjoying such a lovely and loving companion!

He and Mama told in detail of their trip home, and Mama said how happy she was to be here with her loved ones! She also said how excited she was to be starting a new life with her handsome, gentleman husband, 'Edward'. She already realized that life with Dad would always be interesting because of his kind ways and positive attitude!

I was glad we had gone to see Marilyn's sister so soon, because I wanted Mama to get to know everyone as soon as possible. Our happy union and lively conversation lasted well into the evening, and we spent a comfortable night in a charming hotel furnished with authentic antiques. Many movies are made in that area, and the stars always stay there.

We spent the next two days showing Mama all the interesting sights, even taking the luncheon train ride, and discovering that Mama absolutely loved 'traveling around' and seeing beautiful scenery and different places!

The morning we had to leave, we had breakfast with Phyllis and Raleigh, and left with a warm 'goodbye'!

Marilyn and I had lots of work waiting for us at home, and we had already settled down to a fairly regular routine. Mama had begun doing some cooking of her Viennese specialties that I had been missing for so many years, so I was ecstatic!

Our relationship with Mama was as congenial as it had been with Dad, and the house was more than large enough for all. Mama adored the children, and never minded if Marilyn and I both went out for a short while on some business project. This did not happen often, and Marilyn was usually home.

Marilyn loved to cook, but she loved our work more, and was happy having Mama begin making most dinners. Having both Mama and Dad made our lives more blissful than ever!

Another great event in our lives was when Marilyn gave birth to our third little girl, Karen. I thought that maybe this time it would be a boy, but I was not disappointed when I saw that beautiful, perfect little girl. Heidi and Becky were four and three, and adored their new baby sister.

Karen almost became 'Mama's baby'. Mama could not keep her hands off of her. She was constantly holding, rocking, singing to baby Karen, who seemed to grow into the happiest of babies because of it! I'm convinced a baby cannot be given too much attention!

Karen's sweet disposition reflected this upbringing! This is not to say that Marilyn and I neglected Karen. We were actually both at home most of the time, and always gave the girls our full attention. Whatever business, vocation, or interest I would pursue, I would never follow a career which necessitated my being away from my family.

This is one reason why I did not follow a singing career. I was told by several very famous people in the music business that I had a great tenor voice, and I was urged to enter this field and to let the public know of my special singing talent. However, I knew that to really learn music, especially serious opera, would mean giving full-time to studies. This would curtail necessary income for some time, and if ultimately successful, take me away even more from my cherished family.

The other possibility of course was that I might have started a singing career earlier in my life, and I might have been successful in that endeavor. However, I could not have been any happier than I was with my family, and being married to such a fabulous person as Marilyn.

At that time, my number-one consideration was to help bring up my children, and to be there when a father was needed. I always felt I would become successful in art, or in business of some kind.

I was out daily, contacting various businesses, and at one time had been achieving a fair amount of success. As I was driving, I noticed a house with a boat out in front. The boat had a "For Sale" on it, and was an open

For Egon his beautiful blond girls are
a gift from God and a treasure to
behold.

Egon's love - Marilyn, as always
radiantly beautiful and exuberant,
with a positive outlook on life.

sixteen-foot, with the shiniest mahogany front deck I had ever seen! It had a twenty-five horsepower Mercury outboard motor, and was sitting on a nice new trailer.

I rang the doorbell, and a middle-aged man said he had built it himself, and the mahogany decking had sixteen coats of varnish! The price seamed reasonable to me, so I bought the boat. He put a hitch on my car, hooked up the boat and trailer, and off I went!

I arrived home saying, "Well, dear, I didn't get any new business today, but I bought a boat!" Marilyn was not too enthusiastic, but admitted the boat was certainly beautiful. Dad, on the other hand, was immediately excited! He was an ardent fisherman, always ready to 'hook one on', and said, "Let's go fishing right away!" It was still early, about two in the afternoon, and Dad had heard there was good fishing off Newport Harbor, and launching ramps were convenient there. True to her agreeable nature, Marilyn said, "Have a good time!", and gave us her Blessings.

The weather was fine, the boat launched easily, and the motor purred like a healthy kitten. Dad was readying his fishing gear as we faced the length of Newport Harbor to get to the open sea. We wanted to see how the boat would handle out in the ocean, and we had visions of catching 'a big one'! To get there quickly, I gave it full-throttle and the boat was racing along when we saw people in other boats and along the shore, shouting and waving their arms!

Neither Dad nor I knew that there was a five-mile-per-hour speed limit in the Harbor, but were soon sternly educated when another boat pulled alongside and we were told the rules of running a boat in any port. We were a little embarrassed, but slowed to the required speed, and soon were in sight of the open sea.

I had never run a boat in the open ocean before, and was completely unprepared for what we were about to encounter! Dad, however, had been on many ocean fishing excursions, so he was not at all worried. His main concern was to bring home a big fish! As we passed the final breakwater of the Harbor entrance, the sea ahead looked flat, but suddenly we were in the middle of ten-foot swells!

The boat was lifted high like on a roller-coaster, then pushed fast down, only to be caught by another swell and thrown sideways! As I desperately tried to control, the boat, I glanced at Dad, who was calmly taking it all 'in stride', and working away with his fishing line! I somehow managed to keep turning the boat back toward the Harbor, until at last we felt smooth water beneath us!

"I'm sorry, Dad," I said, "but I don't think this boat is made for the ocean! I think we'll have to stick with rivers and lakes." Dad agreed, and we made it back quite a bit wiser, but still glad to know how well the little boat operated in the water.

I do recall one other very nice day with that boat. We knew a family with two children, a year or two older than Heidi and Becky, who lived near Newport Beach. Mama and Dad kept baby Karen for the day, and we met our friends at Newport's Back Bay. In those days, one could water ski there, or simply run a small boat fast in the water for fun! We had a very enjoyable day.

CHAPTER 10

We Found a New Dimension

One of our considerable number of advertising accounts was a toy manufacturer for whom I had been designing and printing boxes. When I was seeing them one day, they asked me if I had access to a sculptor, as the man who had been doing their little plastic toys had become ill. Of course, I said that we had a very good commercial sculptor, and had them show me the kind of clay that should be used for making their production molds.

I had never tried sculpturing before, but stopped by a large art supply store, bought the right kind of modeling clay, and was also given a few tips about making figures that could release from a mold, with no 'hooks' to lock them in. The first assignment was a bendable plastic clown about eight inches high. Somehow, I knew I could sculpt. My fingers soon produced a very cute clown, skinny enough to be bendable, but with ruffs at his neck, hands, and feet, and a really happy-looking, smiling clown-face. Somewhat anxiously, I took the clown in to the client.

To my surprise, they raved about it, and insisted that I keep using the same sculptor for all their new products! I was now working most days, and into the nights to take care of all the various advertising obligations.

One of the partners of the plastic toy company had another business which involved three-dimensional photography. Such photographs were being made popular at that time by a company in Portland, Oregon, called ViewMaster. They produced a 'viewer' into which one slipped a 'disk' of pictures, which viewed as three-dimensional. They sold scenics in souvenir shops, and children's stories in toy stores and book stores, and enjoyed massive distribution. Their viewer was very high quality and quite costly.

My client manufactured a low-priced little viewer, packaged in a box with a set of '3-D' slides. He was selling scenics in souvenir shops, and one day he asked me if my sculptor could make some children's stories, so he could sell to toy stores.

The idea intrigued me, but I realized that to select a story, sculpture small figures, set-up little scenes illustrating the story, set-up lighting, and do three-dimensional photography of high commercial quality, we were talking major time-consuming effort. Marilyn and I discussed the idea that there could be a need for this kind of business, so we developed a plan and even wrote a contract agreement to present to the plastic-viewer company owner.

I set-up a meeting, and presented him with my ideas. At this point, I had to tell him I was the sculptor who had been doing the toys for his other company. At first he appeared quite surprised, but then he smiled and seemed to be happy it was me, because our other dealings had been very cordial.

I told him that I would really like to create three-dimensional children's stories for him, but that such an endeavor would be a major undertaking, and I explained some of the procedures. I also stated and that it would have to be an almost full-time venture, and that I could only do it under certain conditions outlined in an agreement we had written, and which I then presented.

He had been very satisfied with my ability as a sculptor, and I told him that my wife was an artist who would work with me, and that she was also a commercial photographer, so she would be able to do the three-dimensional photography, of the highest professional quality.

The agreement stated that I would produce the children's stories and furnish three dimensional color transparencies for reproduction, to sell in conjunction with his present viewer in a box packaging. I would retain copyrights to the pictures, and besides a fairly substantial retainer, I asked for ten-percent of all gross sales. Further, I would retain the right to market the stories under a different product configuration from his.

While this would have to be almost full-time, I assured him I would still be able to do the packaging designs, and toy-sculptures for his other company, and I returned home from that very first meeting with signed-contract in hand!

Marilyn and I decided that our first story would be "Cinderella", and we set-up a workshop in a room with a built-in bar and a large corner 'booth'. The table-top was 'formica', so clay and paints would easily wash-off. We also had a very large basement storage-room where we built the Cinderella castle, so our large home kept proving to be ideal for us! We found several reference-books, and began designing, and planning to make seven scenes for each story. They would be inch-to-a-foot scale which is standard miniature doll-house size. We thought we could buy some items, but the only things we ever bought were some tiny pottery bowls and a pitcher, at Olvera Street in downtown Los Angeles. Somehow, we made every diminutive item in every story!.

Little Heidi and Becky would sometimes watch, fascinated for hours, and Mama even 'got into the act' when we were making The Three Bears. I had designed and built from 'Balsa Wood' a very cute two-story woodsy house, a little bigger than for people, because it was for bears of course! Marilyn helped glue the hundreds of roof-shingles, and she added green shutters at each window. Marilyn then made all of the furniture, and when she had finished the beds, and painted the headboards with hearts and country flowers, Mama said they looked European, and should have the appropriate kinds of pillows and comforters! She had already been using Marilyn's sewing machine, so they went out and found very small checks and prints in cotton fabrics, and tiny 'seed' beads for 'buttons' on the wee pillow-cases. What fun we all had!

Marilyn had immediately suggested making the people out of wire pipe-cleaners, so we could bend the same figures into different positions for the various scenes. I liked the idea because then I only basically had to sculpt the heads, hands and feet. Marilyn assembled the bodies, and made the clothes. Everyone seeing our first finished films remarked that the figures looked so real, much more so than if the people had been done like figurines.

The filming became somewhat interesting. We first purchased a very fine '3-D' camera, but immediately found it did not work for the close-ups. We kept the camera for shots at a distance of six feet, but had to purchase and learn to use a 'rack', with a good thirty-five-millimeter camera. Marilyn had always worked with large-format films, four-by-five or larger, but was glad to work with 'thirty-five', and had learned about it in her schooling of course. The '3-D Rack' had numbers on it, and there was a formula-guide for how close you were to your subject. It was a challenge, but the results were absolutely perfect slides. deeply three-dimensional!

We both went to present the first set of films to my 'associate'. He seemed astonished to discover what we had produced, and ran all over the building showing them to everybody there, saying, "Look what these kids have done!" Everyone seemed very impressed and shook our hands saying "Congratulations!" We were delighted at their response, and outlined several of the next stories we had planned, The Three Bears, Hansel and Gretel, a space story which we were writing, and The Birth of Christ for Christmas.

When those were finished, we all agreed to begin marketing them. I had all of our films copyrighted, and fortunately had even kept working with several advertising accounts, when quite suddenly, our plastics company associate passed away. He had not accomplished any distribution for his 'viewer' product, and I was convinced that there could be a better product design.

Of course, I also thought of Viewmaster. With them in mind, somehow I began thinking how great it would be if the Viewmaster 'plastic-viewers' could 'talk', and tell a child the story while they watched it! In those days, it was long before small tape recorders and CDs, and we still depended on "78-RPM" records to listen to music.

I found a design engineer, and we developed a small Bakelite record the size of the Viewmaster film disk, and a viewer with a second opening on the side, similar to the one for the film. The most difficult part of the project was getting a small needle to play the record over a small speaker. With some experimentation, however, we were able to use a tiny cone attached to a small round cardboard box, which actually produced a good speaking-voice sound. We were even able to devise a system whereby when the little record was inserted, it would always stay in synchronization with the picture being viewed.

We contracted with a record company to produce the little three-inch-diameter records. Marilyn wrote the scripts and recorded the stories for them. I had a plastics company make a good-looking working model. It was fun to see how this little 'Sound Viewer' (as we called it) worked!

As soon as I had the finished model in my hands, I made a call to the President and CEO of Viewmaster. He seemed enthusiastically interested, even telling me that their design department had been working for two years trying to develop something similar, but had been unsuccessful.

We arranged a meeting in his offices in a town just southwest of Portland, Oregon, called Beaverton. The meeting was in about a week, so Marilyn and I drove up, enjoying a mini-vacation. We took two days to drive the thousand miles, and the next morning were cordially greeted at the

Viewmaster offices.

There were several executives at our meeting, and they all seemed most impressed with my 'Talking Viewer'. They agreed to a twenty-cent per unit royalty, however, they wanted a year to evaluate both the product and it's marketing, for which they offered us $3,000.00. Because Viewmaster was already established as the largest National distributor in the field, I happily accepted their offer.

Because we were to return the next day, to finalize everything, we drove around the countryside, and both agreed we had never seen more breath-takingly beautiful scenery! It was early spring, and everything was so green! Suddenly we saw a new house, set in amongst big, lush pine trees, with a "For Sale" sign posted. We stopped, and a realtor was there who showed us though the well-built, one story, four bedroom, very attractive home with a large view window looking out over hills and a valley. Part of the property, in back of the house was a one-acre pine forest looking like it had come out of one of our fairy tales! The price for the whole thing was about one-fourth that of our home in the Wilshire district!

Marilyn and I were overcome with the beauty of the whole area, and began seriously saying that Portland might be a nice place to raise a family. Of course, there were many things to consider, so after meeting and settling everything with Viewmaster the next morning, we drove the twenty miles into downtown Portland. We were amazed to find some of the largest international advertising agencies, like (then) "Cole & Weber". Stopping in there and another big one, we were immediately assured of assignments in art and copywriting, or even a full-time position for me, and steady part-time for Marilyn which was all she wanted while the girls were small.

I felt like I was back in Montreal where there was a real need for good advertising talent. Later we realized that the Portland area had many major manufacturers with world-wide distribution, such as Hyster road-building equipment, and others equally impressive. As before in our lives, everything seemed to just 'fall into place'! We drove back to Beaverton, and put a deposit on the house in the pine forest.

Of course we loved the Wilshire District house, but it would have been years before we would really own it under my purchase contract. We had enjoyed the three or four years we lived there, and certainly made good use of it as office and home.

Mama and Dad also seemed excited over moving! Maybe our enthusiasm over it was 'catching', but as we packed, and the movers picked up the furniture, we all seemed to have a exhilaratingly happy attitude. Dad and I both had separate good-running cars, and we leisurely caravaned to Portland. I pulled my little custom gem of a boat behind me. Karen was six months old, and she and Heidi and Becky got lots of attention, and enjoyed the trip.

Our belongings arrived about the same time as we did, and we were soon snugly settled in our pretty house in the forest. Marilyn and Dad had some very nice pieces of furniture her mother had selected, including a high marble-top end-table with cameo-like carvings. Onc day we had seen, in a shop window, a white bisque figurine made into a lamp, and although it was costly to us at the time, we both agreed we 'had to have it'! So that table and lamp fit perfectly in the middle of the big picture window where the builder had already put white muslin Priscilla curtains. We were soon known throughout the neighborhood, in fact the whole valley below us, as 'the house with the beautiful lamp in the window'.

The entire property was fenced, so we allowed Heidi and Becky to go outside by themselves, but they called our back acre "The Hansel and Gretel" forest, and kept asking their "Daddy" or "Grandpa" to go into it with them.

The first event in our new home was Easter, and the forest was inspiring for an "Easter Egg Hunt". For days, we kept baskets, bunnies, and pull-toys hidden in a couple of big boxes in the back seat of Dad's car, and had the most elaborate Easter morning ever for those three little girls! We did not hide anything too deeply into the forest, so they were not afraid, and easily found everything! They all seem to still remember the atmosphere of that 'Easter Hunt' in that 'real' forest!

Dad was gloriously happy with enough land for a garden. He had more than just a 'green thumb', he was actually a very knowledgeable horticulturist, and never tired of spending early mornings and evenings creating 'picture gardens' of both edibles and flowers! He and Mama both seemed very happy, with pleasant dispositions, and it was glorious country for Sunday drives which they both loved!

Dad also found the Portland area culturally sophisticated in having symphony orchestras, school orchestras, and almost all children taking piano lessons. He was again immediately successful in his own musical instruments and pianos business, buying, selling, and repairing.

Marilyn and I met with the owner of an advertising agency in Portland, whom we had spoken to on our first visit, and he was glad to hire us both. On the mornings when Marilyn worked, we drove in together and left the car in a downtown parking-structure out of the rain. It was about three or four blocks away from the agency, and there was a grassy park with trees, gazebos, and a paved path down the middle of the street where we walked. Raining or not, the sun was usually shining, and the leaves of the trees sparkled with tiny water-drop-diamonds. It was amazingly beautiful, and we found ourselves settling down into a comfortable and tranquil routine which seemed a welcome change from the, although enjoyable, daily hustle of our business in Los Angeles.

The scenery in Oregon is superb, with profuse pine forests everywhere, and the majestic snow-covered peak of Mt. Hood always in sight. Two beautiful rivers merge in Portland, the great Colombia, and the gorgeous Willamette! Going inland along the Willamette, there are many pretty smaller tributaries emptying into it.

One warm afternoon shortly after we had moved there, Marilyn and I drove on a road along the edge of one of these small rivers. We soon came upon a place where the river widened, saw several small boats, and a sign, "Rowboats for Rent". Again, it was so beautiful! The trees were luxuriant and rocks along the edges of the small river created a splashing sound as the water rushed over and around them.

To <u>not</u> stop and rent one of those little rowboats was totally out of the question! A friendly, elderly gentleman helped us put the boat in the water. Marilyn sat facing me, on a seat across the stern, and I sat on a seat near the middle of the boat, with the oars in my hands, and my back to the bow. I had rowed a couple of times in Canada, and felt comfortable and even elated. This was fun!

The river at this point was smooth and shallow, really just a large creek. As we glided along, I sang a few words of a song to Marilyn,

> "He would row, row, row
> Way up the river he would row, row, row,
> A hug he'd give her,
> And he'd kiss her now and then,
> She would tell him when,
> And he would row . . . "

. . . when suddenly my singing was interrupted! Out of the corner of my eye, I had seen something big splash above the river! I wasn't sure what it was, and I told Marilyn to look behind her, and I said we had better get out of here because I thought I had just seen an alligator jump out of the water! As I made that ridiculous remark, I began seeing splash after splash, and remembered we were in Salmon country!

I had forgot about Salmon swimming up those tributaries to spawn! . It was quite a sight, and an exciting experience to be out among those radiantly beautiful and of course harmless Salmon.

As we returned the boat, I told the man about our experience. He seemed surprised we did not know that we were right on the way to a Salmon hatchery. He said it was an interesting place and that we should drive up and see it. Well, he did not have to twist my arm! A very short distance on up the road, and we were at the entrance to the Salmon hatchery. It was a weekday, and there were no other visitors, so a nice operative led us to where we could look down into several huge cement 'tubs'. Each held hundreds, maybe thousands of different sized Salmon. The last tub contained the largest, which were about to be released to make their way downstream to the ocean. They would return several years later, each to the place where it was hatched, in order to spawn. We of course had previous knowledge of all this, but the hatchery was interesting to see. They had pictures of record-size Salmon being caught at the mouth of the Columbia River.

Both rivers were convenient to our new house, but the summer season for boating was shorter than we were used to in Southern California. That first year, we actually had an early spring, so on one of the first 'warm-ish' days, we took our little open boat with the outboard motor, and launched it in the Willamette. We had left Karen with Mama and Dad, but brought Heidi and Becky, all of us wearing life-jackets of course.

We all fit comfortably in the actually quite luxurious little boat, and because there was no speed limit on the river, enjoyed an afternoon of fast, fun rides! We even stopped in a shallow little cove where the girls enjoyed wading while we fixed a lunch. It was an enjoyable day until heading back, the water became a little choppy, and we all got splashed a bit.

Still, we definitely enjoyed boating, so when driving home we began seeing boat-sales places, we stopped at one. It was called Reinell, and even though it was only eighteen-feet, it had a little cabin for protection from water splash. In the lowest-priced model, the cabin was bare, but the salesman suggested that people put-down the better, thick patio furniture pads so the children could take a nap. Even though it was only a couple of feet longer than our little 'speedboat', it had twice the room inside! With some deck chairs, we could even take Mama and Dad along, so it looked like we would have a much more practical boat! I don't remember the financial arrangements, but I know we arrived home that night with our new Reinell in tow!

Marilyn and I loved our work at the advertising agency, and Mama adored Karen, and Heidi and Becky too. She took care of them on the days Marilyn worked with me in Portland. Reading stories to them helped her in reading English, and she would make Austrian dinners, so our children grew up with both her cooking and Marilyn's mostly American-style.

We were certainly fortunate to have such wonderful, loving parents with us, giving us the peace of mind to fully enjoy our creative work. I still had in my possession all of the color transparencies of the three-dimensional children's stories. Viewmaster could not use them because they already had the same stories, and had staff artists producing theirs at a very low cost. However, one day, I met someone from "The Oregonian", Portland's largest newspaper. He took a couple of the little boxed sets with the plastic viewer and slides in to the paper with him, and they were very impressed. They sent a reporter and photographer to our home for an interview, and to our surprise a scene from our "Three Bears" story was the full-color cover-picture of their next Sunday's magazine section. The story inside was a biography and more color pictures of us 'working' on the props. We became 'instant celebrities in Portland, and to this day we treasure a framed copy of that magazine story! It hangs in our home-office.

I was invited to join the Art Directors Club of Portland, and we enjoyed many of their social events. Portland had a gorgeous opera house showing very fine European productions, and also a magnificent art museum. A famous private collection of sculptured pieces was being sent throughout the Country. At the end of it's tour, it was to become an endowment, one piece to each museum visited. The directors traveling with the exhibit were so impressed with Portland's cultural enlightenment that they selected two fine pieces of sculpture to be returned permanently to Porland's art museum. Marilyn and I   both felt we had found a wonderful place to live, and life was great!

Each weekend, weather permitting, we would take our new boat onto the Willamette River for a little cruise. But with the first really warm, sunny Sunday of summer, came the time to brave the big Columbia! It was already quite a wide river in Portland, being relatively close to it's mouth at the ocean. Boarding our Reinell felt quite secure, with the deeper hull and little cabin, and it was such a nice sunny day. I felt I was using caution by not going up or down the river, and just cruised around a bit, over to the opposite shore. There were small waves which were fun to skim over.

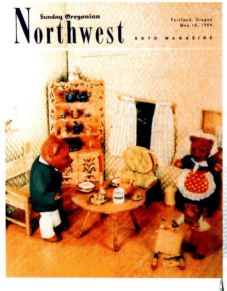

Our publication articles and pictures as it appeared in Portland's major newspaper "The Oregonian".

Egon and Marilyn made many new friends through this exposure and Egon was sought after as a noted artist receiving many accolades and business.

Because it was our first trip on the big river, I thought it wise not to linger too long. Being across the river, we started cruising back to where we launched and parked the car, when suddenly the small waves became large ones, and the wind battered our now seemingly very small boat!

I never knew a river could churn up such large waves, but we were probably not encountering the worst the river had to offer! Slowly, with the waves crashing over our little cabin, we finally arrived at our launchsite, drenched, but thankful we did not capsize! I had already decided midstream, that if we made it across in one piece, we had to get a bigger boat!

I guess, when you are young, you don't give up, you just fight harder! Our next boat was a twenty-one-foot Trojan with a much deeper hull, and two thirty-five-horsepower motors, enough power to move it along at a good clip. It had a real cabin with a tightly-closing door to keep it dry inside, two narrow bunks, a built-in eating area, small galley, and even an enclosed head. There were steering wheels both inside the cabin, and outside on the ample afterdeck. Really a mini yacht!

By this time, we had found that a 'sunny day' in Oregon meant sunny in the morning, but you could bet that there would be a shower or two before the afternoon was over, and I'm talking all year 'round. Hence the watertight cabin on our little 'yacht' and we were now ready to go anytime it was not storming!

So the very next sunny bright weekend morning, we proudly boarded our 'yacht', filled it with gas, and began a trip up the Columbia River to a place called the Dalles. We knew that on the way we would be going through three 'locks' which raise boats to another part of the river, over one-hundred feet higher. They were mostly used by commercial-transport boats during the week, so we found on a Sunday that we were the only boat going through. As we entered the first lock with huge heavy steel 'gates' in front, and the ones behind us closing, we suddenly felt infinitesimally small!

Then what an ominous sight and feeling ensued as water rushed into the lock with great force, lifting our boat until it seemed level with the top of the great gray gate in front of us. As it opened, we cruised forward into the next lock. Going through those locks, especially with a small boat, is an awesome experience, certainly worth doing once in a lifetime!

After returning down the locks, the trip was beautiful and uneventful. except for one eye-opening revelation! We had had to stop for gasoline several times, and the cost of the amount of gas we used in those two outboard motors was shocking! A few trips and we could have bought another boat!

Though inquiries, we were told that an inboard motor had very little gasoline cost in comparison. I guess this is what is called 'learning by experience', or 'learning the hard way'!

Needless to say, we did not take many long trips with that boat, because it was like a money-eating machine! For the next few weeks that summer, we only used it on the Willamette, going to nearby beaches for wading and picnics. But we were in love with the enjoyment of boating, and the rivers were a natural attraction!

So then one day, noticing an ad in the paper, I thought, "This is it!" The ad described a twenty-four foot Chris-Craft (an absolutely top make) for sale with a boat house on the Columbia River! It went on to list 'all the comforts of home' - main salon and galley, head with shower, a stateroom (bedroom) and an inboard motor (low gasoline cost!). I had never thought about a boat house! What a bonus! No more trailer and launching, and the boat would be protected from the elements when not in use! We could even store things like extra life jackets for guests. The possibilities seemed endless, and the real miracle was that the asking price was absolutely feasible!

We made an appointment to look at the boat, and tried not to show how excited we were over what we saw. The boat house was aluminum with several side windows, electricity, good lighting inside and out, and looked brand new, which since it wasn't, meant almost no maintenance! There were already large storage chests with padlocks, for storing things. A cabinet had shelves with varnish, brushes and such paraphernalia which the seller was just leaving for the buyer. There was a wooden deck, the exact shape of the boat, and extending all the way along both sides. All you had to do when returning from a cruise, was to point the bow in, secure one line, jump out onto the deck, lock a security gadget, get in your car and drive home! If you have ever gone through launching procedures, you know the joy we were feeling!

The boat itself looked like a gem, the same 'feeling' as our first little custom craft! Beautiful varnished wood throughout, and while not new, had been cared for to perfection! On a test run, the motor purred smoothly, and even the bilge looked new-boat clean. What a find! Actually, our Trojan was a very nice looking little boat, and we were able to sell it right away, so all worked out well.

We spent many pleasant hours and days with that wonderful Chris-Craft! Many times Marilyn and I purposely went out when it was even raining quite heavily, because we were snug and warm in that boat and boat house!

Although it may have sounded like it here for awhile, boating was far from our main concern. Our attentions were primarily on furthering our careers and financial status.

At a costume party given by The Art Director's Club Egon had joined, we went as an Arabian Sheik and his Harem girl. I used a black makeup eyebrow pencil to draw a moustache and small beard, and we looked-up turbans in the encyclopedia. Marilyn wore a gold-satin formal dress with a long sheer veil over her head, but not her face. She had 'glued' a red ruby on her forehead and we were standing around enjoying lively conversations, with Ginger Ale in our champagne glasses, when we were introduced to an account executive from Cole and Weber, the really large agency in Portland. The next morning in the Oregonian, our picture appeared as part of the write-up about the Art Director's Club event.

A day or two later, I received a telephone call from the Cole and Weber executive we had met, who said something like, "Now I remember who you two are! You had that Sunday Magazine write-up about sculpturing and writing children's stories. I'd like to meet with you both about some of my accounts."

He lived in Lake Oswego, the most exclusive community near Portland, and he invited us to his home, saying his wife wanted to meet us because she had been a school teacher and had enjoyed reading the magazine article about the two of us. She and Marilyn almost immediately became great friends!

After he saw my complete portfolio, and I also showed him that Marilyn had done some pretty impressive industrial writing for our own accounts in Los Angeles, he arranged to hire me at Cole and Weber full-time, and offered Marilyn the same, but she only wanted to work three days a week, all of which worked out very agreeably. When we figured out everything, our income about doubled at that meeting!

We gave notice to the owner of the agency where we had been working, and I promised to do freelance artwork for him if he ever got into a bind. He was a very nice person, and we parted in good friendship.

Marilyn particularly enjoyed this large agency. She became so proficient with the engineer's specification sheets for one International account that when the client came into the agency, they warned Marilyn to 'hide' in the copy-writing offices because they did not want the client to know that it was not a <u>man</u> doing the 'new' writing the client was so impressed with. It

At an art directors costume party in Portland Oregon Circa 1954 there was a romantic association to the concept of an Arab Sheik, emphasized previously by the much publicized marriage of actress Rita Hayworth to Sheik Ali Khan.

Here Egon definitely meats the criteria of an ultimate romantic Sheik, trying to impress a beautiful lady, Marilyn.

was the first time that client had ever been satisfied with the technical copy on certain types of new mechanical products.

Marilyn used to say to me that it's all just logic. You look at the last catalog ad on the product, then scan the 'engineer's spec-sheets' for anything that seemed <u>different</u> than before. To her, it was that simple, but I even remembered some of our L.A. accounts that were almost shocked that she had 'found' their important new feature, when far more experienced advertising writers seemed to 'miss the point'. My high quality artwork was also greatly appreciated.

CHAPTER 11

There's No Reason Why the Farmer and the Cowman Can't be Friends

As another year rolled by, Marilyn and I drove through much of the local countryside. One such excursion took us to a beautiful farming area, just twenty-five miles southwest of Portland. We discovered a quaint little town called Scholls, where there was a real old-fashioned 'General Store' which included a grocery. The town was surrounded by miles of farms, walnut orchards, and dairies with green pastures and healthy, happy-looking cows!

We came upon a pretty-looking farmhouse displaying a "For Sale by Owner" sign. It was a picturesque barn-red with white trim, and there was a small barn freshly painted the same. We could not resist stopping and looking!

The owners, a friendly young couple, showed us around. The house was a two story with three bedrooms. As we entered, we saw a good sized livingroom to the left. The diningoom to the right had a large picture window looking out at a big old Oak tree with a child's swing hanging from it, and the pretty farm country beyond. Upstairs, the charming bedrooms had partly-slanted ceilings giving them a storybook quality! The well built barn was usable for storage, and had stalls for farm animals.

The owners had a little girl, and had fenced the entire perimeter of the property, which consisted of five acres of beautiful big walnut trees. There were also five Black Bing Cherry trees, an enormous Bartlett Pear, some sweet purple "prune-plums", and a giant grafted apple tree, bearing bushels-full of five different kinds of apples! What a little "Treasure Farm" we had found! And the most amazing thing (to us) was the whole place was selling for about one-third the value of the house we were in!

We of course had no idea what living on a 'farm' involved, but I had heard the term 'gentleman farmer' and we thought we could operate the place on that basis, being so close to the sophisticated City of Portland. In fact, a suburb of Portland, called Cedar Hills, actually <u>adjoined</u> The Scholls area.

When Mama and Dad saw the house, we all agreed it was a little small for all of us, and Mama was definitely enthusiastic over buying a pretty three bedroom, two bath, new house in Cedar Hills of their own. It was large enough for them to occasionally have the grandchildren for the night, and Mama liked 'modern' furniture, so we kept Marilyn's 'antiques' which were perfect for the 'farm'. The pretty house in the forest sold quickly at a nice profit, and we bought the farm, and also the house for Mama and Dad.

In our farmhouse, there was a large downstairs 'playroom', and the girls said that their bedroom upstairs, with it's angled ceilings, looked like Wendy's bedroom in their "Peter Pan" book, and they loved it!

Marilyn made the large upstairs bedroom into a 'picture out of a magazine'! First she found a 'Jenny Lind' headboard, and used a charming heirloom quilt as a bedspread. The quilt had a different bird, hand-embroidered in every 'square', and a wide yellow border. It had been all handmade by her Aunt Armgarde and a church 'Quilting Bee'.

Marilyn then set a dressing table into a gable-window alcove, and added a ruffled skirt made from a white petticoat, lavishly hand-embroidered at a very young age by her mother. Some framed botanical prints on the walls finished the feeling of 'Country', but with a 'decorator' flair!

Mama and Dad bought all new furniture that Mama selected, and they got nicely settled. Their house had large lawns, front and back, which Mama loved! She was happy to have Dad plant flowers around the edges, and even a small, cut-flower garden in back, but that was it!

So he was soon out at our five acres every morning, planting long rows of corn and all kinds of vegetables. Now I wanted the kids to learn about farm animals and I actually got a little 'carried-away' trying to acquire at least a pair of each. I forgot we were not Noah's Ark!

We bought small flocks of ducks and geese, and I think two dozen baby chicks. We found a fine large pair of rabbits, a pair of goats, a baby lamb, and a calf that still had to be fed milk from a large bucket that somewhat resembled a baby-bottle. Also a very gentle riding horse named Patch. He was a big brown horse with a white mark on his forehead, and the family we got him from had several children, and had taught him to lie down with his legs tucked under him so kids could climb onto his back. He would then

"CLOSE TO NATURE"
About 25 miles southwest of Portland Oregon, Egon found a farm with this darling little farmhouse, a bit of "Heaven on Earth".

Gentleman farmer, Egon, worked as an artist in Portland. The farm provided a new experience and relaxation.

For education and fun we bought and raised almost every kind of farm animal

... including a most gentle horse named "Patch".

"FARM FUN"
Marilyn used eggs from our chickens, ducks and geese to create our family for an Easter decoration.

Patch would lie down and let the kids climb on his back, then he would gently rise up and take them for a ride.

From left: Becky, Egon Sr., Karen, Marilyn, Egon Jr. and Heidi slowly rise, and leisurely walk around taking the kids for a ride! He was so amazing, the way he seemed to fully understand what he was doing!

All of the animals were incredible! One white duck that Heidi named "Movie Star", was friendly and followed the girls around outside. They would carry a baby rabbit in a small box, let it out on the front lawn and play with it for hours. I recall one amusing incident when a pair of our big grey geese were proudly marching along followed by their little goslings. I tried to come up behind them, but as I got a little too close, the gander turned around and with wings spread, and head and neck stretched forward, attacked me!

I stood my ground to see what he was going to do. I soon found out as he pecked right at me, as high as my waist. It didn't hurt of course, but I found it comical and actually was proud of that protective gander! So I pretended to be scared and backed off, walking away slowly as I saw him, ever so proudly, prancing on his way with his family.

We were completely inexperienced 'farmers' but enjoyed the whole thing immensely, especially because we were not depending on income from it. Dad was enjoying planting his garden with almost every kind of vegetable nature had invented, and we enjoyed bountiful meals from it. But somehow his garden grew and grew and grew! One morning I saw he was digging in the animal area almost to the little barn where chickens and ducks were nesting on their eggs and the baby calf was in a stall.

"Dad," I shouted, "No! No! We have to separate the 'farming' area from the animal area! The animals need enough room to feel free!"

Dad agreed of course, and I immediately began building a nice looking wire fence separating the areas. Dad was happy. He just changed crops from time to time when space became sparse. So it seems in our case, the 'farmer' (Dad) and the 'cowman' (me) definitely remained friends! In fact, Marilyn just mentioned reading about making low-salt dill pickles, and the next thing we knew Dad brought in from his garden, baskets full of small green gherkin cucumbers and armloads of fresh dill!

Our General Store had given Marilyn a pamphlet about freezer-storage being easier than canning, because they rented freezer lockers. The first thing that got us 'hooked' on doing it was those scrumptiously sweet black-red cherries filling five whole trees all at once! The store also sold throw-away paper cartons to put things in, and the locker rental was next to nothing!

All the next winter, I would stop by the locker on my way home, and many nights we had cherries with whipped cream for dessert! We bought our milk at a nearby dairy, and with the extra cream, made all our own butter and had all the whipped cream we could use. Marilyn invented a quick way to make the butter with a Mixmaster, and she served it in pretty little glass dishes with lids.

She also read books and books on the care of the animals, and it took her a full two hours every morning, but she loved the animals too, and kept them super clean and well-fed. There were cats with kittens already there when we bought the place. They were not pets, but ran wild to keep down vermin, and we were told not to feed them. However, there was a sheltered place where Marilyn left a large panful of the best dry cat food, and a bowl which she filled with milk three or four times a day. When our chickens grew big enough, we gave them 'the run of the place', and they soon discovered the catfood and the milk which they seemed to like better than their own food.

When the chickens were six months old, we kept the hens for laying, and I think three or four roosters, but then I took the rest of the roosters to 'the rendering house'. When I took them in, they weighed them and said they had never seen six-month-old fryers that big! I think they each weighed seven or eight pounds!

We had already been enjoying fried rabbit dinners, breeding the rabbits every four months. When the bunnies were three months old, they got quite wild, so the girls did not mind when one morning they had disappeared, especially when they were told that there would be new little bunnies to play with soon! When I would pick them up on my way home from work, the packages looked just like I had bought them at a supermarket, and I would stop and put them in our freezer locker at the 'General Store'.

Then there were the walnut trees! Our five acre place was probably the smallest but we were on 'the list' of growers, so in the spring, a man with a tractor came by to plant a cover crop of rye and wheat, then later to disc it into the ground around the trees. This served as fertilizer for the walnut trees, and of course, God supplied plenty of rain for the trees to absorb all these good nutrients. Then in the fall when the trees shed their bounty, along came a group of transient 'pickers' with their own big burlap sacks for gathering the walnuts from under the trees.

We had heard rumors that some transient workers could not be trusted, and we were fairly well isolated on our little farm. Although fields of crops surrounded us, the nearest house was about two miles away, and with our little girls running around, we bought a small but effective firearm called a

'38-Special'. Marilyn wore a heavy denim jacket with big patch pockets which hid the gun, and she even took lessons in shooting it.

I also got a shotgun, and a '22-Rifle' with a 'Scope', but am very glad to say we never found the need to use any of the weapons. One day, however, a neighbor who had twenty acres in walnuts adjacent to our property, came over and asked me if I would mind taking my rifle and shooting some of the squirrels that were 'helping themselves' to the walnuts.

I said, "OK", and the next morning was a Saturday, so I took my rifle and didn't have long to search. There were several squirrels having breakfast at the nearest tree to the house! I aimed, and had a cute little squirrel centered in my scope, but it was impossible to pull the trigger!

As I lowered the gun, I thought that it seemed like there were enough walnuts to share a few with the squirrels, and I went back into the house to enjoy my own breakfast.

Now to continue the story of harvesting the walnuts. Each day, the pickers filled a large open truck which we had rented, and which had to be driven by six o'clock to the 'co-op' warehouse on 'the other side of the mountain'!

Dad offered to drive, but we planned that he would bring Mama to the farm every morning before he left for work, because if he could not get back in time, Marilyn would become the 'delivery gal'! This way, Mama would be there to stay with the children if Marilyn had to drive, and anyway, the whole walnut picking time was only for two weeks.

The rental trucks had no cab doors, so the driver could quickly 'exit' if the truck started to roll over the side of the mountain! The road was usually muddy from rain, so Marilyn would slip and slide, trying to stay in the deep ruts made by other trucks. I was working in Portland and was not fully aware of the 'fun' my poor but wonderful wife was having, delivering those pesky walnuts! I was gratified that both Marilyn and Dad came through all trips unscathed!

Unfortunately, the little money profit from such a small walnut crop was not enough to put honey in your tea! Even considering the small government subsidy check we received later on, and all the 'fun' experiences (!), we decided to ignore our 'orchard' from a commercial standpoint. Of course we would have all the walnuts we could eat, and Mama had a walnut cake recipe that became 'legend' in our family!

When we needed a second car for Marilyn to drive, we bought a real "Woody Wagon", completing the 'picture-farm' look! On some days Marilyn drove Heidi and Becky to school, then dropped Karen at Mama's house, and drove into Portland to pickup copywriting jobs from the same account executive at Cole and Weber. He was always glad to get her writing when she had time, and she wrote two large flower-and-seed catalogs which seemed tedious, but Marilyn always said she enjoyed it!

I drove daily from our farm in Scholls to work in Portland, and somehow, I guess just eating well and sitting a lot at my art table, I gained twenty pounds. I decided to inquire about Badminton in Portland and found quite a large following for this sport. They played at the exclusive Multnomah Athletic Club! I found I could play there as a guest, and soon made friends with some of the best players.

However, Badminton is a fast game when played competitively, and being twenty pounds overweight made it impossible to win against the top players.

So I bought a fabulous Italian lightweight racing bike, and rode every day to Portland and back, with an accumulated fifty miles over a fairly steep and long hill. I began eating lunch every day at a healthfood store in Portland, following strict nutritional guidelines. I not only lost the twenty pounds within two or three months, but became much stronger and felt exceptionally well.

Playing Badminton became a joy once more, and I was soon one of the best players in all of Oregon.

My singing voice had also greatly improved, and I gave some thought to renewing my resolve to seriously study voice, even thinking of doing something professionally in this much loved endeavor.

Living with her husband in Portland was a famous singer, Brunetta Mazzolini. In those days, one of the most popular weekly radio programs was on Sunday nights, and was called Chicago Theater of the Air, with Bruno Walter conducting the Chicago Symphony Orchestra. Whenever Bruno Walter needed a soprano singer for his program, he always had Brunetta fly to Chicago, and he always introduced her on the air as the world's most perfect lyric-soprano voice. She also sang in productions at the Hollywood Bowl every year.

Because she was dedicated to the world of music, Brunetta did some very limited and very selective voice coaching, and Marilyn went with me one evening when I auditioned for her. After hearing me sing, and having me do some scales and try to sight read, she discovered that my knowledge of music was limited, and my voice needed coaching-lessons. She said however, that in her opinion, with study, I could have the 'greatest tenor voice alive today'.

With this encouragement, I began taking lessons from her, three times a week after work. She was a masterful musician who also played piano, and was a perfectionist in her own opera style singing, and equally demanding with her students. Her own voice, besides being naturally clear and beautiful, had tones like a finely tuned instrument, perfect in sound and key.

Brunetta had me sing scales for her, up and down, again and again, and kept stopping me as soon as just a tone or two did not satisfy her perfectionist's ear! As the weeks went on, I noticed a vast improvement in my control, range, and quality of tone. Even Brunetta seemed to become more and more impressed with my singing, with how effortlessly I could extend three octaves in full tenor voice, and reach 'high-C' with ease.

She even began talking about wanting to take me to Chicago to meet Bruno Walter. An amazing little side-note here, is that I did not know at the time that my paternal grandfather had married Bruno Walter's sister! With his sister's last name the same as mine, the family connection would certainly have been discovered if we had met, and who knows where it all might have led?

I continued Brunetta's coaching lessons for about three months, and have always been grateful for them. Even in that short a time, I know my voice became much more 'professional' sounding than ever before.

I began to realize, however, that to pursue singing as a successful career, I would actually have to give up my commercial art profession which provided us with necessary income. If singing were prosperous, it would require traveling and being away from my family. No! The most important thing in my life was my wife and my children, and I wanted to be with them every day!

So I decided with some sadness to forgo this direction, but singing was a great physical and mental part of me, and I've never been long without a song!

One day Marilyn called me at work and said a salesman was offering a 'Health Insurance' policy that had maternity benefits which paid an amount that was about three times as much as the premiums would be, even for a year. The maternity benefits would become valid when the policy had been in effect for nine months. Regardless, Marilyn and I were both enthusiastic about having another baby, so we took out the policy. Nine months and one week later, Marilyn and I went to check in to Portland's gorgeous maternity hospital.

It was a few minutes before twelve a.m., and we were told that if we could wait until after midnight we would owe a half-day less to the hospital. Knowing there was a total-benefit limit, we thought this was a good idea, and though mild contractions were quite regular, Marilyn was comfortable, and said we could take a walk for a few minutes.

As we left, the lady at the desk called a warning, "Don't eat anything!" However, right there on the corner by the hospital was a bright and welcoming deli, and we both sat down and had Pastrami sandwiches and cole-slaw!

Now Marilyn had found that in Portland, doctors were old-fashioned and did not believe she really could 'deliver' without pain. Calling though the 'phone book, she found an M.D. who had just got out of the Navy, and had never delivered a baby! He was perfect, even ordering one-gram of calcium intravenously, which she asked him to do, and which was ready and waiting for her when we checked in. Her contractions were strong, but she said they just felt like interesting movements inside of her, with absolutely no pain!

I sat in the waiting room, and very soon a nurse came in with a cute, bundled-up baby, eight-and-a-half pounds at birth. She said, "Mr. Reich, you have a baby boy!" After three girls, I couldn't believe it, and said, "Really? I've got to see!" So she opened the blanket, and there was a perfect little baby boy, and he was beautiful!

The nurse suggested I meet Marilyn at her room, and I got there just as she arrived. Her first words were something like, "Oh my goodness!" because hanging on the drapery rods on display were a long white-floral quilted robe she had made, and a long nightgown with a hand-smocked yoke from a very elegant store in Portland! Even her floral satin make-up case, and white Marabou slippers were displayed on her bed!

Marilyn had chosen a four-bed room, not to save money, but she always loved company! The other three ladies were fast asleep, but the nurse told us that in the bed across from Marilyn's was the editor of the Society Section of the Oregonian, Portland's largest newspaper. When a nurse opened Marilyn's suitcase, to hang her things in a closet, the lady-editor had been up for a night feeding, and insisted such an exquisite maternity ensemble must be left out to be enjoyed by all! In fact, it seemed that word got around, and nurses were stopping by from all over the hospital, to peek in the room!

Marilyn went right to sleep about four in the morning, and slept until almost ten, when she put on her nice things, and walked down the hall to a pay-'phone to call me that she was ready to come home. She enjoyed the next couple of hours, nursing "Egon, Jr." and conversing with the other ladies in the room.

At the farmhouse, Mama and Dad awaited our arrival, and they and the girls were overjoyed with the beautiful baby boy! With all our experience and knowledge of nutrition, he slept through the night within a few days, the same as the girls, and was as bright and healthy as a baby could be!

Besides, even at a very young age, our little boy was mostly smiling and already showed his pleasant and agreeable disposition which he has kept to the day of this writing, his forty-seventh year on this planet!

CHAPTER 12

400 Miles Long, 100 Miles Wide, 3 Feet Deep - Approx. . .

The birth of our son occurred on June 8, 1955. I was still riding my bicycle daily, to and from work, and although it's really not an important fact, was easily winning games against some of the best Badminton players in Oregon. I never entered competitions because they were too time-consuming.

On one occasion when I was at the Multnomah Athletic Club to play Badminton, I got into a conversation with an interesting man, named Syd, from Florida. He was in Portland on business, and he was successfully producing a three-dimensional advertising product which showed '3-D' color transparencies through a cardboard viewer which was eye-adjustable, and amazingly bright and clear!

He already had contracts with Ford, General Motors, Sears Stores, and many other major companies, and he showed me a brochure with pictures of his very impressive manufacturing plant in Fort Pierce, Florida.

I told him of my undertakings in the '3-D' business, and mentioned my existing children's stories. He seemed very interested, and we planned to meet the next day. To our appointment, I not only brought the transparencies of the children's stories, but my updated art portfolio as well. The result of that meeting was that he kept insisting that I had to come to work for him!

He offered me an excellent salary to be his Corporate Art Director, and was willing to guarantee he would produce and market my stories with his viewer, and give me additional 'royalties' on that. I told him that what he was suggesting would involve a major move for my family, but that if he would draw up a written agreement, I would give it serious consideration.

The Viewmaster Company still had my 'sound-viewer', but had sold their entire corporation to a large conglomerate, and there were no signs that they would produce my invention in the immediate future. Marilyn and I both were extremely tempted with the idea of seeing our '3-D' children's stories on the market!

Syd had returned to Florida, but in only a few days, called that he had a Corporate Agreement ready, and could I meet him at the Multnomah Athletic Club? Of course we met, but he understood that I needed some time to make such a major decision, and also would have to give notice to the agency where some national accounts had become dependent on my commercial illustrations.

We had lived in Portland for four years. Egon, Jr. was turning two, and we had recently driven down to see the newly opened Disneyland. I guess the children knew about it from television, and of course they loved it! I remember we had a suite at the Disneyland Hotel for $9.00 a night, and the biggest thing there was the 'Chicken of the Sea' Pirate Ship, but when we saw those gates as we walked in the first day, Jr. started running (toddler-style) and we could hear him saying over and over, "Diddyland! Diddyland!"

We had to admit it was a 'magical' place! While it was not in Florida, it was the reason we had recently driven down to Southern California, and that could have been why both Marilyn and I (and even Dad too) began discussing the fact that we did not feel 'at home' in Portland's general atmosphere.

We missed warm days at the beach! Oregon's beaches were always too windy. The river beaches were nice, but summer only lasted a month or two! We found ourselves picturing Florida having the atmosphere we missed from Southern California.

While Dad and I both were doing very well financially in Portland, we were not becoming wealthy, and the opportunity of accomplishing bigger things with our '3-D' project was of course our main consideration in deciding to make the move. So it was fortunate that the emotional aspects all seemed to fit together, and it was with a spirit of adventure and anticipation that I turned in my resignation at the advertising agency. We put the properties on the market and began packing!

My two weeks went quickly, but selling the houses and packing would take longer, so I would fly ahead, begin working, and find lodgings for the family. Fort Pierce was small, on the east coast of Florida, one hundred miles north of Miami and fifty miles north of Palm Beach. I took the plane to Miami, and the train to Fort Pierce. Syd picked me up at the station, and we drove directly to his plant.

It was a well-organized operation, with about a dozen people working, printing, die-cutting, and assembling his product. He had prepared a very nice office for me, and there were several assignments waiting for me to design and illustrate. The cardboard viewers were printed with each manufacturer's full-color designs and messages. Waiting for Marilyn to arrive, I kept busy, and did many nice designs for major manufacturers, all of which were very well received.

It was almost three months before Marilyn had sold the farm, boat and cars. She put half the furniture in storage, and some onto a moving van and was ready to come with the children. There were still some things to complete concerning the sale of the properties, but Mama and Dad stayed to finish those, and then they planned to drive across the country.

Marilyn always loved trains, and when she found it would cost $1,400 to fly with the four children, and a total of $200 to take a gorgeous "Domeliner" across the northern route to Chicago, and what the brochures called 'Trains Famous for Southern Hospitality' the rest of the way, she knew how she wanted to make the trip! I had purchased a car (Cadillac sedan), and had planned to drive to Miami to pick them up from the plane, but this way they would arrive right in Fort Pierce.

Marilyn thoroughly enjoyed the train trip! She planned everything. It was to be for five days, and they would arrive in Fort Pierce at four in the morning, but on a Saturday, so I would not have to go to work that day.

She took everything for the trip in two small suitcases, one of which was mostly filled with games and books. To go at that price, she went coach, but was told a pillow and a blanket for every passenger would be given for sleeping. She also took five real-down pillows which compress very small, but puff-out huge when released. She was told that the trains were not crowded at night, and that each of them would have a full double seat for a 'bed'. The first two days to Chicago were mostly spent in the high 'Vista-Dome', watching deer and herds of elk through that amazing north country!

They discovered the 'Club Car' while waiting for the 'Dining Car' the very first time. The 'Club Car' had an open carpeted area in the middle where the girls could open a board game and sit around it to play. The food in the 'Dining Car' was wonderful, and the waiters were more than cooperative at 'dividing' meals, and helping Marilyn feed the children well at a low cost.

A half-day 'layover' in Chicago was supposed to give time for a bus tour of the city, but the train's arrival and departure did not comfortably coincide with the bus schedule, so they found a park across from the station, and the children played on swings and ran around the grass for a few hours, which I'm sure was time better spent than sitting on a bus!

Leaving Chicago, Marilyn found the 'older' trains had an advantage. The passenger seats could 'flip' and face each other! With a suitcase in the middle, this made twice as big a bed for Heidi and Becky. Every night, Marilyn was able to have all the pillows she needed to make comfortable beds for all, including herself. She said she never slept better than on that rocking, moving train!

I arrived at the train station to meet Marilyn and the kids about an hour ahead of schedule. Actually, I was excited to see my family again, and I wasn't sleepy anyway. While sitting on a bench in that little station house, waiting for the train to arrive, I found myself contemplating something I was seeing which was unsettling to me.

It seemed that in Fort Pierce, in the year 1957, discrimination was shockingly apparent! I was not used to seeing signs reading,

"White Rest Rooms"   "Black Rest Rooms"
"White Water Fountain"   "Black Water Fountain"
"Benches for Whites"   "Benches for Blacks"

All this seemed terribly stupid and insulting to me, especially because I had also heard a white, so-called 'big-shot' say he would get a 'nigger' to do some menial task that needed doing. This statement struck me as if he had said it to me, and it felt very uncomfortable! Although now, I am certain that in Fort Pierce, as well as everywhere else in the United States, these bizarre, almost silly discriminatory practices have long since been eliminated, and are even illegal.

But why do people want to cause others to hate them? The only emotion that insults can bring forth is hatred. I can't emphasize enough, the wise advice from the Bible, "Do unto others as you would have them do unto you." This philosophy leads to compassion and nullifies aggression.

I like to think it's better to have a friend, rather than to make an enemy. However, that does not mean one should accept aggression. Quite the contrary, aggressive individuals or evil regimes who intend harm to innocent people must be dealt with harshly. Unfortunately, it is because of the attitudes of a certain segment of individuals, that human society is often at war!

My thoughts were interrupted as I noticed people gathering to meet our train. I saw that it was almost time for my family to arrive! I felt thrilled and excited as the train pulled into the station. I soon saw Marilyn waving from a window, and I climbed aboard, finding the children all still asleep. I picked up my two-year-old boy with a hug and a kiss. A dear, sleepy little voice simply said, "Hi, Dad!", and he fell back asleep in my arms.

I had found a new duplex and rented the whole thing, half for us and the other half for Mama and Dad. The furniture had already arrived, including boxes with sheets and towels, so I had made the beds, and 'my family' was very quickly settled in their new home!

Mama and Dad soon finished up everything in Oregon. Some of their furniture had arrived with ours, but they still had their bed and some things, so they rented a cross-country trailer, and leisurely drove all the way to Florida! They kept in close touch with us all the way, did a lot of 'sightseeing', and really thoroughly enjoyed the trip!

We tried to settle-in in our new environment, and it really was a different environment that we had expected! Fort Pierce is on the edge of the famous (or infamous?) Okeechobee Swamp! It is a massive section of Florida where mosquitos and a multitude of other biting-bugs thrive along with snakes like deadly Water-Moccasins, and of course Alligators. In fairness, there were also some beautiful birds and other nicer wildlife.

Daily, small tank-trucks drove the streets of Fort Pierce, spraying mosquito repellent, but one still had to use an unpleasant-lotion on all exposed body parts! As diligent as we tried to be, we all suffered some bites, and little Becky had an allergic reaction, suffering itchy lumps the size of eggs on her arms! Becky also was fascinated by some two-inch sized grey toads that were all around the yard, and she used to catch them and pet their little heads. Now don't tell me about 'old wives' tales' because her hands were soon covered with small warts! The doctor's 'cure'? Stop touching the toads, of course!

Of course, there was also a sort of strange beauty about the place. In fact, Marilyn kept saying she felt like we were on another planet! I once heard Florida described as being 400 miles long, 100 miles wide, and 3 feet deep, which might explain the fairly good-sized pond in back of the property where "Joe" lived. Joe was a six-foot-long alligator who answered to his name. As long as you threw him some bread or other food scraps, he didn't come after you, but accepted the morsels in good stead.

Our yard was completely enclosed by a strong, new chainlink fence, but it did not keep out snakes, and shortly after we moved in, Marilyn went into the laundryroom one morning, and saw a huge yellow snake, perfectly

Handsome Egon Jr. at four months old.

... and at his first birthday with admirations from sisters, grandma and grandpa.

Moving to Ft. Pierce Florida in 1957 near the edge of the Okechobee Swamp, provided a myriad of mosquitos, snakes and alligators, but the fishing was good which Marilyn's dad enjoyed. He usually brought home a generous bounty.

"The Chairman of the Board", Egon Jr. enjoying his second birthday.

At McKees Jungle Garden's (near Ft. Pierce) nature abounds with playful Macaws and giant alligators.

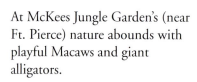

Little 2-1/2 year old, "Hercules" Egon Jr. proudly lifting up a big fish.

coiled, on a high shelf above the washing machine. It was so high that Marilyn did not notice it until they were almost face-to-face, and it looked so comfy we just left it there. However, that very day, we went to the local animal shelter and came home with a cute, lively little Terrier. He did his job well, as he scared all the beasties away and let us know in no uncertain terms if someone or something came into our yard.

We were also 'over-run' with some very small frogs. The laundryroom was in a separate cement-block structure near the kitchen door, and as quickly as Marilyn could fold clothes from the dryer, and bring them into the house, we still found frogs among the clothes! I had to turn-out my socks every morning because there were almost always one or two cute little green frogs inside!

Marilyn's arrival had been in June, and summer in Florida is the rainy season. Marilyn soon learned that when it started to rain, usually about three in the afternoon, we felt it was prudent to unplug our appliances for an hour or two, because more often than not, even a short rainfall could be accompanied by lightening. We saw on several occasions two to three foot long lightening bolts shoot out of our electrical outlets on the wall! It was not supposed to be dangerous, but could 'blow-up' even the refrigerator if it was still connected to a wall plug.

Of course we soon adjusted to Florida, and began fully enjoying life as always! We went to the beach both in Miami and Palm Beach. The ocean water was warm, and it was shallow with only very small breakers.

A few miles north of Fort Pierce, near Vero Beach, was "McKee's Jungle Gardens". It became one of our favorite places to go on a weekend, because they exhibited rare birds, various beautiful, tropical plant-life, parrots and colorful macaws flying free among the trees. The birds would follow tourists along the various paths. The girls wore tennis shoes, and whenever we went there, one big colorful macaw found it imperative to untie Becky's shoe laces! It did it so deftly, a person could not have done it as quickly! We always laughed and enjoyed this exuberant and adorable performance by that beautiful macaw bird!

There were also several pens with cement walls about three feet high which housed huge alligators. On one of our visits, as I passed by those pens, and saw a monster lying about four feet from the wall, not moving a muscle. I shouted and whistled at him to make him move, to no avail.

There was a long, thin tree-branch on the ground nearby, which I picked up, and I gave the alligator a little nudge on the head. I touched him lightly, not wanting to hurt him, just get a little action. Well, I got action alright! He opened his immense mouth, hissed a low, graveling loud tone, rose up on his feet and shot towards me as fast as lightening! I never thought those huge creatures could move so fast! I backed-off equally fast, and of course the wall stopped him. I never bothered that neat beast again! Actually, I love alligators! They make such beautiful watch-bands, purses, and so forth, so I am glad they are no longer on the endangered species list!

When Mama and Dad arrived and got settled, Dad loved the place, mainly because of the fabulous ocean fishing! He could take an early-morning boat, be back about ten, and we often had a huge, gorgeous fish for dinner! In fact, he began catching too many, so he built a 'smoker' out in the yard, and even passed around packages of tasty smoked fish to the neighbors!

We never experienced a hurricane, but one morning when Dad was out on a fishing boat, they saw a 'waterspout' in the distance and heading toward them! A waterspout is caused by a 'whirlwind' over the water, so strong that it pulls water up in the air, a hundred feet or so, and everything on the surface of the water with it! Fortunately the captain of the boat had enough presence of mind to immediately turn toward shore, and outrun the wind!

We were all amazed the next day when we saw a picture of that enormous waterspout on the front page of the local newspaper, and thanked God that Dad had made it back home, safe and sound!

As Christmastime approached in Florida, the rains stopped and the days were clear and sunny, yet balmy and never too hot. This was what Marilyn called 'ambition weather', and she used her good 'Speed Graphic' slide-camera to take portraits of the children, and wrote a poem for our Christmas card.

We had been attending a small Presbyterian church, and I sang solos with the choir. At the Christmas Eve service, the minister read Marilyn's poem. He told us later that he had been sitting in his office trying to write something about children for his Christmas sermon, when our card arrived. He said he really felt it came in answer to his prayer for inspiration.

The little Christmas Card poem was as follows . . .

Their Cherished Angels....

From left, Heidi 8, Karen 5, Becky 7, Egon Jr. 2-1/2. Marilyn and Egon Sr. were blessed with four healthy, beautiful and intelligent children, from then till today, 2003 and beyond.

This picture was from the Reich's Christmas Card in Florida 1957, and a poem (see text of book) by Marilyn, was read by their local minister as part of his Christmas sermon.

Angels of Christmas

As the twinkling stars still shine
A Christmastime, at Christmastime,
So are the Angels of Noel Night
With us too, their eyes so bright
As they gaze at the sparkling
Christmas Tree,
Saying dear little prayers,
Then dancing with glee,
For Children, so pure,
Symbolically fine,
Are surely <u>our</u> Angels
Of Christmastime!

Egon, Jr. had 'asked Santa' for a rocking horse, and we ordered one from Miami with heavy springs, and the wild action that little boy wanted! Of course, the girls had to have equal gifts, and the only other one not readily available was a bed and a dressing table for a large (eighteen-inch) bendable ballerina doll that Becky wanted. The doll came with a wardrobe, but needed something more for 'play value'.

I had met a man named Luther who had designed and built some of the machinery for the plant where I worked. I knew he owned a grapefruit orchard, and we had talked about our walnuts in Oregon. I also knew he had a complete machine shop at his home, so Marilyn had me ask him if he could build her a doll's bed, dresser, and bench, if she gave him the dimensions. He finished them forthwith, and Marilyn painted them white, then added little pink roses.

When they were finished, we drove out to show them to Luther, a young man with a wife and two small children. When he saw the pieces all painted, he called to his wife, saying, "Look, Honey! Look what I made!" So we continued to have special fun, and each Christmas seemed like the best ever! We also became good friends with Luther and his family, and, by the way, he grew the sweetest and most flavorful grapefruits in Florida, or anywhere!

After about a year and a half, the company where I worked was suddenly experiencing a drastic reduction in production. It seemed that the companies who were using this type of advertising were not getting enough results for the dollar-amount being spent. Large, formerly-repeat orders were being cancelled. This caused a crisis among the stockholders of the company who had invested in the machinery and the construction of the factory-building. Of course, because of these circumstances, there wasn't any way they could, or would want to undertake a new project such as my three-dimensional children's stories.

At a stockholder's meeting, it was decided to close the operation and sell all the assets. I met several of the stockholders who agreed to pay my salary until the place actually closed. In general they were very good people, and they all felt apologetic to me. Fortunately we had made a good profit on the sale of the farm, and because I had sufficient earnings from working, we had not used any of our reserve monies.

As much as we liked some of the interesting things about Florida, we nevertheless felt we would not be disappointed if we decided to leave.

In fact, it seemed like our attitude whenever we were making a change in our lives, was that it would be exciting, and life would be better than ever before! So we began to plan our new direction with much enthusiasm! We had many choices. We could go to New York where we knew there was a major advertising market, and artists did well. But it was not in our hearts! No, we wanted to go back to California where Marilyn was born and we knew we loved to live there! So, 'sink or swim'; it was, "California, here we come!"

CHAPTER 13

♪ . . . and Make the ♫ San Fernando Valley My Home. . .

We had enough money. Dad and I had two good cars, and we decided to save the moving van expense, and rent two big one-way trailers. Most of Marilyn's antique furniture was still in storage in Oregon.

Dad and I were both strong, and we enjoyed loading all our belongings into the trailers. We planned to leisurely 'caravan' together across the 'Southern Route'. Mama and Dad had come to Florida from the north, so this would all be new to them, as well as to us, and we intended seeing 'everything' on the way!

Leaving Fort Pierce, our first stop was Silver Springs in about the middle of Florida. What a fabulous place that was! There was a water-skiing 'ballet' show, many exhibits, and some amazing 'free' playground equipment for the children that resembled carnival rides! They had a 'snake show', and when they asked for a volunteer from the audience, Heidi was the first one up, and she got to have a huge snake wrapped all around her. Of course, she loved it!

The 'Springs' were crystal clear, like little lakes with massive green lawns right up to the very finished looking, man-made, cement-with-rock edges. Absolute perfection! The most memorable part of all the shows for me was a giant catfish! At the edge of one of the springs, a guide tossed a large loaf of bread into the water, and in one second, a huge, whiskered mouth grabbed and swallowed the whole thing! I had never imagined that kind of fish getting that big!

We stayed two whole days, and then were on our way through the Florida 'Panhandle', Alabama, Mississippi, and as we came to Louisiana, we thought we should take a look at New Orleans' historically interesting areas. But as we entered the city, we discovered that Mardi Gras was in full swing! The traffic was so heavy we could hardly move, and especially with our trailers in tow, we just wanted to get back out onto the highway! We were lucky because as we continued through New Orleans, we found ourselves on Bourbon Street and I'm sure we saw a very representative row of beautiful old buildings, ornate wrought-iron balconies, and all!

Every mile of our trip seemed to provide us with interesting and beautiful sights. Mama was absolutely thrilled, actually getting to see 'all of the whole United States', as she put it. She had never dreamed she would be doing this much traveling, which was her very favorite thing!

We drove through the cities of Dallas and Abilene in Texas, then on to New Mexico. We drove a short distance out of our way to visit the famous Carlsbad Caverns, certainly one of the most impressive sights one could ever experience. In fact, photographs don't do it justice, and to describe it is almost futile!

We entered the caverns through a big opening in the earth, and found there were elevators to take us down 750 feet, to the level where a tour was just starting.. There was a path with a rail to hold onto, electric lights throughout, and even a gift shop! Marilyn and I, as well as Mama and Dad, certainly saw nothing wrong with the humanization of conveniences brought into this masterpiece of nature. It did not seem to deter, nor even disturb, the millions of bats in "Bat Cave"!

We were told that the Caverns had become a National Park in 1923, the year I was born, and that the tour was three miles long. We soon came to "The Great Room" of the Caverns with a ceiling of almost 300 feet, and saw amazing stalagmites and stalactites as long and as tall as sixty-five feet, and the lights shining on them produced a rainbow of colors!

The guide told us that the stalactites were the long, pointed columns which stuck 'tight' to the ceiling of the caverns, and the stalagmites stood on the floor and 'might' reach the ceiling someday! While he may have meant this as humor, I found it an excellent way to remember which was which!

There were pools of water below our path also displaying the pinks, white, and yellows from the minerals. I lifted little Egon onto my shoulders so he could see over the heads of the crowd of people around us.

The guide of course told how those huge, pointed columns were formed by the dissolving action of water on limestone, drip, drip, dripping for millions of years!

It brought out the realization that our world and the universe lives by a different time-frame than an individual human lifespan. Somehow, it gave me a comforting feeling, to think that the gentleness of little drops of water had the power to create tall rock-hard columns.

Our guide then asked us to stand still and not talk for about thirty seconds while he turned out the lights. He wanted us to realize that this was all happening in absolute black darkness. The dark seemed intense and so did the silence. In that thirty seconds, I thought I heard only one drop of water plunk onto a stalagmite, and possibly the faint swish of a far-off flying bat, but that was all. We left the Caverns exhilarated, and definitely humbled. I had carried little Egon a good part of the way, and my arms hurt a bit, but I didn't mind. As the saying goes, "He ain't heavy, he's my (in this case, bundle of joy, son!)."

On the trip, we had stopped early enough every evening to find a nice motel, have a good dinner together, and enjoy a full night's sleep. After the time spent at the Caverns, and feeling we were getting close to our destination, we decided to not do any more 'sightseeing', and drive to Los Angeles as directly as possible.

We still had to go through Albuquerque, also Flagstaff, Arizona, but then we really began feeling excited as we passed through Needles, then Barstow, and we were home!

The first morning back, we drove around the city, and found that real estate in Beverly Hills and the Wilshire District had increased drastically and besides, the homes were getting very old. Realtors all said, "Everyone's moving to the San Fernando Valley. The houses are new, and lower in price!"

We discovered that the general move to 'The Valley' actually started with several movie stars, Bing Crosby, Bob Hope, and others building large homes and ranches there. The Valley had several community names, such as North Hollywood and Van Nuys (southeast), all the way to Granada Hills and Northridge (northwest), but it had all been incorporated into the City of Los Angeles, so the schools and city services were 'big-city' efficient.

The best thing was that it was actually all 'close-in', even the farthest parts only about a half hour from any Los Angeles area.

I may have been somewhat influenced by Bing Crosby singing, "I'm packin' my grip, and I'm leavin' today! Cause I'm takin' a trip California way! I'm gonna settle down and never more roam, and make the San Fernando Valley my home!" That song seemed to give the Valley an appeal and a certain charm, and when we looked at several new housing developments, they were all quite nice.

The entire Valley had been overbuilt, so every new house was a good value. We liked the northwest where we were told the summer weather was a little cooler because of a breeze along the small mountain range that bordered the Valley to the north. We found one new development with a particularly pretty yellow and white house with decorative brick planters in the front, and a very large back yard. We really loved that particular house, and there was a sales office nearby. We were able to buy it at a reasonable price, with a low down payment, and the street it was on was called Danube Avenue. Marilyn joked, "What a coincidence! We may not be on the Danube River in Vienna, but Danube Avenue in California isn't a bad alternative!

Mama and Dad found an absolutely charming and very reasonable rental, and renting seemed like a good idea for awhile until Dad saw if he needed to be right in Hollywood for his business. Their house had an 'outdoor arbor' completely covered by a massive lilac, and we will never forget the many times we enjoyed the beauty of those flowers, and that very fresh, mild fragrance as we had summertime meals, or even just lemonade on a Sunday afternoon.

Meanwhile, I learned how to put in a lawn at our new house, and Marilyn filled the brick planters with fragrant gardenias, and put a pretty lemon tree with a birdbath by it, in front by a big Colonial-style corner window. A neighbor built a handsplit cedar-stake fence between our two properties, and Marilyn trained an orange Bougainvillea along a part by the front sidewalk where the fence was low.

Bougainvilleas were just beginning to come in different colors, and we had strangers ring our doorbell to ask what that plant was, and to remark what an artistic and impressive garden we had!

We sent for the furniture in storage in Oregon, and soon the house felt like 'home' and was all gorgeous with Marilyn's 'professional' decorating.

While outside one day, I met a neighbor from about four doors down. He was a big, husky, nice-looking man who introduced himself as Dan Blocker. He said he was an actor, but this was just before he started in the Bonanza series. He and his wife, Dolph, had four children about the same age as ours, and we got to know his whole family.

I liked Dan. He was a very pleasant and congenial person, and he often asked me over when the whole cast of Bonanza was at his house. I always enjoyed talking with every one of them.

I even got involved for awhile with some Bonanza publicity, and designed and produced some promotional items for them. The studio producing the Bonanza series was also a fun place, and I liked the Bonanza publicity agent. They only did a few things I could help with, but he continued to call me when they needed something.

An interesting thing about the big back yards behind the houses on Danube Avenue, was that an alley ran behind them, about three feet higher than the rest of the otherwise level lots. This gave us a hill, or a bank straight across the back of the backyard, with a good, heavy, solid wood fence all across the top. We had put in a lawn on the flat part, and were starting to terrace, and plant flowers on the hill.

Then one day we saw some of those above-the-ground, round swimming pools. The largest size had a ladder into it, and could be maintained with a 'vacuum' and chemicals like a built-in pool. None of the children had learned to swim, so it was the safest kind of a pool to have while they learned.

The height of the largest size pool was almost the same as the height of our hill, and it occurred to me that if I cut a curve into the hill, the pool would fit into it and not take much space from the level yard.

Much to my chagrin, I found that the dirt of that hill was hard-packed clay, almost like as solid rock! Cutting a large half-circle out of that was the most arduous physical labor I had ever encountered, but I was determined, and with pick-axe and shovel I attacked the hill! It seemed like every hour's work only got me another 'inch' toward completion, but finally, the pool was set perfectly into place!

The hill was a little higher than the pool, so I cut and paved some steps up the hill along the curve of the pool, for jumping-in! While it took a lot of sweat and time, it could not have been a greater success!

The four kids found a way to make the water 'whirl', so then they could just float, calling it their "Merry-Go-Round" pool! We found 'pool toys' and games of all kinds, and shouts of 'Marco Polo' were heard 'throughout the land'! I think we had them take actual swimming lessons at a nearby park, and I know they were soon all good strong swimmers!

Marilyn and I used the pool too. I think it was only about three laps across, but it was cooling and relaxing. Marilyn soon found that soaking in the cool water for only a few minutes, kept her comfortable for a couple of hours of outside work on a hot day. The kids and I loved the heat of the Valley, and Marilyn had air conditioning in the house, so we managed.

When we first moved back, I took a job with Stamps-Conheim, the largest local company producing a catalog of advertising-clip-art Both the newspapers and companies with their own advertising departments subscribed to their weekly publications, often referred to as 'canned art'. Such companies were supermarkets, discount stores, and even department stores. The 'art' was mostly 'seasonal headings', such as illustrations of Santas and whole Christmas scenes, Easter bunnies, eggs and baskets, Thanksgiving cornucopias, and so forth! There were also many 'generic' products, like a photograph of an appetizing dinner plate showing a T-Bone Steak for a supermarket to enhance it's meat ads.

I inquired about Marilyn doing this photography for them, and after giving her a tryout job, they had her do a list of them every week. She totally created the setups, used small spotlights and her good Speed Graphic Camera, handing me sets of printed eight-by-ten glossies for me to take in. Her photos all showed very impressive beef roasts with garnishes, and other delicious- looking food displays.

I kept looking for something that would pay a higher salary, when I heard of a lithograph printer in Hollywood, which filled the entire main floor of a large building. As the story went, the whole second floor was an art studio called "ModernArts", which was very stable because it could exist nicely on the art for just the big printing company downstairs.

I made an appointment to meet with the owner of the studio, who took one look at my art portfolio and hired me on the spot. There were two long rows of art tables, and artists with various types of skills, some even accomplished illustrators like myself, and there seemed to be enough work for everyone. The place actually had a pleasant atmosphere, and I felt I fitted in quite well and was soon enjoying doing a better type of art than the newspaper-catalogs.

Here again I soon encountered the fact that printing-customers think art should be 'free'! Especially a printer as big as the one we worked with, had found they could charge enough to just 'include' the art, but then they tried to get 'ModernArts' to charge them as little as possible! The owner of the studio was a nice fellow, and was trying to be funny whenever he handed a job to an artist, always with his little saying, "Here's another quicky and a cheapy!" It didn't matter if it was a two-day illustration or just a line draw-ing, he meant we should work as fast as possible. Being all experienced artists, we did our jobs fast and efficiently.

Something else unusual about this studio was that there were two Para-keets flying free! One was yellow and green, and the other a light blue. One would land on the edge of my art table, walk over and chew on the end of the pencil I was using for drawing! They had many such 'tricks', and we all loved those little characters!

One day, I heard they needed another paste-up artist, and Marilyn had been saying she would like to try a full time job. Egon, Jr. was about to start full-day kindergarten, and Mama was willing to stay with the children after school, from three until about five-thirty when we could be home. She was used to making a nice dinner every night for Dad and herself, so she even suggested she have dinners ready, and we could all eat together.

It all seemed possible, so Marilyn started riding in to work with me every day. Such fun! And in just a few weeks, Marilyn became the fastest paste-up artist they had ever had! She could 'eyeball' the whole thing so accurately that when she finished, she just checked it with a T-Square and it was done!

As usual, it was not Marilyn's nature to 'rest on her laurels', so when she had spare time, she began noticing an art-filing system that an 'efficiency expert' had been hired to create. There was a partitioned corner of the stu-dio where large bins for the art storage had been built, and Marilyn noticed that when artists went in there, they stayed 'forever', muttering to them-selves!

The problem was that when a new job could be done more quickly with a previous similar job for reference, the old job was filed by name, and no-one could remember the <u>name</u> on the prior job. After asking the artists what they always <u>could</u> remember about old jobs, and analyzing the forma-tion of the bins, she presented a plan to the studio's owner to re-arrange the art storage bins by annual quarters. He said, "Do it!", and the change worked wonderfully!

The next little 'problem' Marilyn could not help noticing was the owner, himself, sitting long hours over the artists time-sheets. Years before when we had our own accounts, she had got used to doing the billing for the artwork, and was well aware of the various aspects, even that the size of the entire printing job enters into it.

Somehow, one day the opportunity presented itself, and she offered to work on some of the time-sheets with him. The result was that he bought a desk for his 'reception room', and had a partition built behind the desk to hide an art table. He put Marilyn at the desk like a receptionist, but doing time-sheets. When she would finish the billing, she would do paste-ups, and still jump up and 'play receptionist' if a client walked in. The owner was in his 'Glory'! He had tried to get help with the time-sheets before, but had given up, and he even told me that Marilyn did them better than he did! And he now had a gorgeous receptionist for his art studio besides!

The poor owner! This all happened in a short time period of about four months. Things were not going well on the home front! School had started in September, which is when Marilyn started working. All went as planned with Mama for a couple of months, but then she caught the flu, and we had to get other baby-sitters. We could not seem to find 'Mary Poppins', and I'm afraid our children were rather like the ones in that story!

One day in early December, we had a serious conference with the children. Another baby-sitter had just quit, and Marilyn said something like, "We'll have a bigger Christmas, more presents if Mommy keeps working!", when Egon, Jr. pipes up with, "I just want a plain old balloon, and Mommy!"

Well, that did it! Marilyn gave notice and worked another two weeks. but I think the owner of ModernArts kept calling until about March, before he would really believe Marilyn was not coming back!

Always busy, Marilyn had already become involved as a group leader in Camp Fire Girls 'Bluebirds' for Heidi and Becky. She was even a director in a 'Bluebirds' summer daycamp, writing and directing a play for the final day program. The play was taken from the old German story called "The Bluebird" which had inspired the name of the younger Camp Fire Girls.

Marilyn's group co-leader, Aline Patton, became a lifelong friend, along with her husband, Bob and their two daughters. Bob was a Nature Science professor, and I remember one Saturday we took the Bluebird Group to a nearby mountain area for a nature hike, where the trees were particularly lush, green and beautiful. I was inspired to sing the song, "Trees", and the little jiggers seemed to be impressed with my rendition of the song, because they all listened intently without making a sound, then clapped a little and marched happily with us into the forest.

Meanwhile, the opportunity presented itself to purchase a lovely, larger home in an up-section of the Valley, Northridge. This gave the kids separate bedrooms and there was a large built-in swimming pool. The children were strong swimmers by then, and the pool provided good exercise and recreation for all of us.

The first new neighbors our daughters met were Girl Scouts, and our girls wanted to join their 'Troop', so Marilyn went into Girl Scout Council and became the 'Crafts Lady' for the entire San Fernando Valley!

She also became involved with a publicity caper resulting in her picture being in the Los Angeles Times Society Section several times, partially related to the Girl Scouts, and partially with the International Needlework Guild, an important, century-old, World-Wide charitable organization which had originally started in England. On occasion, she still wears a lovely, small cloisonne pin from the Guild.

Heidi's elementary school 'graduation' was nice, a party with punch and cookies, but nothing to make it special, so the next year, Marilyn decided to become more involved with Becky's. She made Becky a dress of light blue polished cotton. It had a gathered circle-skirt with three petticoats.

Together with some other ladies from the PTA (Parent-Teacher Association), Marilyn planned the event. She cut from cardboard, a giant, six-foot high, curved-edge picture frame, painted white and gold, to stand on the stage in the school auditorium for taking pictures.

Marilyn also made a very cute refreshment-table centerpiece, a styrofoam 'doll' in 'cap and gown' made of royal blue crepe paper, stepping through a small version of the white and gold picture frame. She designed little white graduation hats, and 'miniature diplomas' tied with royal-blue ribbons, which the ladies made, to scatter along royal-blue banners down the center of each table. The whole room looked decorated, and the students took home little souvenirs of the happy and enjoyable event!

When Marilyn asked the PTA for volunteers for a workshop to make the party favors, one lady who came was named Kathy Green, and she and her husband, Seymour, became our very good friends.

Kathy was an unusually nice person, was talented in art, and enjoyed many different hobbies like sewing, gardening, gourmet cooking, and more! Because she was a gentle, friendly, and creative person, Marilyn found her a compatible good friend.

Also, an interesting fact, Kathy was part American Indian with long dark hair and a beautiful face, which provided the inspiration for Marilyn to paint a large oil-portrait of her in an authentic Indian costume. The painting turned out beautifully, and is loved by her family to this day. I was especially proud of it.

Kathy also had a beautiful singing voice, and was singing professionally in a nightclub where she met her husband, Seymour. He was the Chief of Police of Manhattan Beach, just south of Los Angeles, and part of his job was checking the clubs, and he always said that he fell in love with Kathy the minute he saw her!

Seymour and I also became good friends. He was a jovial fellow with lots of entertaining jokes, and was also quite talented in music. He had a beautiful ukulele, and often played the accompaniment for my singing.

At one time, Seymour had a small Chihuahua dog he 'taught' to 'sing'! I must admit that funny little dog did a lot of howling with his nose straight up in the air, and Seymour claimed he could 'sing' several songs including "White Christmas". Oh, yeah! Anyway, Seymour was fun, and always welcome at our home.

In back of the Northridge house, by the pool, there was a large paved area with a brick barbecue and we often had friends over for get-togethers which always seemed to include music!

I remember one particular evening, we invited several notable guests for a musical poolside party. Marilyn had put lamb shishkabobs on the barbecue, as part of a delectable dinner, and Seymour brought his ukulele to accompany Kathy and me in some singing.

Marilyn had also met Virginia O'Brian at a PTA meeting. She lived nearby with her children, and we had been invited to her house one Sunday afternoon, with our kids. Virginia, for readers who may not know her name, was a famous singer and actress in many movies. She had leading roles in movies with such stars as Judy Garland and Red Skelton.

Easter at the Reich's first home after returning to California - on Danube Avenue in the San Fernando Valley.

Young Egon Jr., Marilyn and Egon's mother (Mama). To the right Heidi, Becky and Karen.

Below, friends Kathy and Seymour Green.

Kathy was part Indian (Native American) and Marilyn painted this portrait of her in costume.

Always clowning, Seymour insisted his little dog was singing White Christmas with him. Although unrecognizable, the little dog did howl up a storm!

Marilyn had asked her over that evening, not really knowing if she would want to join-in with our 'musicale', but she and Kathy 'hit it off' immediately, and she not only sang several songs, including one of her amazing 'dead-pan' versions, but she also told some interesting anecdotes about being self-taught and how she got into the movies!

What an evening we were having, but there's more yet! I had met a man from Hawaii who right at that time was on a television series called "Hawaiian Eye", playing a very big part, that of the Honolulu Chief of Police. He not only came to our party, but he brought his beautiful wife, his Hawaiian guitar, and they sang "The Hawaiian Wedding Song" as a duet. They also sang several other songs, in the most beautiful 'harmony' I've ever heard.

A young artist from Mexico City worked at Stamps Conheim when I was there, and we became friends with his wife and two adorable little children. His name was Alfredo Sanches and he was not only a very talented artist-illustrator, but he was also a excellent musician, playing fabulous classical guitar. He loved the music of Johann Sebastian Bach, and could play from memory every note that Bach ever wrote.

It was quite a thrill to hear him play classical guitar with such feeling and fluency. Some classical music, when played even by good orchestras, can sound mundane, but listening to Alfredo, sensitively plucking the strings of his guitar, made every note of anything he played sound beautiful!

He enjoyed playing accompaniment to my singing, and had taught me every word of the famous ballad, "Granada", in Spanish. I never really remembered what the words meant, but I could correctly pronounce the whole song!

Alfredo also came and played at our musical party, and we had a lot of fun with so much musical talent that evening. Marilyn had asked the Pattons and several other friends. The atmosphere was congenial, and the music was exhilarating!

Music brings joy to everyone, and our lives are much enriched by it, and it provides us with grace and appreciation of a wonderful life!

Mama and Dad were doing well, taking trips every weekend. We usually took the kids someplace like "The Date Festival" in Indio (in May), or some event, even once the State Fair in Sacramento, or up to Lake Arrowhead, or just for a day at the beach. We all loved the beach!

Dad was doing well in his business, and had renewed part-business friendships with several movie people.. One in particular, was Jimmy Durante, who every Christmas sent Dad a package containing all of his new recordings from that year.

CHAPTER 14

The Pledge of Allegiance

Meanwhile, my mother and I were both eligible to apply for United States Citizenship, and in order to pass the Citizenship test in those days, one had to be able to answer over a hundred questions. I believe if you missed five or six, you had to re-apply, and at a later date take the test all over again.

There were several nightschool classes available in various highschools and colleges, for learning the United States history required for the Citizenship test. Mama and I registered at one of those classes, and I began attending with her, but besides my daytime art job, I always had some sort of business project I had to work on in the evenings. At first, I thought I could find time to learn from Mama's study papers, but I always seemed to be too busy.

Mama went right ahead, took the test, and got her Citizenship. When I saw the questions she had to answer on a written test, I realized that I would have to complete a course, following a pattern of concentrated studies. I really planned that as soon as I finished the project I was working on, I'd re-enter the school, and the next time I would finish and get my Citizenship!

I was about forty-two years old at that time. Well, one business undertaking led to another, and at the age of seventy-six,. I finally found enough time to achieve my long-coveted United States Citizenship!

I was still fearful of those United States history and Government questions, but I was determined to do all the learning and whatever was necessary to pass the test!

Now having enough money, I hired a very knowledgeable lawyer, Mr. Colyn B. Desatnick, who specializes in Immigration and Citizenship affairs. I felt I might need help with filling-out 'forms' and other potential legalities.

To my surprise, he informed me that the tests had been modified, and no longer consisted of so many questions. Furthermore, because I was over age sixty-five, and had lived in this county for more than twenty years, I would only be asked twenty-five questions.

He provided me with all kinds of booklets about our Constitution, and important dates of historic events, and so on! He also gave me a list of twenty-five questions that would likely be asked. I studied and carefully took many notes, in order to memorize all the answers.

The day of my Citizenship examination finally arrived, and although I felt quite confident that I was ready to face this critical test, I took my attorney with me for support!

We entered a small room, and were seated by a small desk, behind which sat a very nice middle-aged man, the 'Examiner'. His first comment was that the test could be conducted in 'my language'! He undoubtedly meant German because he knew I was originally from Austria, but I was quick to reply that <u>English</u> was 'my language'.

He seemed pleased, and we began the test. He asked me a couple of personal questions, verifying his records, and then asked, "What is the significance of our Fourth of July celebration?"

Of course I knew the question referred to the Declaration of Independence, and that the document was formally accepted by the Thirteen Colonies on July 4, 1776.

After I answered that question correctly, he said, "You passed!"

Wow! What a trip! One question and I passed! He must have figured that because of my confident, but courteous manner, I could easily have answered all twenty-five questions. I was almost sorry I couldn't prove my knowledge, but extremely happy I passed!

There was only one other procedure to finalize my Citizenship, and for me to receive my Certificate of Naturalization. I was required to take part in a ceremony with about five-thousand people at the Los Angeles Convention Center, and to take the Oath of Allegiance before a Judge of the United States Supreme Court. I must admit the ceremony gave me an unexpected elated feeling of joy!

The speeches by various notable persons were short but inspiring. In all, it was very enjoyable, and it made me proud to receive my Certificate.

Marilyn and our then-adult children and their spouses were all there to make it a memorable celebration. Our darling daughter, Karen, had bought a special leather folder for my Certificate, which I thoroughly treasure. We all then went to lunch at the famous Farmer's Market in Hollywood, which held long-time memories for our family.

I want to thank Mr. Desatnik for the expert help and peace of mind he gave me, actually making the whole procedure a really pleasant experience.

While working as an artist, marketing our Three-Dimensional Stories was constantly on my mind. We treasured the color transparencies which represented many months of miniature work.

I began spending evenings designing a clever viewer which could be cut from a single sheet of cardboard. It could be squeezed flat, and would have a spring in it to pop it open. The set of transparencies for each story would fit nicely on a card that would slide through the back of the viewer. Picturing the shape of the viewer and slide-card together inspired the thought of a small book. As a book, it could have pages printed with the text of each story, so they could be read to a child while the youngster viewed the color pictures.

My slot for the viewing card was deep for stability, and had frosted light-diffusion plastic on the back. Working on it almost every night, I designed book covers for all of the stories, and Marilyn and I wrote six to eight-page versions of each. I did layouts for the typesetting, with delightful little illustrations on almost every page.

I was able to buy a set of three-dimensional transparencies for a souvenir book on California. Marilyn did some research and wrote very appealing text for it. I also did a full-color illustration for the cover, showing distant mountains with a field of California poppies in the foreground.

To mass-produce the book would require some very specialized machinery, and at least a small factory. The cost? As with all marketing projects, there are many aspects to consider which can make the difference between success and failure. But, nothing ventured, nothing gained! (or lost?)

I did not have enough money to undertake a new business alone, but a friend who saw my finished book sample was impressed. He owned a medium-sized factory in an unrelated field, and said he could invest a few thousand dollars, and would have a room in his building we could use. We agreed on an equal partnership, and I was to do all the production and marketing.

Well, the little books, about four inches by six inches in size, turned out beautifully, and I worked late every night, finishing all art and supervising the printing. Things were going well, and I was able to sell the books to almost all the major department stores in Los Angeles. We had even designed and produced a nice display rack for them.

The stores, however, began insisting that the books sell at a price too low for us to make a decent margin of profit. We tried to reduce our production costs, but found they were actually going up instead! In fact, our budgets were exhausted! We sold our inventory, and agreed that if it ever became feasible to sell the product at it's correct retail price, we might give it another shot.

I still have some of those quite-beautiful little books. Our son, now in his forties, recently met someone who still has a set that he has owned and treasured since he was a child.

Of course, I am sorry the books did not become a successful venture. but I learned much! I especially learned that any project needs to be very thoroughly analyzed, and sufficient foundation needs to be established, to even begin to assure success.

While holding my art jobs, I always pursued some business, assignment or project on the side, working evenings. But whatever my small successes or failures were, I had one conviction, and that was to never blame others for a failure, even if a blame could be made. I can only learn from my mistakes or failures, if I place the responsibility for them squarely on my shoulders.

Birthdays, Christmases, summers, winters came and went, and our busy, happy family grew energetically, and except for a few of the usual 'sniffles', remained very healthy.

With our swimming pool and air conditioning, and always enjoyable evening temperatures, we had got somewhat adjusted to the heat of the Valley, and we very much enjoyed many of our activities there.

However, something shocking occurred which ultimately changed our lives for the better!

Heidi seemed to be growing up a little too fast when at age thirteen, she

3-D STORY BOOK®

A **NEW** AND REVOLUTIONARY STORY BOOK FOR CHILDREN

This outstanding value complete with illustrated story pages, 3 dimensional color film, printed slide card and unique self-opening viewer in gorgeous full color bookbound cover!   for only $1.29 RETAIL

Numbers Available

101 CINDERELLA	103 THE THREE BEARS	many other stories in production
102 HANSEL AND GRETEL	104 SPACE POLICE	
	105 THE BIRTH OF CHRIST	

Actual size of book 5" x 7"

2 doz. to carton
Weight 7 lbs.

Open Book and take out Slide Card and Viewer. A Viewer and Slide Card are in every book.

Viewer pops open automatically. Story also printed on Slide Card.

Read from beautifully illustrated pages while viewing 3-dimensional Color Slide.

To put Viewer back into Book, simply squeeze and slide into clip. Envelope on inside cover holds Slide Card.

... An Interesting Venture and Learning Experience!

Illustrated are some of the children's Story Books, which we produced with three dimensional color film picture cards and 3-D viewer.

Beautifully designed product, and well received, but which provided some lessons in business finance.

began to notice boys! Of course, maybe it was the other way around. She was already tall, had long blond hair, and besides school activities, there was a little neighborhood shopping center nearby, where we sometimes allowed all four kids to go together to an afternoon family movie.

We were very concerned parents and provided stern guidance, but always with a generous portion of love. No hanky-panky, swear words, nor bad behavior of any kind was tolerated. Marilyn and I believed strongly in setting good examples. Not like in some families where, "Do as I say!", not "Do as I do!" was the accepted rule of the day!

One Saturday, Marilyn and I were both home when the 'phone rang. We let Heidi, being the eldest, have an extension 'phone in her room because young girls seem to enjoy long conversations with school friends. On this occasion, Heidi and I answered the 'phone at the same time so she did not hear the click of an extension pickup, and she was not aware that I was listening.

What I heard shocked me into some sort of unexpected reality! There on the line was the voice of an older boy she must have met and seen without our knowledge. The conversation was very intimate, and soon became vulgar and totally disgusting with swear words directed against parents, like, "Parents are a bunch of s _ _ t!", followed by other four-letter words, including the 'f-word' and others even worse!

Heidi did not respond in kind, but listened as the boy told her to go outside and he would pick her up, and she meekly said, "OK! I love you!"

At that point, I burst into their call, telling Heidi to hang up the phone immediately! She hung up, and I went into her room and confronted her with the obvious questions. His name was Devon, he was seventeen, he lived a few blocks away, and his wealthy parents traveled a lot and left him home with a housekeeper, a car, a motorcycle, and no supervision!

Without even taking the time to properly explain, I had Marilyn jump into her car and drive over to Mama and Dad's house with all the kids.

Just seconds after Marilyn drove out of sight, the doorbell rang. As I opened the door, I saw that Devon was not short, but slight-of-build, and behind him stood five big thugs sneering at me! In a rude voice he asked, "Where is Heidi?"

I replied, "Heidi is not here."

When I heard him say next, "I'll give you five minutes to get Heidi or we're coming in!", I quickly closed our big, heavy front door, and immediately 'phoned the police, advising them of the thug's ultimatum.

In less than five minutes, a police car drove into our cul-de-sac (like a dead-end) street, I opened the door and saw the five 'pals' run 'like the devil', but Devon was either on drugs or drunk (the police found empty beer cans in his car) started to argue and even pushed one of the policemen! It did not take the policemen long to handcuff that irate 'thug' and shove him into the police car.

I drove over to Mama and Dad's house, and told the family all the weird details! Everyone was shocked, and we realized Heidi was going to have to be watched every second of the day and night!

Next, I went and bought a twelve-gauge shotgun, not to kill that thug, but to scare him if he ever came around again! We went home, and the rest of that day was uneventful.

The police must have released Devon that night, because Sunday morning I heard a motorcycle racing back and forth on our street. I had left my car out in our front driveway, and with my new rifle in hand, steadied my elbows on the top of the car. As Devon came toward our house again, I kept the gun pointed straight toward him. It must have looked like a cannon to him, because he took-off like a scared rabbit, and we only saw him once or twice after that, cruising the neighborhood. I certainly seemed to have diminished his bravery.

It was almost impossible to watch Heidi every second, so we decided to take drastic measures and move away to a completely different area. During summertime, the kids favorite thing had been to go to the beach, and of course that's where Marilyn always wanted to live, so one weekend, we took the kids and drove to Malibu. It seemed isolated, with nothing nearby for the kids to do.

We then sort of 'worked our way' down the coast, Santa Monica, Marina del Rey, even Long Beach, but could not seem to find an atmosphere we liked until we got all the way to Laguna Beach, about a hundred miles from where we were living! Well, wasn't moving far away what we really wanted?

Besides, Laguna held great appeal for us with numerous art galleries, wonderful beaches, beautiful scenic surroundings, and convenient schools close by. The shopping area was like a little 'Main Street', called Forest Avenue, lined with huge old trees, brick sidewalks, enchanting little shops, and a European-style bakery where one could sit and have coffee with a pastry. Even the hardware store at the upper end of the street was quaint, with the same feeling as our 'General Store' in Oregon!

It seemed like we had found the 'best of both worlds', the charm we had loved in Oregon, but right here in the Los Angeles area, the perfect place for us! And of course when the kids saw that the beach was within 'walking distance' from the entire town, they could not have been more excited!

A friendly realtor suggested we rent for a year, to give us time to 'get acquainted' and to sell our home in the Valley, and he took us straight to the most picturesque house in all of Laguna! It was big, Bougainvillea vine-covered, solid wood and well-built against the side of a hill, four stories high, plus a terrace with a barbecue higher than the top roof! All with spectacular, panoramic views of the ocean!

It was big enough for all of us, including Mama and Dad. We loved it and so did the kids, because although it was on a pretty residential street, it was actually right down in the town itself! The livingroom, three stories up, had a broad corner window with the best view from anywhere in the house. We put our big grand piano right in it, and looking out day after day, watching the spectacular sunsets over the ocean, Becky used to sit and play wonderful concertos, or songs like Exodus for me to sing.

I know I used to say that I wouldn't mind if girls could grow up from age thirteen to twenty in an instant, but I do have to admit there were many memorable happy times during those years!

However, now many years later, Heidi just recently told me a story about something the kids did on the day we were moving into that first house in Laguna. It was wintertime, and while the weather in Laguna was warmer than the Valley, it was still chilly, and the ocean was cold, so no-one was swimming.

But our kids were so excited to be near the beach, they all secretly put on bathing suits under their clothes, and trekked the couple of blocks down to the water's edge. They took off their clothes and for a few minutes went body surfing in the frigid waves. Heidi said she overheard a couple of 'locals' passing by make some remark about 'crazy tourists'!

Now it seems funny to me, but had I known it then, some punishment would certainly have been dished out!

Anyway, we all loved the move to Laguna, and were glad we rented for awhile, because there was more to Laguna than one realized at first. There were homes, and even housing-tracts from bottom to top, all over the surrounding hills, and also South Laguna. One section, called "Top of the World", would probably have tempted us at first, but driving up the long, curved streets to get there was not fun, and within the year, we found a great, new house to buy, just a block from the highschool, and a block (the other way) to the largest supermarket in town!

Being a tourist town, it had very fine hotels, the greatest restaurants, and many civic programs. The most important event was the "Festival of the Arts" where many famous artists living in Laguna annually display their latest works in beautifully constructed, partially-open surroundings.

Inside the festival, there is an open-air theater, somewhat smaller than the Hollywood Bowl, but similar. Every year during the summer months, on a large stage, there is created an almost breathtaking show, unrivaled anywhere in the world. It is called "The Pageant of the Masters".

Famous old-master paintings and sculptures are reproduced with real people as the figures, clothed in costumes exactly matching the paintings. The backgrounds and foreground pieces are carefully constructed, and painted as they appear in the original picture. The stage is bordered with a giant, ornate gold frame, and down in front, there's a full symphony orchestra!

The show starts at dusk, and as stage-lights come on and the first incredibly beautiful, simulated 'live' painting appears, the orchestra plays classical music as an excellent announcer's voice comes over a loudspeaker, describing the painting, giving a little bit of it's history, and usually some interesting stories about the artist who painted it.

During this time, the performers must stay completely still, simulating the real painting, but in glorious three-dimension! The beauty of this is really hard to describe, sitting under the stars on a warm night, enjoying fresh sea-breezes, listening to magnificent music played by a real symphony orchestra, and seeing fabulous, life-size versions of the most beautiful famous paintings, all brightly lit and exquisitely exhibited!

There are usually twelve or more paintings and sculptures created for the nightly show. The participating 'actors' are all volunteer residents of Laguna! As soon as one show ends, the one for the next year is soon cast, and work and rehearsals for it continue all year 'round. All of our children appeared in many of the Pageants. When one or more of our kids were in it, we were given passes for the dress rehearsal.

We soon found the schools to be treasurehouses of activities in music and art that the girls especially enjoyed! Egon, Jr. was twelve, in his first year of Junior-Highschool, and there was a new one just north of the town, and everything seemed to be going along just fine.

Unfortunately, a very sad thing occurred while we were all living together in Laguna Beach. Marilyn's father, our beloved Dad suddenly died in his sleep. He was eighty five years young, and we all loved him dearly. In my mind he will always remain one of the greatest men who ever lived. His kindness, helpfulness and gentleness are often recalled in all of our pleasant memories of him, and he lives forever in all of our hearts.

At another of our 'family meetings' it was generally decided that because Mama was living with us and was always aware of the children's activities, Marilyn and I could both work to augment our income. Actually, the kids were all old enough to be on their own, and had almost too many activities, including their own horse! Karen had bought it from a friend with her baby sitting money. It was a black Arabian jumper, quite old with some stubborn quirks, but still beautiful, and a smooth, graceful runner. All the kids loved him, and took turns riding him for miles along the beach by the boarding-stables just north of town.

One Saturday, we were enjoying a leisurely drive along the ocean south of Laguna. As we turned off the highway to buy gas, a block or so away, I noticed a really nice looking big discount-department store, called "Value Fair", which suddenly gave me an idea. If I could get a job in their advertising department, it would be a lot closer than Hollywood, where I was still working.

I went into the store and asked for the manager of the advertising department. I was told. "This is part of a chain of stores, but you're lucky! The General Manager and the President happen to be here today, which is unusual!"

I introduced myself to the General Manager, whose name was Joe, and mentioned that I was an artist with department store experience, and that I was interested in working closer to Laguna Beach where I was now living. Whereupon, he told me that they had opened several new stores, and they were looking for an Advertising Manager, but that their general offices were located in East Los Angeles.

I reasoned that although it was not real close to Laguna Beach, it was still quite a bit closer than Hollywood, and the position sounded interesting. So I asked Joe if I could meet with him Monday morning, at his office, and show him some of my work. He agreed, and we pleasantly shook hands, and I looked forward to our meeting.

I was cordially greeted that Monday morning in Joe's office, and after seeing samples of my work, offered me the job at a considerably larger salary than I was making at my present job in Hollywood.

We proceeded to discuss the various functions and approach to selling of their various stores. The image, although 'discount', needed to show somewhat more sophistication. I was happy with that, and anxious to put my creative talents to work!

I left my job in Hollywood on good terms, and charged ahead with my new and exiting responsibilities! Their program necessitated producing two twelve-page newsprint mailers every week, each containing eighty or more different advertised products, and needed some clever attention-getting headings and designs throughout!

I did the whole thing from start to finish, including directing the printing, which necessitated on many occasions my being at the printer's until two in the morning. I would then rush home, get up again at six a.m., stop at a coffee shop, and be ready for work the next day!

Fortunately, I was still young and healthy, and made up some of my lost sleep on the weekends. But my earnings were very good, and fortunately they were soon able to hire some help for me, so the late nights were getting much fewer.

When I first went to work for Value Fair, I met a friend who worked with a Discount Store Chain, called Unimart. He told me that they were looking for a Public Relations Manager who could also 'play secretary' to the Corporate Director of Advertising.

As Public Relations, she would be expected to write answers to all complaint letters, write news releases, and completely plan and execute all 'Grand Openings' which, in 1965, were almost like a neighborhood carnivals!. All this, not just for the Unimarts, but also for 126 Food Giant Markets, and the Builder's Emporium Home Centers!

I thought it sounded like a job which could make use of Marilyn's versatility, and said so to my friend. At her first interview, she was hired, and only had to drive to Santa Fe Springs, about twenty minutes closer to Laguna than my job. We usually caravaned in two cars, but often were able to meet for lunch.

The children were all in school, and Mama was there taking care of their immediate needs. They did their homework, had other school activities, even tennis, and of course went swimming at the beach. A strict time schedule was adhered to and everyone had enjoyable times. Marilyn and I made enough money to meet the needs of the children, and supply them with various sports activities to keep their energetic little beings in good mind and spirit.

The children were always the most important part of our lives, and although we strictly upheld moral principals and insisted on proper behavior, as well as respect for others, we always attended to their needs and rewarded good efforts.

Heidi and Karen excelled in art, and Becky was very talented in music. She had developed a strong, beautiful voice, and got lead parts in school performances, especially in light operas. Becky also loved to play the piano, and some afternoons when I was home early enough, some of the boys from the highschool 'Glee-Club' came over. Becky always enjoyed showing off my powerful tenor voice, and played accompaniment for me to sing some songs for the benefit of the boys.

Egon, Jr. was as fine a young boy as you'll ever want to meet, always friendly and polite to everyone. He was a tall, strong boy for his age, and aggressive bullies backed-off from tangling with him. He became friends at school with a boy whose father owned a yacht brokerage on Newport Bay. We sometimes let Egon go with him after school, and he taught Egon how to sail all kinds and sizes of sailboats.

It was not long before Junior saw a single-sail catamaran in the harbor, called Aqua-Cat. It was a small, light, easy-to-handle craft, and he 'desperately' wanted one! The agency for them was on Newport's 'Upper Bay', which connects to the main bay under a Coast Highway bridge, and is a nice sheltered area for smallcraft. Luckily we found that this little catamaran was only two or three hundred dollars, and for a small fee, he could store and launch it right there by the bridge.

So every day after school, he rode his bicycle to Newport Beach, a distance of about nine miles, and greatly enjoyed learning to 'fly a hull' and the many catamaran sailing maneuvers. He of course was always home before dark, and did his homework after dinner.

After about a year of sailing the Aqua-Cat, he began entering local races, several of which he won. Then one day, he casually remarked, "Dad, there's a catamaran that's so fast it beats everything in the water, and it's called a Unicorn." I went to see this 'Speed Demon', and was thoroughly impressed!

The hulls were long, thin, and very pointed at the bow. All catamarans have a canvas decking, but this one seemed to be made of a stronger nylon-type material, and the mast was higher than any I'd ever seen on a 'cat'. It looked like a craft from outer space which would fly away if you didn't tie it down.

Well, that thing cost over three times the amount of the Aqua Cat, which we would sell, but Junior agreed to also get a paper route to help pay for the Unicorn. I felt it would be a good learning of responsibility to help pay for a coveted item.

This got him into racing earnestly, and we had to join a yacht club so he would have 'colors to fly' and be able to enter International races. We found a new, smaller yacht club where he could also keep this larger catamaran.

The yacht club had a low monthly fee, but a requirement that members pay a fairly good sum for monthly 'services' whether used or not, and these so-called 'services' included eating in their dining room! So a few times each month, Marilyn, Mama, and I, and sometimes some of the kids, were 'forced' to enjoy some lovely lunches or dinners looking out at Newport Bay!

I guess that living near the ocean, and especially beautiful Newport, boating sort of gets in your blood, because one day I stopped by a yacht sales agency 'just to look'. Of course, right in my barely possible price range, they had an absolutely beautiful forty-foot Owens, with shiny mahogany decking, chrome rails like new, and twin 'Chevy' 200-Horsepower engines, powerful enough to reach Catalina in forty-five minutes. (It was a two hour cruise on the 'Big White Steamship'!)

The little yacht's main salon had a couch that became two 'bunks', a large 'dinette' that made into a twin-bed, and a complete electric galley with a large enough generator for all the electricity we could ever use. There was also a 'head' with a shower, and a separate master stateroom.

When we were also offered a permanent mooring on a close-in channel with a large parking lot on Coast Highway, it became our yacht and a beach house all rolled into one! We named it "Caldean", ancient Greek for "Follower of the Stars".

There never was such a boat! It had controls inside as well as dual controls on the flying bridge, ship-to-shore radios, a large afterdeck for lounge-chairs, but also with a fully-automatic live bait tank, plus outrigger

Egon Jr. at the age of his Catamaran racing days. Shown here Egon with Egon Sr's. cousins from New York, Rose and Walter Gruen, a most pleasant and congenial couple.

Egon Jr. rigging his "SPEED DEMON" Unicorn Catamaran.

The Reich's home on Linda Isle (Newport Beach) with private dock (at low tide).

The "ULTIMATE FUN MACHINE" a Hobi 16 on the dock at their house.

The Reich's "Owens" cruiser, a party boat, fast and elegant.

poles for fishing Marlin!

Marilyn and I thoroughly enjoyed the boat as a weekend 'get-away', and we had many great day-cruises along the coast, and to Catalina with all the kids and their friends aboard! Junior continued doing well in catamaran racing, including Internationals held in San Pedro, which is the big Los Angeles' Harbor. We would watch those races from the Owens, and sometimes we were a committee boat, making sure all racers followed the laid-out course correctly.

Marilyn and I were both doing well and enjoying our jobs, when suddenly the company where Marilyn worked sold-out completely to Vornado, a Chicago-based, National retail conglomerate. Many changes began taking place, one of the first being a new Corporate Director of Advertising, Marilyn's 'boss'. He only saw Marilyn listed as Public Relations Manager, and very soon informed her that in a meeting with the Vornado executives, they insisted that in their corporate structure, Public Relations did not exist, and Marilyn was to be fired.

Marilyn had become familiar with food manufacturers' radio and television allowances, which could give 'free advertising' to the market chain, but had to be correctly 'qualified'. She had heard that the food industry was new to Vornado, and that the new Advertising Director had only been with non-food companies, so she discussed the possibility of her being in charge of radio and television advertising for the company.

The new Director arranged a meeting for Marilyn to fully explain the thing to the Vornado Vice-President/General Manager of their new Western Division. The meeting lasted well over an hour, and as they were walking out, Marilyn overheard the Vice-President say to the Ad-Director, "If we had about seven Marilyns, you and I could play golf every day!"

The result of the meeting was that Marilyn was made a full Corporate Vice-President, in charge of radio and television buying, producing all cooperative advertising commercials, and it also involved working closely with the buyers in arranging product-purchases with connecting allowances. The entire operation, the way Marilyn pushed it, became so big that within three months she had a secretary and an assistant working under her. She was also getting to know all of the radio and television sales and production people, as well as representatives of many major food manufacturers.

Sometimes I stopped by her office on the way home and met some of these people, and as we got better acquainted,, we asked some of them out on our boat on weekends. I also became acquainted with some of the company executives, and Marilyn and I were invited to various dinners and parties.

On one such occasion, quite a humorous thing occurred. A top executive in charge of the San Diego food stores invited us to join him and his wife for dinner at a theater-restaurant. On stage, a so-called 'hypnotist' asked for audience participation, and I volunteered.

As he began his act, those of us who did not pretend to 'go to sleep', were called 'not good subjects for hypnosis' and escorted off the stage. He then had each of us in turn do something 'under hypnosis', and when he came to me, he asked who I had always wanted to be, and I replied, "Mario Lanza."

Our host did not know of my singing ability, and after the 'hypnotist' made a few gestures toward me, he said, "You are Mario Lanza! The stage is yours!"

Whereupon, in my best full-tenor voice, I sang, "Be my love, for no-one else can end this yearning, this love that you and you alone . . . "

I finished with huge applause, and when I returned to our table, Marilyn had not 'said a word', and our host insisted I had been really hypnotized! Even though I explained to him that I sing that way all the time, he kept insisting that no-one could sing that good without being under hypnosis!

Another really funny thing, was that before I left the stage, the 'hypnotist' quietly asked if I would join his act as a regular participant in all of his performances. I politely declined!

While we enjoyed working for big companies, I kept thinking about the fact that a large chain like Food Giant was able to qualify for a big dollar amount of television advertising, because of volume purchasing, and smaller market chains could not take advantage of such allowances, because even the smallest radio buy was higher than their purchasing-volume could generate.

Another thing Marilyn had done for Vornado was establish a 'house' advertising agency to receive the fifteen percent 'agency commission' from the stations. She and I constantly discussed the details of her work because most of them were so interesting.

CHAPTER 15

A New Enlightenment

Finally I had an idea! If I could combine several small to medium-sized market chains, and advertise them together, it should generate the volume equal to a large supermarket chain, thereby qualifying for certain advertising allowances. The first thing I had to clarify was how I could advertise several products on one radio announcement without conflicting with FCC (Federal Communications Commission) regulations.

I explained my idea to the General Manager of one of the top Los Angeles radio stations. He had become a good friend, and after pondering a few minutes, he came up with a brilliant idea. I could establish an umbrella company, under which I could advertise various products on one announcement.

I thought of the name "Southern California Manufacturers and Retailers Association", "SCMR" for short, which satisfied everyone, and I soon had <u>five</u> supermarket chains <u>under contract</u>, including the then smaller Albertsons.

This opened up a whole new horizon for us! Marilyn also saw the great potential in all of this, so she resigned her position with Vornado, and we worked as a team in our new company, SCMR.

We also established an advertising agency, called "Rex Advertising" in order to earn the accepted fifteen percent agency commission from the media. We chose the name, "Rex Advertising", in honor of Marilyn's royal grandfather, August Rex.

We rented a nice suite of offices right in Laguna Beach, overlooking the ocean. Although I did quite a bit of daily driving, we still were almost always close to home.

Our new business enterprise became very successful, and I was able to help food manufacturers obtain shelfspace for their products in the stores. The supermarkets were happy because we generated extra profits, by way of free advertising for them.

All of us loved our life in Laguna, when overnight the town seemed to become a haven for outcasts, squatters, and young girls and boys in outlandish hairstyles and torn 'Levis'. They swarmed in from all parts of the country, and it seemed Laguna Beach became a 'melting pot' (and I'm sure they were smoking plenty of 'pot'!) of the 'Hippie' cult!

They were lying in the streets, the beaches, all over the place, stoned out of their heads! Hanging in groups, singing and playing weird instruments out of harmony, and worst of all was the large amount of open drug use and sales which was going on!

The 'Hippies' even began accosting older, decent people, anyone dressed conventionally, right on the street. One morning, Marilyn arriving at our office in a business suit, had one of those disgusting characters, probably high on drugs, step in front of her and spit in her face. We were both horrified over how Laguna Beach had changed!

The drug cult behavior was beginning to infiltrate the school, and we were of course concerned about the influence on our children. We began looking for new living quarters away from this horrible 'Hippie-Den' Laguna had become!

This all took place in the 'sixties', and I am happy to say that as of this writing, Laguna Beach has long since returned to it's original artistic charm, and we now enjoy visiting there again.

Marilyn and I, as well as the children, still enjoyed spending time on our boat. It was always docked on a channel of Newport Bay, across from a very exclusive section of homes, called Linda Isle. Every house had it's own waterfront terrace with a large boat dock. While relaxing on the deck of our boat one day, I noticed a 'For Sale' sign on the house straight across from our dock. I contacted a realtor, and bought that quite elegant house. So, all we had to do was drive our boat across the channel, and we were home!

This house was large enough to use one of the downstairs rooms as an office, and still had plenty of room for all. Besides our boat, the dock had room enough for Egon's catamaran, and a small sailboat called a "Kite" we bought for Karen. On several occasions, I enjoyed watching Karen with the little sail nearly touching the water, speedily sailing across the bay.

Linda Isle consisted of beautiful homes, and not only gave us the many pleasures of boating, but also the opportunity of meeting new and wonderful friends. One of such neighbors were Rosanne and Richard Valdes. Richard owned a yacht manufacturing company, Columbia Yachts, then later, Lancer Yachts, and presently, Mediterranean Yachts. All of his yachts, from twenty-six feet to sixty-five feet, have always been of the highest quality, beautiful and expertly designed. Rosanne, his lovely wife, besides being the mother of their six wonderful children, is a congenial, sweet, and artistically talented lady. We are proud to have in our possession some of her art, which she has so generously given to us. Our lives certainly have been enriched by our friendship with them and their family.

As time went on, Heidi had been in a local college for one year when she turned eighteen and got married to a nice young fellow who had a good job with the post office and was very athletic. They both enjoyed swimming and other watersports.

Becky married her highschool sweetheart when she turned twenty. He was very handsome, and by then had a well established pool construction business. Both girls lived nearby, and we all enjoyed visiting with each other.

About a year after her marriage, Becky presented us with our first grandchild, a beautiful little girl named Victoria. Two years later, Vicky helped welcome her baby sister, Melody. Both girls were absolutely 'living dolls', very smart and talented, and we enjoyed them so much!

"Out of the mouths of babes!" There were many instances when our little grandchildren said or did cute things! One Fourth of July, we were all together watching fireworks at the beach. Vicky was still under two years of age, and she was sitting on my shoulders. As each burst of lights filled the sky, we would point and say to her, "See, Vicky! Another one!", and again, "Another one!" over and over. When the show was over, and we were walking back to the cars, I still had Vicky on my shoulders, when she excitedly pointed to the sky and said, "Anunner one!". We all looked up toward where she was pointing, and there it was, a full moon!

When little Melody was only five, she was reading simple books, but the amazing thing was that when she read aloud, she used dramatic expression, like a trained, experienced actress! I made several tape recordings of her readings and still treasure them. She was, and still is so pretty, the song, "A Pretty Girl is Like a Melody" could have been written about her!

Our kids were mentally well balanced in school and in everything they did, perhaps because Marilyn and I were always there, and tried to set good examples for them. I also think the sailing served as an emotional stabilizer. Maybe it was a little of both.

Egon, Jr. had learned to like fishing from his grandpa, and often asked if we could go fishing on the big Owens. The 'price' for going fishing on the Owens was for him to 'swab the deck' and generally put the boat in sparkling clean condition. He didn't complain much and always performed this chore to perfection.

He usually took a school-friend along, and of course, the Captain (me) had to go along as well. First, we always had to go to a fuel-dock and fill-up with fuel, then buy live sardines for the circulating bait tank, and we were ready for the 'high seas'! About ten miles offshore, we would stop the engines, and the boys would cast their lines.

On one of these fishing trips, as we quietly floated along, I jokingly said, "I hope you don't catch a whale!"

Just as I spoke these words, not more than four feet from the boat, a dark gray pointed mountain emerged up from the sea! Then it immediately vanished back below the surface of the water!

The boys excitedly asked me if I had 'seen that whale?' I told them I couldn't have missed it, and that it must be bigger than our boat!

I had visions that if he didn't like us, he could probably upset our boat, but I guess they are somewhat docile creatures and he was only curious, because he stuck his head out of the water several more times, each time a little further away. We were relieved, but at the same time excited over such a close contact with that wonderful creature of nature!

Marilyn and all the kids and their friends enjoyed many very special trips on that convenient and comfortable boat! Going to Catalina was always enjoyable, and often exciting when we encountered large schools of Dolphins or Porpoises. Although our boat was fast, they would keep up with us, moving from one side of our boat to the other! If I tried to maneuver the boat into the middle of their group, they quickly all moved together on one side again! They are amazingly intelligent and beautiful creatures!

Sometimes, as we crossed the channel, we saw ominous fins cutting through the surface of the water, and there was no mistaking who they belonged to! We were all glad to be aboard a sturdy, safe boat as we watched the Sharks swimming in large circle-patterns. Unlike the Dolphins, they paid no attention to our boat.

Getting closer to the island. we always encountered another rare phenomenon, only found in a few places on the globe, and the Catalina Channel is one of them! They are Flying Fish! I had heard about Flying Fish from Marilyn and her dad, who used to see them when Marilyn was staying at Catalina, and she and her dad crossed the channel frequently. But to imagine Flying Fish, unless you believe in fairies and mermaids, is almost impossible!

To actually see them is an amazing experience! They are a little over twelve inches long and a shining silver color! They shoot up, about four feet out of the water with their wide, wing-like pectoral fins broadly outstretched, and actually fly alongside the boat for fifty to a hundred feet before slipping back into the water. They are particularly beautiful at night when boats shine lights which attract them. Their 'wings' take on an iridescent, shimmering translucency as they swiftly glide along with the bright beams of light!

It was always peaceful, anchored in the Catalina Harbor, or in one of the sheltered Coves on the lee side of the island. Catalina is a large enough island to give secure protection from the untamed sea. There was a feeling of adventure, along with the great beauty of the sea, so one needed to be ever alert for the unexpected!

I recall one trip we took to San Diego, a cruise south along the coastline of about seventy miles. Marilyn, Karen, Egon, Jr. and I did not start off until late afternoon. We enjoyed relatively calm seas for that time of day, staying about three miles offshore.

By the time we reached San Diego Harbor, it was pitch dark and a fog had rolled in, bringing visibility down to two or three feet. We knew the entrance to the Harbor was at the south end of a long jetty made of huge, sharp boulders. I had Karen position herself on the very tip of the bow, holding tightly to the secure chrome railing.

I thought I was quite familiar with the length of the rocky jetty, so when I believed we were at the harbor entrance, I slowly turned the boat inland. Almost immediately, Karen let out a loud yell, "Dad, you're going to hit the rocks!"

I quickly set both engines in reverse, and just made it away from possible disaster! A short distance further south, we began seeing buoy lights, and were able to find our way to the docks of the hotel where we always stayed.

That hotel catered to boater-guests, and provided fun activities for kids and adults alike, including rentals of various water-sports equipment. Or, we could just board our boat and cruise the harbor. There were huge Navy ships moored right nearby, and one time we pulled in close to an Aircraft Carrier. Looking up from under the long, protruding decks, gave a view not otherwise possible to see! The height and enormity of this beautiful ship was breathtaking.

We had had several years of enjoyment with our boat when one incident made me decide that the ocean is best left to the fish! It was a calm, sunny morning as we cruised toward Catalina, and our less-than-an-hour crossing was enjoyable and uneventful, except for our usual sightings of Dolphins, and those ever-present Sharks.

We all had the famous Calamari-burgers for lunch, and enjoyed the island until about four in the afternoon, when we boarded our boat for the return journey. The sky had become somewhat overcast, and there was a slight northerly wind blowing. I thought it was nothing to worry about, but a few miles from the Catalina shore, the wind picked up, and huge swells developed which seemed to come from all sides! I knew to point the bow into the wave, but as soon as I cut into one of those huge swells, another would hit the side of the boat, sending it listing dangerously close to completely capsizing!

No matter what I did, trying various speeds, and making full control-use of both engines, even that big, heavy, forty-foot boat was being tossed around like a cork in a tub of water!

There seemed to be no let-up in the force of the wind and the size of the waves, which had begun crashing clear over the top of the boat! We had on our lifejackets, and were saying our prayers, when we sighted shore! The swells were still large, but had somehow become manageable!

When we could get our bearings, we saw we were twenty miles south of our usual destination-point! I still had to fight the swells all the way back up to Newport Bay. Late-day return trips always took a little longer than the forty-five-minute morning crossings, but this had taken over three hours! We were just thankful we made it 'in one piece'!

At that point, Marilyn and I decided to become 'landlubbers', also Marilyn said she didn't mind at all giving up being the 'Galley Slave'! We loved taking little trips to the local mountains, and to visit Marilyn's sister, Phyllis, above Yosemite, or even take a trip to Northern California to see the redwoods. So we sold the boat and bought a medium sized motor home, a GMC with extra-large windows all around, and a streamlined, aesthetic design. It also had air-cushioned rear wheels, comfortable, adjustable seats, and even the driver's area had the great big windows all around for excellent viewing. A 350 horsepower engine allowed it to climb all mountain highways with ease.

There were two swivel 'lounge chairs' for passengers, plus a thickly padded 'dinette' which could convert to a bed. The 'kitchen' was complete with a full-height refrigerator and a microwave oven which worked on either 110- volt or 12-volt power.

A double-bed room was at the back, and a bath with a shower had a clever doorway arrangement that could form a temporary 'dressing room'. Lots of closets and storage cupboards were all around, and we had our own generator producing 110 volts, plus a bank of several batteries for 12-volt usage. Everything, even the inside lights, worked on either voltage system. There was a large water heater and extra big water tanks. Our two gasoline tanks held sixty gallons, giving us quite a traveling range.

Although the boat provided us with many memorable and educational experiences, the motorhome proved to be more fun, and allowed us to conveniently travel to many interesting places. One trip we will always remember was a business trip to Portland, Oregon. We took the inland, fast highway up there, but wended our way along the coastal route on our return trip. The distance from Portland to Los Angeles is a thousand miles, a two-day trip, but coming home along the coastline, we took ten days.

We had never visited the giant redwoods, which are another sight so amazingly beautiful, they are hard to describe. Even seeing a color movie of them, can't compare to actually being there and perceiving the incredible height of those sky-touching trees and their enormous trunks with deeply-cut, ruddy-red, thick bark! You must touch it to actually feel and discover and understand the beauty of those behemoth trees!

To see the redwoods, we had driven a short distance inland from the mountainous shore-area, just south of Crescent City, California. At one point, we stopped the motorhome in a wide 'turnout' along the two-lane road. There were no other cars around, and I walked into that very quiet

The Reichs' home away from home in the all comfort "GMC" motorhome. Visiting incredibly beautifully displays of the power of nature.

"TREES OF MYSTERY"

A scenic attraction within the beautiful giant Redwoods, in Northern California.

It's worth a visit!

"Cathedral Trees" formed by nine living trees, so tall they seem to reach to the heavens.

These trees stand in quiet serenity, for those who are lucky enough to see and experience this phenomenon. One of the biggest living giants, thrilling to just touch.

Along the Northern California coastline.

forest, dwarfed by those wondrous trees. There were large ferns and other healthy green plants and bushes all around with a soft ground-cover of finely granulated redwood bark, achieved by nature over thousands of years. Everywhere, we saw fat squirrels with shiney coats, jumping to and fro, and birds singing with bell-like clarity! It was a symphony of nature's most lovely creations!

One giant redwood tree was lying on the ground with thick, powerful roots exposed, probably felled by lightening eons ago. The thick roots were like steps for me to climb up onto the tree, and the trunk was so broad, it seemed as if I was walking on a flat surface, rather than a round one. My shoes are twelve inches long, so I carefully stepped-off the length of the tree, which was 306 feet to the top! Marilyn and I both felt very privileged to see those breathtakingly beautiful trees!

Seeing and experiencing all the wonders the world presents to us, makes one pause and reflect on how and why all this is so. Life is like a window which opens at birth, and one wonders why it must close. Perhaps a better analogy would be, for us to be grateful for any time our window is open. At least this is the healthier attitude, bringing us happiness, rather than sadness. I know that both Marilyn and I are thankful for every minute our window of life stays open.

I also feel quite sure there is a greater purpose for us going through life, which is why there are things that give us a sense of morals and an inherent knowledge of right from wrong.

Although we sold our boat, we still enjoyed our home on the bay, and Egon, Jr., and Karen still made good use of the boat dock. Karen's 'Kite' had the reputation of being the most difficult small sailboat to handle, so she particularly enjoyed her expertise with it. Junior still raced his Unicorn Catamaran, so he gave me quite a surprise one day when he announced he wanted to make another change, to a 'Hobie Cat 16'. He explained that the Hobie 16 had two sails, a 'main' and a 'jib', so it was more maneuverable. Here, I thought he'd never part with his Unicorn, but I soon saw he really did have more versatile fun with the Hobie. He was still able to race, and Hobie Cats had become so popular, there were also beach picnics and other social activities.

CHAPTER 16

The Road to Success

Marilyn and I also enjoyed working from our home, and always were a good working 'team', as we saw our food marketing business flourish. Many clients (food manufacturers) sought our assistance in helping to market their products.

One such client was a well-established, large but local, white-bread baking company. They were having trouble holding their shelf-space in the super-markets, and when their president called me, we arranged a meeting at his plant in Los Angeles. He was a very congenial person named George, who explained that the bigger markets were all buying bakeries of their own, and producing 'house' label breads. This pushed other brand-name breads either totally off the market or reduced their shelf-space so drastically that many major brand breads were losing money!

George's fine, older baking company was seriously affected by these actions of the supermarkets, and he looked to me to come up with a possible solution. I was well aware of what was happening, and was also aware of a strong trend toward nutrition and whole-grain breads. When I discussed this with George, he showed me a line of "wheat" breads they had already tried to bake and sell. They were small, one-pound loaves, rather dry, and not even well marketed. Of course, they were not selling!

I told George that to force the supermarkets to carry his products, so as to increase sales, he would have to take the following steps.

First, he would have to have a label with something on it of vital interest to the general public, and something the supermarkets could not copy!

Secondly, it would have to be an extraordinarily good tasting loaf of bread. Thirdly, it must be large, a one-and-a-half-pound loaf! And last, but not least, it must be really whole grain.

George had no idea how he could accomplish all this in one loaf of bread!

Especially, requirement 'Number One' seemed almost impossible! So, I asked George to give me a few days to come up with the answers.

The most highly respected name in nutrition at that time, 1971, was Adelle Davis. She had many medical degrees, but had also spent years in research beyond basic medicine, into bio-chemistry and nutrition. Several books she had written, all based on medical research, had sold over fourteen million copies, and her many television appearances made her name known to 'everyone'.

Now, Adelle Davis was a very close friend of ours, dating back to when she knew Marilyn's mother. We often visited, and she wrote about my good diet in one of her books, and I also did some illustrations for her book called, "Let's Have Healthy Children." Adelle Davis was a brilliant person who absorbed herself in her work, primarily for the good of humanity, and was forever helpful if someone was in need.

She used to get up at midnight, to write until seven or eight in the morning, when she would make breakfast for her husband and two children and begin her busy day of nutrition-consulting with a large number of patients. She said she had to write at night because it was quiet, and the telephones did not ring. She ended her day with patients at four, and read medical journals until dinnertime. She had a lady come in daily to fix dinner.

Adelle wrote the first Macmillan textbook for highschool nutrition classes, and was President Eisenhower's personal nutritional consultant. Marilyn and I loved and respected her greatly, and one time at her house, I met Tom Brokaw who was there for an interview.

But now referring back to my conversation with George at his baking company, and my 'Number One Requisite' of having something on the label of vital interest to everyone that the supermarkets could not steal nor copy! My thoughts continued with, "What would meet these requirements better than the name 'Adelle Davis' on the label of an outstanding, genuine nutrition-bread!"

Even though we were very good friends, my first call to Adelle about my idea of using her name, was met with a definite, "No!", because she had never commercialized her name, and had very strong feelings about never wanting to. She also said she had no interest in any monies from any such venture.

However, because of our close friendship, she agreed to meet with us to discuss some of my other ideas. Marilyn and I drove to her home at the appointed time, and she greeted us warmly as usual. Knowing she absolutely did not want to endorse any product, I kept thinking of other ways to use her name, and pointed out to her that her name carried with it an assurance that anything connected with it must be trustworthy! Her name could help promote nutritionally-valuable food products, and therefore increase the buying of <u>good</u> food right at the food-source! At that time there were very few good-tasting 'real' whole-grain breads on the market.

She agreed with our theory, and I could tell my next thought was actually turning the tide! One of Adelle's most famous books was, "Let's Cook It Right", an amazing 'gourmet' cookbook, with a 'healthy' version of every famous recipe! So I suggested that instead of calling the bread, an "Adelle Davis Bread", it would simply say, "Made from an Adelle Davis Recipe".

I incorporated this statement in a dignified manner within a small oval design of wheat. We all agreed that this use of her name had far more salespower than simply another famous-name product, of which there were many. Somehow, it even sounded more appetizing!

She next, very firmly stated that she had turned-down offers from many, many companies, simply because she did not feel she could trust their integrity in the production of food products. She asked us if we intended being personally involved with the manufacture products showing her name, because she said we were the only people she knew that she felt confident would make trustworthy products. We assured her we would not only constantly be involved, but would always get her approval of all ingredients, prior to producing or marketing the breads or any product.

I then suggested a royalty based on number of loaves of bread sold, and again she stated that she did not want to personally benefit financially. My next idea was to form an 'Adelle Davis Foundation' to receive the royalties which could be used to further studies in nutrition. This idea greatly appealed to her, and Marilyn sat right there at Adelle's typewriter, and together we wrote a simple agreement which we both signed. Marilyn and I had some experience in the correct wording of Agreements and Contracts, and one time the little paper we wrote that day, proved it's legality in a court action, due to someone, not Adelle, trying to dispute our Agreement.

At this same time, I also needed to create a name for our breads, and after various considerations, settled on the name, 'Better Way'. I was able to obtain a Trademark for the name for the breads, cereals and other baked products.

Now having a signed Agreement to use the name, Adelle Davis, I went back to George at the bakery. He was very impressed, and almost jumped for joy when I told him I would help produce the product, design the label, and also be involved with the marketing. Of course we both understood, I also intended to share in the profits.

Before actually arriving at a plan as to how I was to be involved, we needed to develop a bread. I needed to be enthusiastic over it's taste, and it's appearance was of the utmost importance also.

I very soon learned that a large white-flour bakery, such as this was, with big machinery, producing enormous quantities of bread at one time, found it very difficult to bake a bread with all whole-grain flour. Adelle would not approve the use of any white flour, and even to this date, most 'wheat' breads contain considerable amounts. To hide this fact, the baking industry is allowed to call white flour, 'wheat flour'. Only 'whole wheat flour' in the list of ingredients gives the assurance that it is what it is meant to be.

The reason for this, is that the bran and the wheat germ make whole wheat flour heavy, so it is difficult for the bread to rise. White flour rises much more easily, which aids in mass production.

However, with the help of George's 'Master Baker', a formula was developed, containing extra wheat germ, and other good ingredients that should make what promised to be a wonderfully nutritious loaf of bread! On Saturday (bakery 'down' day) they tried a test-run of 200 loaves, the smallest 'bake' possible in that huge equipment. From an expense point of view, it was imperative that the first test-bake be successful. Result ? Bread almost as flat as pancakes!

The same formula, at home with a small oven, produced a gorgeous loaf of bread! So they adjusted timing, plus mixing procedures, and after the second, third, and even the fourth try, George informed me that they had thrown out 800 loaves of bread and couldn't afford to continue testing. It was the firm opinion of the 'head baker' that a loaf with all those ingredients like extra wheat germ, and no white flour, probably couldn't be done!

But I had confidence, and asked to sit down with him and analyze what we could do to get a good loaf of bread! I strongly felt that it just had to be a matter of finding the right proportions, the right balance between ingredients, including even minute amounts of salt and sugars. After quite a long discussion, I discovered that one of the most vital ingredients in holding up the bread during and after baking, was wheat gluten, which is 75% pure protein, and high on Adelle's list of approved ingredients. I suggested adding considerably more gluten to the bread, and we made a few other minor adjustments, all of which should help somewhat, and it seemed at last that we might be on the right course!

I was determined, and George agreed to continue using his bakery if I would stand the cost. It actually took five or six more Saturday test-bakes, but we suddenly had a beautiful looking bread which was moist and tasted better than any other bread on the market! We were really, finally on the road to success!

I had also had several meetings with a large National bakery, called American Bakeries, whose Los Angeles plant was very close to George's. They had 140 trucks, compared to George's 45, and they wanted to distribute our new bread line, but their baking-capacity was filled at the time. So I arranged to have George's bakery bake the bread, which increased his production to the capacity he needed, and American Bakeries would do the distribution.

To build our business on a good foundation, we incorporated with the name, "Better Way Foods, Inc.", a name for which I also received Copyright and Trademark protection. As soon as people saw we were using the name, Adelle Davis, in conjunction with our product, we were approached by several people wanting to invest in our company.

I was not willing to sell more than ten percent of our total stock, and I did sell about that much. I made certain that I only sold to persons who proved in writing that the nominal investment given to Better Way would not cause any hardship to them, should the company experience difficulties.

The breads were an immediate success, selling over twenty-thousand loaves the first week, with no prior advertising! Of course, the name, Adelle Davis on the bread, drew people to it like a magnet! But to maintain high <u>repeat</u> sales, the bread would have to be good enough on it's own merit, and I drove to the bakery daily, making certain that it was. We started with several varieties, such as Wheat Nugget and Seven-Grain, plus others!

*"The Road
To Success"*

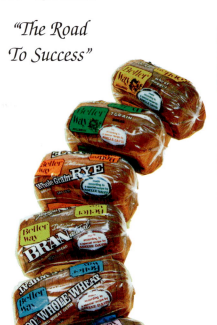

Egon formed Better Way Foods, Inc. with nationally distributed breads and cereals. At a booth at a food convention, daughter Karen and friend manage the promotion.

The complete line of breads as they appeared in the Chicago market.

Egon's wife Marilyn was vice president and controller of Better Way Foods. Her competent financial leadership helped the business become and remain successful.

Two views of the Better Way mixing plant in Newport Beach. It always received the highest commendation from health department inspectors.

If the bread wasn't an excellent product, enjoyable to eat, no matter whose name was on the wrapper, there would not have been continued repeat sales, and Better Way Breads have proven themselves Nationally, for over thirty years!

Because of the breads' immediate success, it soon became necessary for American Bakeries to do the baking of the breads themselves, but they had 'served their purpose' for George! They had helped keep him in business until he could arrange for a very successful sale of his bakery to a large cooperative grocery distribution company.

With the breads so successful in the Southern California area, I wanted to increase distribution all over the country. American Bakeries had baking plants in many cities of the United States, and as they took over the baking of the breads locally, I developed a closer relationship with their executives.

I was told that the most acceptable manner of association with large National bakeries would be for me to develop a bread mix, which I could produce myself. It would be sold to the bakeries with a basic formula and baking procedures, and 'Better Way' bread wrappers, as a 'Franchise Bread'.

We opened our own 'Dry Mix Bakery' plant with two-thousand pound 'dry ribbon blenders' and even a 'hammer mill' to make some of the flour for the 'Seven Grain' variety. We rapidly grew in various areas, but it wasn't without a lot of work. Besides supervising production, and producing various advertising promotions, I had to travel quite a bit.

We hired two full-time bookkeepers, but Marilyn soon found she had to learn 'Accounting', to protect us from 'uncaring' accounting firms. The plant operated efficiently and in good order.

It was about October 1973 when suddenly Adelle Davis died, which grieved us terribly and shocked the whole nation! Of course, no-one lives forever, but Adelle, in her seventies, was doing some bone and mineral absorption experiments which necessitated taking a number of X-Rays. Doctors concluded that it was possibly because of this that she contracted cancer.

I always suspected that the long hours she spent writing, reading, and generally benefiting her patients may have caused abnormal stress, and might have been a contributing factor in her illness. But it was never noticeable, because every time we saw her, she was her usual relaxed, very pleasant and happy type of person.

Her books remained in demand, continuing their important contribution to humanity and the furthering of nutritional knowledge. We continued to use her name on our products, and they remained very successful. Because of their quality, they stood on their own merit.

CHAPTER 17

"Feeling Our Oats"

Then one day, a day we always depicted to be somewhere in the future, suddenly became the present. Our daughter, Karen, announced she was getting married. We were aware of the nice young man she was seeing. He was in the construction business, and had bought houses at a good price that needed renovating, then sold them at a good profit.

Karen was talented in interior design, and even knew how to hold and use a hammer! They found compatibility and love, and we helped them have a beautiful wedding at a church in Newport Beach, called St. Andrews which Karen selected because it was all light-blue inside!

They bought a new house high on a hillside in Laguna Beach, and a year or so later, presented us with our third beautiful girl grandchild, named Deanna, and two years later, precious baby Jenny. The grandchildren were all such happy blessings!

Egon, Jr. was now a handsome young man, six-foot, four-inches tall! He had been dating a girl he had known since highschool, and they had a beautiful church wedding with a garden reception at the lovely home of the girl's parents in a nearby neighborhood.

Junior was going to college with plans to become a dentist. He and his wife both worked and earned sufficient to support themselves and live comfortably. Their first child was also a girl, Erin Melissa, who had natural light red hair like my mother's. This gave us five granddaughters, so when Junior's next child was a boy, it was an exciting day! They named him Egon Tyler Reich III, and to avoid confusion, we called him by his middle name, Tyler.

Realizing our bread business was becoming bigger, and in need of help in management of sales and production, Egon, Jr. said that he would like to work with me in building the company. I was pleased because he was, and still is, a very intelligent person, and I needed someone on whom I could depend completely. It became wonderful to work with him, and he could relieve me of many problems and responsibilities. We progressed with further distribution and new products I had in mind.

One such product became a National best-seller. It developed in the following manner. In the mid-nineteen-seventies, there evolved a craze over an oat-type cereal product young people called "Granola". The stuff being sold was mostly oats with some raisins and a few nuts thrown in. Among the recipes I had from Adelle Davis was a product she referred to as a health cereal. I had tasted it some time ago, and was very impressed with the flavor and high nutritional content! I decided to jump on the 'Granola Band Wagon' with this cereal, and called it simply, "Better Way Granola". I even improved the recipe somewhat with a better baking process, and had a 'granola' product far superior to anything yet on the market.

It consisted of only about twenty-percent oats, with large equal amounts of wheat germ, sliced almonds, sesame seeds, non-fat milk, and other high protein and flavorful ingredients. When baked correctly, it tasted so good, nothing to this day has come on the market to compare with it.

To test-market this product, I designed attractive clear bags, so the product could be seen, because it not only tasted delicious, but was appetizing in appearance. I had produced about 200 cases. Each cardboard case contained twelve packages, and I decided to take five cases in my car to a small healthfood store near our home. The owner knew who I was, and I asked him if he would mind if I would put out some little paper sample-cups with a few 'nuggets' of my new granola in them for customers to taste the product.

He agreed, and although his little store did not have much foot-traffic, there were at least a dozen or more customers during the couple of hours I was there. To the proprietor's amazement (and mine!), every customer (I mean, each and every one!) that tasted my granola, bought at least one bag!

The store owner said he had never seen a response like that with anything, and bought the five cases from me, then and there! As he re-ordered another five cases less than a week later, he remarked that it was the best selling item in his whole store, and that people 'must be inhaling the stuff'!

Next, I approached the largest healthfood distributor in Los Angeles with my product, and he rejected it, saying that they had their own granola, and it was not selling very well.

That same day, I bought two Ford vans, and asked my daughter, Heidi, and my son-in-law, Randy (Becky's husband), if they would want to try selling directly to healthfood stores from Santa Barbara to San Diego. I offered them a good commission, and they both agreed to give it a try, if only to help me out, and get the product started on the market.

Well, a strange phenomenon occurred! Every healthfood store, large or small, experienced the same 'buying-frenzy' as in that first little store!

Suddenly, we began getting 'phone calls from stores, saying they were 'out' and needed more immediately! The word actually spread all over the country, and distributors were contacting us, from California to New York and Florida, and all States in between! I don't think there was one town or city in the United States where we didn't sell our granola with great success!

The Los Angeles distributor who had turned me down, now begged me for it! Although Heidi and Randy were doing well, with their little vans, we all realized that it was 'bucking the system', and they were glad to have helped me get the product started, and they had made a few extra dollars besides. So I got out of the distribution business almost as quickly as I got in, and I contracted with every major healthfood distributor in the United States!

Another item of interest was that our competitors were not happy, including the biggest, Quaker Oats. They had their own granola product which was dropping in sales, so they decided to make a product 'like ours'. They had millions of dollars to spend on advertising and flooded the market with their new granola, but of course, it was far inferior to ours and did not make a dent in our sales volume!

The President of Quaker Oats, aggravated at that, and knowing that I bought all my oats from them, called me one day and bluntly stated, "We're not going to sell you any more oats!"

Fortunately, I was immediately able to purchase the highest quality oats directly from a mill in Oregon, at even a slightly lower price.

The granola craze continued for several more years, and our product remained in great demand. We also were making progress with the distribution of our breads. Although I began my working-life as an artist, I enjoyed running a business. There were difficult times, even very difficult times, but there were also the elating times when problems were solved or overcome.

There were the times when I had the privilege to meet top executives in large companies, some with great insight and talent and who have remained my friends to this day. One such person was Bill Ennis, an executive with American Bakeries, who was instrumental in establishing our breads in Oregon and the State of Washington. I have dealt with many good managers, but Bill and I had many things in common so we really enjoyed our conversations.

Marilyn and I visited with him and his wife. I still did quite a bit of singing in the evenings, and continuously made tapes of my singing to orchestral recordings, I found out that Bill belonged to a theater group, and performed singing also. We exchanged tapes, and I was very impressed with his voice and presentation, and he was enthusiastic about my recordings.

Bill also had a great sense of humor, and every time we talked, we had a few laughs. He was Irish and he knew I was not, so every St. Patrick's Day he would send me a funny card, usually with a Leprechaun, in which he 'made me' an "Honorary Irishman for the Day!" I always thanked him, and even sent him a St. Patrick's Day card in kind! One time I heard that the early settlers in Ireland came from the Czechoslovakian regions of Europe, and because my ancestors came from Czechoslovakia, I told him I might be Irish too, and we might even be related! Well, he said that there is probably a little Irish in all of us, and I am inclined to agree.

What I must now sadly write is that Bill suddenly died of a heart attack, which was a great personal loss to me. As a close friend, and fine family man, I know I am among many who miss him greatly. I will never forget that cheerful Irishman who will always hold a special place in my heart.

Besides working to build our business, I also kept my eyes and ears open to opportunities in real estate. I did not have the time to aggressively pursue real estate investing, and I would not have wanted to deplete the cash flow from the bread business, but I was always anxious to analyze a special or unique property availability.

One such property drew my attention, right where we were living, on Linda Isle. It was a new, distinctive house, built, furnished and beautifully decorated by the Chairman of the Roadway Inn hotel chain and his wife. Tragically, just before they were to move in, his wife passed away.

Alone, he did not want the house, so he asked a friend on the island to sell it for him. I noticed a small 'For Sale' sign on the house with a telephone number. When I called the number, a neighbor came over and showed Marilyn and me the property. The house was larger than ours, and Marilyn was amazed that the furnishings were all 'her style' which she called 'elegant Colonial'.

The owner was anxious to divest himself of the property, so the selling price was attractive, and I jumped at it! Amazingly, it included all furnishings, custom brocade draperies, even a German Stroh original crystal chandelier! For a short while, we made mortgage payments on two houses, but that made the move unhurried, and we soon sold our first house.

Living in that beautiful house was most enjoyable, with it's exit via Newport Harbor, directly to the open sea. Our young sailors (our kids) continued doing full justice to the boat dock, and our lovely place on the bay.

We also enjoyed inviting friends and business associates for terrace parties, or a day at the private Linda Isle swimming beach, clubhouse and tennis courts.

After living on Linda Isle in Newport Bay for several years, we saw values of homes considerably increasing, especially this type of waterfront home. One day, I was approached by a direct buyer with a generous offer.

It so happened that Marilyn and I had been looking at a very rare and exclusive estate on upper Newport Bay. (It was originally built by Ruby Keeler, a famous movie actress and dancer, who was also at one time, married to Al Jolson.) The property consisted of three acres with massive lawns and gorgeous landscaping, a 6,000-square-foot Colonial house, a forty-foot swimming pool, even horse stables down by the entry-drive.

We knew that an investor had bought that place four years before, so we went to the realty office who specialized in those estates to see if one in that vicinity was for sale.

Well, I guess as the saying goes, timing is everything! The agency owner was sitting at his desk preparing a full color ad, because he had just that morning listed the very place we had fallen in love with four years before!

Although considerably higher priced than our Linda Isle home, I found that the profit derived from the sale of Linda would enable us to purchase this fabulous estate! So without blinking an eyelash, I said, "Cancel the ad. The property is sold!"

The realtor took us out to see the place, which we found had been some-what abused by renters, but was as fabulous a mansion as we remembered! When we got home, I called our buyer, and told him we would

"BAYCLIFF"
The Reich's ultimate home on Newport Bay. A lovely 3 acre estate overlooking the upper bay and natural bird sanctuary.

Part of the expansive 6000 square foot ranch style house, with a half acre of front lawn.

Summer or winter the 40 ft. pool was always ready for swimmers.

The estate had a beautiful playhouse for the grandchildren. Egon Jr's Erin is shown here.

A rose garden...
...and a stable for horses.

accept his offer if I could take the chandelier, draperies, carpeting, and of course all the furniture. These were all exquisite and expensive, and were now needed to restore the Back Bay estate to it's former elegance. The gentleman agreed to my terms, and we soon found ourselves moving into that beautiful custom estate!

Our chandelier, the brocade draperies, and the carpeting all perfectly enhanced the large rooms of the mansion. The Linda Isle house was almost 5,000-square feet, so all the furniture was large and arranged perfectly in every room! I remember saying to Marilyn that within a year, our new estate would be worth a million dollars more than we paid for it!

Interestingly, we had only just got settled, when a gentleman drove up our long drive, bordered by cypress trees, and said he heard this place was for sale. He was a prominent builder in the area, but was interested in it for his own home. When I told him that I was sorry, but he was too late, that we had just bought it, he asked if I would mind telling him what we had paid for it. When I told him, he said, "You stole it!" Actually, for prices at the time, we had paid a fair amount, but he undoubtedly meant that these rare properties would quickly increase in value.

Even then, there were very few properties in Newport Beach with that much land, and especially overlooking the Bay! We really loved it there!

Every room had big picture-windows overlooking expansive lawns and the bay, with an abundance of trees and gardens. Outside of the large living-room window, Marilyn designed and had the gardeners 'create' a pretty little rose garden, with a charming cast-bench, and a sundial in the center.

The house itself was 6,000-square feet, all on one level. It had a high-beamed ceiling over a thirty-five-foot-long game-room, where we put our large pool table. There were many built-in party-serving areas, both inside and outside in a semi-enclosed terrace, including two brick barbecues. One barbecue was out on some gorgeous wood decking by the huge forty-foot pool. It was a circular firepit-style where the kids spent many summer evenings roasting 'hot-dogs' and marshmallows. Junior even used to bring friends over after a day of fishing, and barbecue their day's 'catch' out there.

There was also a custom-built, two-story playhouse, which had an enchanting front porch, and window boxes with brightly colored flowers in them. Marilyn furnished it with a table and chairs set, a complete kitchen set, even a sink (with a water 'tank' in back of faucets), and baby dolls with a crib, a doll buggy, even shelves, books and the like. We still had little grandchildren who spent many happy hours playing in that darling little house!

Marilyn had a sewing/hobby room in the 'south wing' of the house, next to a large guestroom with a door to the central yard with the pool. We had twin beds and a crib in that large room, and huge closets full of sleeping bags, for any number of the grandchildren to 'sleep-over'.

Mama had what was almost a separate apartment, and I think the only piece of furniture we needed to buy for that whole house was a beautiful little mahogany desk for Mama's room. She picked it out in an antique store, and it is still one of our 'treasures'.

Our 'master suite' consisted of two large bedrooms, a dressing room and two bathrooms, one with a large tile shower, and one with a built-in tile whirlpool bath, plus amenities such as a built-in massage table and a built-in 'vanity'.

There was a large kitchen with a 'snack-bar' and a cleverly designed 'wall of cupboards', plus a full 'butler's pantry' with lovely glass-door cupboards. Marilyn put those to good use, because besides our 'good' china (antique German Dresden) which we displayed in a large cabinet we had bought for the diningroom on Linda Isle, we had a very pretty green English Staffordshire set we used for family gatherings. Our service for sixteen filled the cupboard.

To go with such an elegant estate, of course we had to have an aristocratic cat, and no cat was more aristocratic than the one we purchased, a proud and gorgeous Abyssinian, we named Bes Ra Sehket. The 'Ra' meant 'God', or in her case, 'Goddess'. 'Bes' was an 'Imp' or little jokester. Sehket meant cat (or mountain lion, which she looked like in miniature!).

Bes Ra had a habit of jumping up, onto the kitchen sink, between the butler's pantry and the kitchen. I drew an imaginary line, beyond which Bes Ra was not to go, and enforced that line by removing her from the sink if she stepped beyond it, saying, "You're in the wrong place, Bes Ra."

After I had performed this action several times, all I had to do was say, "Bes Ra, you're in the wrong place!", whereupon she would give a little 'hiss', but right away jump off the sink.

This was usually followed by a hug from me, and a "That's a good kitty!" Anyway, she was as beautiful as she was smart, and we were all enchanted by her.

CHAPTER 18

My Kind of Town Chicago is . . .

At that time we had a well-organized flour mixing plant in an industrial area of Newport Beach, only ten or fifteen minutes drive from our home. We also had our main offices there. The bread franchise business was growing, and together with the Granola sales, enabled us to purchase a beautiful four-bedroom house in a very nice neighborhood in Costa Mesa for Egon, Jr. and his wife to live in. They needed to get settled with their two fast-growing darling children, Erin and Tyler.

We had bread contracts with bakeries in Los Angeles, Arizona, Oregon, Washington, New York, and Florida, and I was most interested in associating with a major bakery in Chicago, a prime market where we were not yet selling the breads. Chicago was an interesting market, with several of the biggest National bread companies distributing their products there.

However, there was also one very large local bakery which still dominated Chicago, and was well-liked and respected by the general public. They were owned and run by a very fastidious family, under the name New Process Baking Company, and their basic line of breads were called, Holsum.

I was fortunate to meet their Vice-President, General Manager, a man of vision and foresight, whose name was Bob Kaliebe. Bob liked our breads and our marketing concept, and chose to start production with two varieties.

It has been my experience through various aspects of life that some people who talk a good story, and there are some who are do-ers. They take the ball and run with it! Bob was definitely one of the do-ers!

Our "Better Way Breads" showed excellent acceptance, so four more varieties were introduced. This gave the line large displays, and therefore created good sales! Of course, they were producing an excellent product.

It gained the attention of a local newspaper, who conducted their own 'blind taste test' against other major brands. "Better Way" was chosen the favorite, and soon became the best selling 'specialty bread' in Chicago!

We enjoyed a long and happy relationship with Bob's Chicago bakery, which lasted even beyond the time when Bob's bakery was sold. Actually, the bakery has been sold a couple of times since then, but "Better Way Breads", to this date, are a successful part of the Chicago bread market.

I have always respected Bob Kaliebe throughout the many years I have known him, and he remains one of my few, but dearest friends.

To reach most of our major markets, our bread mixes were in hundred or fifty pound bags, with an 'order' usually totaling forty-thousand pounds, and adding a very high shipping cost to the mix. Trying to keep my prices to the bakeries as low as possible, I investigated the possibilities of purchasing large diesel trucks to do our own shipping.

The dealers selling those amazing vehicles assured me that after delivering our product, we could easily 'pick up a backhaul' as the truckers called it. In order to accommodate a greater variety of such loads we would be bringing back into California, I bought three fifty-foot freezer/refrigeration trailers with three Peterbilt diesel trucks (called cabs or tractors), all big ones with 'sleepers' (a bed behind the drivers' seats).

At first, they looked like shiny new 'toys' to Egon, Jr. who immediately rushed out and got a truckers' license! He actually did make some of the mix deliveries to Chicago and New York, although he very soon found it was not all 'fun and games'! There was a lot of paperwork, keeping an accurate driving 'log", obtaining permits or licenses to drive into every State, and then there were many truck scales causing delays.

Anyway, that wasn't the worst of it! To get backhauls from New York, truckers drove to the big produce mart in the Bronx. Criminals, knowing truck drivers had to carry some cash, hung around there. Most drivers carried guns for protection. Junior was so big and strong, he always thought he was invincible, but on one occasion, he had parked the truck to wait for a load, and had his back to the street because he was looking through a tool compartment. Suddenly he had a premonition that someone was behind him. He grabbed a large wrench, and quickly swung himself around, just as an equally big guy was lunging at his back with a large pointed knife!

He only averted getting stabbed by a split second reflex action, whereby he swung the big wrench he held in his hand, towards the assailant, who realizing he meant business, ran away as fast as he could.

This incident shook up Junior greatly because he has never been an aggressive person, and the thought of having to hurt someone bothered him as much as the worry of getting hurt himself. When he called and told me about the incident, he pretty much said he thought this would be his last trip!

Theoretically, the cost of the drivers, and running the trucks, subsidized by the 'backhauls', should have made delivering the mixes far less costly than 'common carrier'.

However, there were small accidents and costly mechanical 'breakdowns' almost constantly, and I had 'lots of fun' hiring drivers! There were drivers arrested for driving under the influence of alcohol, and finally one episode that made me give up the delivery business entirely!

One winter day, it was snowing, and a driver leaving Chicago with an expensive backhaul of frozen ducks, fell asleep! He careened across a snow-covered field, sliced a power pole in half, rolled down an embankment and landed in a good sized creek.

I got a phone call, about two in the morning, from a sheriff somewhere in Illinois, asking when I was going to get my truck out of their creek. He said that our trailer was on it's side, and frozen ducks were floating down the half-frozen creek out of sight!

Well, I didn't get any more sleep that night, and after arranging long-distance, the lifting and towing of my equipment to a local truck-stop, found out that both truck and trailer were 'totalled'!

I was insured, but it still cost me several thousand dollars to 'bail out' of the whole incident After replacement of the equipment, and because we had always kept our trucks in good working order, I was able to sell at not too great a loss. Under no circumstances did I want to continue in the trucking business, and using 'common carriers' proved simple, and without too many headaches!

There are of course always things to be learned from any undertaking! I recall one interesting experience when we hauled a full load of frozen Alaskan Halibut from Seattle to Los Angeles. They loaded those huge, hundred-pound fish from floor to ceiling, front to back, with no wrapping of any kind, right into my bare freezer-trailer.

After unloading at a freezer-warehouse in Los Angeles, the truck drove directly back to our mixing plant. I was there when the driver opened the big back doors of the trailer, and we were hit by the strongest fish-smell one could ever imagine! I thought, "There is no way we can ever use this trailer again, especially for bread mix!"

I called the fish warehouse and complained that my trailer was ruined! Their answer was, "No problem!", and proceeded to tell me to buy several large cans of ground coffee, and spread it about a half-inch thick over the entire floor of the trailer. I was then to close the trailer tightly overnight, and they assured me that in the morning all the fish smell would be gone.

I did as he said, and sure enough, the next morning we opened the trailer doors and were greeted by only a slight odor of coffee, and not even the slightest smell of fish! I was thankful to have learned that trick, and it was a lot cheaper than the cost of a new trailer!

Being an artist, one would think that life should be relatively peaceful, and if your work finds a market, you can even make a good living without too many frustrations. So it was for me, a person, who as a successful commercial artist for the first thirty years of my professional life, found solitude and a measure of satisfaction in the work I was doing.

My temperament, however, told me to forge ahead into the world of business, with it's frustrations, hard work, late hours, salesmanship, even seemingly insurmountable problems. All these were some of the inconveniences I had to come to grips with.

Of course, such nerve-wrenchers can actually be part of a formula for success, <u>if</u> the undertaking is based on a good idea, built on a solid foundation, well investigated and analyzed, and most of all in most cases, sufficiently financed.

My concept was solid and my execution well done, proof of which was the success we enjoyed! I must confess, however, that as an artist, not only by choice but by nature, I had to use tremendous willpower for my character to change into a super-salesman and negotiator. Even the production, and the procuring of the various items required to complete the finished product, presented a new and difficult activity for me.

While I had to work hard and ponder over many problems, I admit I found great pleasure when my efforts bore good results. Other very happy memories come from some of the difficult times of running my business, when certain people were exceedingly helpful and made my problems seem to vanish.

One such person was a man whom I am lucky to be able to count as a dear friend to this day. His name is Dan Richter, and I hope he will forgive me for writing his real name here, but Dan always was, and still is one of those persons who makes you feel comfortable.

Whatever business dealings you had with him, they would always be as agreed, so you could relax and know his product would be good, on time, and without his problems being brought into the equation. Besides, Dan is the most wonderful conversationalist, and a real artist in his own right. Dan builds model ships, and is amazing at building furniture. He is a self-taught good pianist, is highly intelligent, and of very fine character.

We only met Dan's very sweet and darling wife once or twice, but 'behind a good man is always a good woman'. I know from remarks Dan has made, that their relationship is as loving and true as Marilyn's and mine.

Dan and his family live in the midwest, and one of my greatest enjoyments is when I pick up the 'phone and give Dan a call, or when he calls me. Dan has a dog, a Beagle named Barney, and I always enjoy hearing the way Dan describes their activities and adventures together! I would imagine that Barney does things pretty much the same as other dogs, but the way Dan tells about his antics, you could enjoy listening for hours!

I am certain that if he would put his words into print, no-one would want to be without a book about "A beagle named Barney" by Dan Richter. Dan is retired and keeps busy, so my prodding him to write about Barney has not born fruit! Anyway, the world is a better place because of a dear friend of mine, called Dan.

Marilyn and I kept very busy running our business, and we were extremely happy how well our products were accepted.

Our happiness was marred by the sad occurrence when my beloved mother had a stroke and passed away. We all loved her dearly, and the children could always find comfort in her sweet and loving ways. She had worked hard when she was young, and her hands were never idle! It became tradition for her special walnut-torte cake to be the official birthday cake in our family, and when she was not cooking up some Viennese delicacy, she was sewing, knitting, crocheting, or even doing exquisite oil paintings of Aus-

Egon's darling mother shown here with one of her incredibly delicious walnut-torte masterpiece cakes.

Granddaughters Vicky and Melody, daughter Becky with husband Randy, all loved great grandma's birthday cake.

These are reproductions of some of Egon's mother's paintings and needlepoint work. Picturing Vienna and Austrian scenes. She didn't start painting until in her 70's. Never having had any formal training, her work reflects a simple but pretty charm.

trian scenes. Her paintings took awards in several local art shows.

She had the most beautiful handwriting, which was admired by all who received correspondence from her. In retrospect, I wish I had spent more personal time with her, but the business and the children took most of my attention, even though she lived with us and we were always close to her.

Of course, the loving married years she spent with Marilyn's father were beautiful and memorable. She and Marilyn were always very close. Marilyn took some art classes with her, which was when Mama started painting, and also joined a local women's friendship club with her. The club had a lovely monthly luncheon with entertainment, as well as a handcraft-group, and a travel section which Mama particularly enjoyed. She went on many day-trips to places like art museums or theater, and 'overnights' to the Grand Canyon and the like. So her many later years with our family were rich with fun activities. We all still miss her and remember her in loving thoughts.

My sister, Lotte, had flown from Vienna to visit several times, which were joyous times for everyone. Lotte is a clever, lively and fun person to be around.

The last time she visited, just shortly before Mama passed away, she told me that Austria had finally been mostly re-built from the ravages of World War II, some fifty-fife years before, and suggested that Marilyn and I visit her in Vienna. For all these many years, I had honestly had no desire to ever visit Austria again.

Somehow, I had deep fears that history would repeat itself, and I might be caught and stranded in another sudden political upheaval! However, I had another very close and dear relative, a cousin named Walter Gruen, who also had to flee from the Nazis. Walter lived in New York with his darling wife, Rose, and he wrote to me, assuring me that Vienna was beautiful again and that there were absolutely no dangers anymore. In fact, he had had his own business for quite a few years, importing Austrian-made products, and he traveled there on a regular basis.

He also said that the food in every restaurant was exactly the same as when we were young, and that cinched it!

CHAPTER 19

The Duke of Norfolk Lives in My Castle

The business was running smoothly, our production-manager was experienced and trustworthy, and Egon, Jr. was there as manager of the whole operation. Our daughter, Karen, had been working for us in the office, and she kept track of inventory and ordering materials and supplies, and we also had a competent bookkeeper.

So Marilyn and I decided to plan our first trip to Europe! We found that lower airline rates started in September, and also decided that it would be the best time of the year for traveling. We would have missed the summer heat, and there was no danger of winter storms that early.

There were no direct flights to Vienna, and connecting flights were either from London, England or Frankfurt, Germany. A couple, who had been long-time friends of ours, had recently moved to the southern seacoast of England, and we thought it would be nice to visit them. I also have a cousin, Susie Gates, living north, near Manchester. Then, we could even visit my Uncle Josef Reich, who is about my age, and lives in Cambridge, where he had been a nuclear scientist with the university there.

So we really wanted to spend some time in England, and made reservations with British Airways to Heathrow in London, and with Austrian Airways to Vienna. The anticipation was as exciting as the trip itself!

I had bought our tickets directly from the airlines, so they probably thought I was a seasoned traveler, and somehow I missed getting the information that only two suitcases were allowed per person.

As we packed, we reasoned that because of the vast distance we would be away, we needed to be prepared for all eventualities! Marilyn felt that in the fall, it could still turn quite warm, and we knew the high mountains would be very cold, so not really knowing what to expect, we took everything! From Marilyn's 'white-champagne' mink coat to sheer georgette blouses, our closets looked almost empty when we were finally <u>packed</u>!

With our respective passports in order, tickets in hand, and seventeen pieces of luggage, we arrived by limousine at the Los Angeles International Airport. We must have looked like real traveling novices, because the ticket agent commented that she had never seen two people with that much luggage. I guess we thought we were moving to another planet!

When we were all safely aboard in our reserved window-seats, we settled back, preparing ourselves for the eleven hour, non-stop flight to London. We left in the early evening, and the closer we flew to the east, the quicker the darkness of night arrived, and then conversely, the quicker the sunrise and daylight appeared!

We slept only very little during that first trip, and we welcomed the several refreshment 'breaks' as well as an excellent dinner and hot 'kippers' and omelette breakfast! We were 'singing the praises' of British Airways all the way! I also feel we are all very fortunate to have such wonderful flying machines as the Boeing 747!

We arrived about eleven a.m. London time, and were helped by a friendly porter to our luggage. I rented a large Mercedes sedan, and with the help of the porter, loaded all of our suitcases. A generous tip to the deserving porter, and we were on our way!

On our way? Yes, but! Our destination was The Ritz Hotel in mid-town London, and we had a detail-map from the car-rental agency. However, there was one slight flaw! Everybody was driving on the wrong side of the road!

The steering wheel of the car I was driving was even on the wrong side of the car! It was as if I had to turn my whole brain around to be able to stay on the side with the rest of the cars!

Another problem was that the map showed the streets going where we wanted to go, but being an old city with narrow streets, most of them were marked 'One-Way". The map could not show this, because we found out later that some were one way in the morning, and the other way for heavier traffic returning home in the late afternoon!

One street I needed to take was not accessible, and the alternate took us in the wrong direction, further away from the hotel, so I had another idea! There were big, black taxicabs everywhere! I hailed one that came alongside our car and asked if he could lead us to The Ritz hotel. He said, "Follow me!", and after a few confusing turns, we were there! I paid and tipped the taxi driver, and we all were happy.

Our friends had driven up to London and were at the hotel waiting for us! We enjoyed a late lunch with them in the most beautiful diningroom we had ever seen in our lives! We even actually tried to buy one of the oval-backed chairs to ship home, but they would not sell it to us!

Everyone advised us to go immediately to bed to sleep-off the 'jet-lag', so we went right to our room. Now we had down pillows at home, and even a down comforter for the few really chilly nights in California, but that bed at The Ritz was the softest, puffiest down we'd ever felt, above, underneath, and all around you - like floating on a cloud!

Our friends were there the next morning, anxious to show us the Harrod's Department Store we'd heard so much about. Walking into Harrod's is like walking into a different world, but still very much on earth! To try to describe the variety and fabulous displays can never do it justice, so my message to everyone who reads these pages, is, "Please, just go there!"

London has much to offer, but Harrod's is one of the most unique sights! The most impressive part of Harrod's is called "The Food Halls". The walls are gorgeous, decorated tiles, and there are fresh foods exhibited in ways so beautifully imaginative that only with personal observation can one comprehend and appreciate the extent of the artistry in their displays!

That afternoon, we took a taxi to 'Madam Touseaud's Wax Museum which is all about England. We saw Henry the Eighth, as well as the present queen with the whole royal family, all standing there so lifelike, you felt they were talking to you personally, as you read about each on small posters.

There is also a celebrity room with every famous person who ever lived! Then we gave a glance at the famous dungeons with an imaginary Jack-the-Ripper, but found ourselves much more impressed with the 'upper floors'!

However, I did want to see the real Tower of London and the Crown Jewels, so when a taxi driver said the 'tours' were only twenty minutes long, and ran continuously, we let him take us there too. Very impressive! With no time for a complete bus tour, we then had a taxi take us by Westminster Abby, Big Ben and the Parliament Buildings, and Buckingham Palace. The driver pointed out many famous statues and other historical sights, and we saw part of Hyde Park, and lots more that I really don't remember anymore.

We were anxious to be on our way, because we were next going to visit our friends on the coast of southern England. They were not far from a small town called Adundel which was the area of one of the most romantic and beautifully kept castles in all of England. As one enters the little town of Arundel, one seems to be immediately transported back in time to the sixteenth century!

There are small houses, several hundred years old, built mostly out of stone, with big, heavy old wooden doors. Everything is kept very neat and clean. There are quaint antique shops (Marilyn found an 1860 Meissen figurine just in from an old estate, in one of them), a bookstore, a jeweler who carried some old jewelry, a pharmacy, a small market, and several small, old hotels.

We stayed at the oldest one, the Norfolk Arms, who boasted that Henry the Eighth had visited there. It is a most charming British museum piece in itself, and the main building is said to be at least four-hundred years old. In the surrounding grounds, small, very pretty, newer 'cottages' were built, where we stayed.

The Norfolk Arms had excellent food and service, and compared to London prices, was quite reasonable. The dining room in the Norfolk Arms was beautifully adorned . It had heavy, old dark wood paneled walls, hung with colorful banners displaying British royal Coats-of-Arms. The whole place had a genuine look of Medieval times, and you could imagine, if you wanted to, Henry the Eighth looking over your shoulder.

The Norfolk Arms, as well as the whole village, is tucked against one of the massive stone walls surrounding the grounds of Arundel Castle. To walk through the castle is an almost reverent and spiritual experience, because of the beautifully-kept rooms, furnishings, and many original paintings, all dating back to Medieval times. They reflect those times so vividly that one cannot help but imagine oneself being drawn into those mysterious days long past.

The stone structure of the castle and it's moat are creations of beauty and sixteenth century design, while the original tower, or 'the keep', dates back to the eleventh century! To enter, you cross a small foot-bridge over the moat, and pass on through the original heavy wooden castle gate, with all the sharply pointed bottom posts. You find yourself picturing movies of castles with men fighting in suits of armor, except this was, at one time, all real. There are even many early suits of Armor displayed in the castle.

Arundel is one of the few castles still occupied and used by it's resident, the Duke of Norfolk, whose family has had possession of Arundel for over five-hundred years. Inside the castle one sees walls filled with magnificent paintings by Reynolds, Van Dyke, Gainsborough, Holbein and many other master artists.

There are over a thousand acres of beautifully-kept green lawns and huge old trees, all giving a feeling of serenity, an ethereal atmosphere of peaceful loveliness to that very, very special place, which is forever etched in the memory of my mind.

I recall one endearing remark, one of our friends made to me, as we were walking through the park-like grounds toward the castle, "Egon, this is your castle!", to which I replied, "Yes, I know and I approve, but I'll have to start charging rent to the Duke of Norfolk!" Of course, I knew she meant it was a special kind of castle I would really love, and I thanked her for the compliment.

There are those who fantasize about 'time-travel'. Well, if you want time-travel in full consciousness and enjoyment, visit Arundel. Incidentally, this southern coastline part of England is where most of the legends of England took place. Robin Hood's Sherwood Forest is quite nearby.

After that 'experience-of-a-lifetime' visit with our friends and seeing Arundel, we found that Cambridge was north of London on the map, and chose our driving route. I surprised myself by getting somewhat, if not totally used to driving on the left side of the road.

Cambridge is another unusual place! It seems like the whole town consists of the Cambridge University. Actually, the University consists of several so-called, Colleges. Then, each College is a whole group of beautiful old Gothic style buildings, with turrets, columns, some almost cathedral-like, all with a central green lawn, big trees and colorful flower-beds.

Again, one has the feeling of traveling several centuries back in time, and one marvels how beautifully these ornate structures have been kept and survived.

We had come to Cambridge to visit one of my father's brothers, my Uncle Josef who had been a nuclear scientist at the university there, and one of the developers of the atomic microscope.

My paternal grandfather was a widower later in life, and as mentioned earlier in this book, his second marriage was to Rosa, the sister of Bruno Walter, the famous Chicago Symphony Orchestra conductor. He was also the star of the "Chicago Symphony of the Air" a Sunday night radio show broadcast on NBC for many years throughout the United States.

When the Nazis came to Vienna, their son, Josef, had been able to go to England and join the British army. He had married a lovely English girl, named Eva. Today, a display in the London Museum of Science and Industry shows a model of his nuclear microscope. He took us on an interesting tour of several colleges, and introduced us to some of the younger professors.

Josef was the most interesting man to talk with we had ever met! He firmly believes that nuclear power should be used more extensively than it is, and that it is no more dangerous than electricity or gasoline, if properly controlled. He says we have just got used to taking the proper precautions with electricity and gasoline, and because nuclear precautions are new and strange to us, we are afraid.

We enjoyed our visit with Josef and Eva. They lived in a two-hundred-year-old house built totally of stone, which was quite interesting, but had all the upgraded modern conveniences.

We also met their son, Christopher, and his darling wife, Susan, who lived nearby in an attractive red brick house with their two lovely girls, Bryony and Francesca. Josef was rightfully proud of his granddaughters who were bright in school, and talented musicians.

It was a very pleasant and exciting reunion because I had not seen Josef for many years, and he had never met my wife, Marilyn.

After our two enjoyable days in Cambridge, we got an early start for the long drive north to the industrial city of Manchester, where my cousin, Susie, lived nearby. She is the daughter of my father's younger brother, my Uncle Emil. Emil and his wife, Mitzi, were able to escape to England when the Nazi's came into Vienna, but they had to leave Susie with my mother who kept her with my sister, Lotte, for several years during the war.

Susie was eventually able to join her parents in England, and she became an English teacher. She married Bill Gates, who had a little girl also named Susan, and they had a son, named Michael who graduated from Oxford and is now married to a lovely wife in Finland, and has several children.

My Uncle Emil and his wife, Mitzi, had owned a farm, but when he retired, bought a large house which had been the vicarage, next to a beautiful old stone church, surrounded by lovely grounds with green lawns, trees and flowers.

By the time of our visit, Emil and Mitzi had passed away, and Susie and Bill had found comfort in that lovely place. As with Josef, it was so wonderful seeing Susie again after so many years, and her handsome husband was a very friendly person. They were both retired, and Bill loved working with wood. He gave us a beautiful little handcrafted wooden tray which we still greatly treasure! Susie was keeping busy writing a book about a very well-conceived, creative reading system for small children, which she had developed when she was teaching English to youngsters in a private school for diplomats and other foreign dignitaries.

We keep in touch by mail. Susie writes long letters, mostly about their grandchildren, which is good, so Marilyn can write back about ours!

Marilyn and I stayed in a large hotel in Manchester, and driving back to London, I felt almost adjusted to 'wrong-way' driving. I had timed our trip to arrive at Heathrow Airport about four hours before our departure for Vienna, Austria! This gave us time to leisurely check in and return our rental car.

Egon's most beloved castle "Arundel". Of all the castles in England Arundel is the one that comes closest to resemble a Fairy tale castle. It's unmistakably Medieval British and although originally reaching back to the year 1,100 historically unique, it is still to this date occupied by the present Duke of Norfolk.

CHAPTER 20

Wien, Wien, nur Du Allein . . .

The flight from London to Vienna took only one-and-a-half hours. This was my first trip back to Vienna, which I had left almost fifty years before!

I knew the war had left much of the city devastated, and although many years had passed, I wasn't sure just how completely re-built I would find things. If they had rebuilt, would it be the same 'beautiful ornate style' of yore, or 'plain and drab' modernized? I even found myself wondering if I would again see cobblestone streets and the streetcars running along them.

I secretly hoped that everything would look just like it did when I left Vienna! I loved all the old buildings, the big, old trees, the ornate churches, all representing in my mind the whole culture of art and music. Vienna had an atmosphere one had to experience in order to understand.

The short flight from London to Vienna went quickly because we were served a full course dinner with Paprika Goulash, tasting exactly like my mother used to make. Also, Marilyn could not believe the delicious flavor of the Vienna coffee, with it's delightful fragrance wafting through the cabin of the 'plane!

The sights from the airplane window were breathtaking! The sunny weather brightened the various lavish greens of farmland below, interrupted by sections of lush forest!

We landed at the new Vienna airport, rebuilt and very modern, making embarking convenient and easy! I was amazed how practical and accessible they had arranged all travel needs such as car rentals and luggage pick-up (with a porter and a cart)! As we left the luggage area, there was my sister, Lotte, with her husband, Hans, and my cousin, Fred, all welcoming us with open arms!

Lotte carried a large bouquet of beautiful flowers for our hotel room, and we were all overjoyed to see one another! Cousin Fred was born in Vienna as I was, and was the son of my father's eldest brother, Sigmund, who had long ago moved to Sweden. Fred, who had spent most of his life in Canada, had recently sold his business there, permanently retiring back in Vienna. Fred was a tall, handsome and very friendly person, ready to help us and to show us around!

After much happy hugging, and briefly discussing our itinerary, I rented a Mercedes sedan, large enough for all of our luggage. I had made reservations at Vienna's finest hotel, The Imperial, mainly because I thought it would have the most authentic Viennese atmosphere.

We knew there was a hotel called The Vienna Hilton, but I thought a Hilton would be like the ones in the United States. Not that there would have been anything wrong with that, but we wanted to experience the differences of being in another land.

So, I followed my sister in her car to the Hotel Imperial, and we were told that there had been a mix-up in the reservations, and they did not have a room for us. They offered to call and reserve a room for us at the newest hotel in Vienna, the Biedermeyer, which turned out to be absolutely charming! It was Viennese-Art-Deco in styling with very high quality shiny wood furniture, and was right in a part of downtown Vienna, surrounded by shops and cafes!

Our reservations there were only for a couple of days, when the Imperial would have a room for us, so we checked-in and unloaded our luggage there, but then asked where we could find the most 'authentic' Viennese restaurant to have dinner. Interestingly, we were told that the most famous chef in Vienna had recently been hired by the Vienna Hilton for 'The Prince Eugene', their main diningroom.

We all jumped into my car, and drove the few blocks to the Hilton. To our surprise. 'The Vienna Hilton am Stadtpark' had the most Viennese atmosphere you could ask for! As we entered the lobby, there was a small all-girl orchestra, playing beautiful Strauss waltzes! The girls were wearing long white dresses with big, full skirts, and the conductor played the violin and danced as she 'conducted'!

We just sat there in the lobby for awhile, listening to their enchanting music! I told Marilyn that when I was a child, every Sunday, just such a ladies' orchestra, much larger, but dressed the same, would walk and dance along the streets of 'Old Town', playing the same as were hearing them

Arrival in Vienna...
Although not much sleep was
had during the 11 hour flight,
Excitement and exuberance
overcame temporary jetlag.

As they arrived in Vienna, Marilyn, with
her little scooter (Amigo).

Cousin Fred, Sister Lotte bringing
bouquet of flowers with husband
Hans to greet them at the airport.

Egon's favorite
Hotel, the Hilton
at Stadtpark.

Peacock's prancing and
flying loose in
Stadtpark, adjacent to
the Hilton Hotel.

Music and dance
hall at Stadtpark.

then!

Across the lobby, there was the entrance to a most elegant and beautifully decorated restaurant, The Prince Eugene. There were many old original masterpiece oil paintings on the walls, one very large one depicting Prince Eugene in uniform, on a horse. Prince Eugene is a revered Austrian historical hero who successfully defended Vienna against the onslaught of the Turks in the seventeenth century. He was given a castle by the Emperor at the time, which is now a historical museum with many fine murals and oil paintings, as well as grounds overlooking Vienna with breathtaking views!

The ambiance of the Prince Eugene restaurant was impeccable, with beautiful wood tables and chairs, and linen tablecloths. The china and silver were the finest. Of course, any restaurant could boast these amenities, but the food was really Viennese! It was also so delicious and fastidiously prepared and served, it had to be incomparable to anywhere in the world!

I have patronized many fine gourmet restaurants in Canada and all over the United States, and many were certainly excellent; however, to me the Prince Eugene at the Vienna Hilton was the ultimate! So there we were, having made reservations at the Imperial to find the Vienna atmosphere and the cuisine we wanted, and having avoided what we thought would be an Americanized Hilton!

What a surprise when the Vienna Hilton fulfilled both requirements beyond our highest expectations! Everything seemed 'meant to be', because when I inquired at the desk, they had just had a cancellation, and we found we could stay there the entire time! We cancelled both the Biedermeyer and the Imperial, and checked in at the Hilton, where they brought a large crystal vase to our room for Lotte's lovely flowers, and we placed them on a small, low table in the room. It gave a lovely touch to the enchanting atmosphere of our 'home' in Vienna for the next two weeks!

That first night in Vienna with my sister, Lotte, her husband, Hans, and Cousin Fred, as we were enjoying the fabulous dinner in the Prince Eugene diningroom, we made plans for the following days.

Lotte and Hans had kept the apartment they owned in town, but were retired, and actually living about fifty miles south of Vienna, in a beautiful little village in the country. The village is named, Sieding, and it is nestled at the foot of the magnificent, high Schneeberg (Snow Mountain), which is also a popular ski-resort area. We planned to drive out to Sieding the next day, and Fred was also going to drive and meet us there.

Marilyn and I slept well, surrounded by down pillows , down comforters, and even down featherbeds over the mattresses, every bit as luxurious as the Ritz in London, and we awoke early the next morning. Our room was on the eleventh floor, overlooking the city of Vienna and the Stadtpark (City Park) below. The Stadtpark is probably the most beautiful park in Vienna with green lawns, big old trees, and an abundance of colorful flowerbeds, all reflecting in mirror-lakes along the middle of the park which extends for miles along a part of the city. There are charming stone bridges, and many stone statues of famous composers, artists, and one particularly impressive monument showing Johann Strauss, standing full-figure in a sculptured arch, with violin in hand.

Beside it is a large gazebo where part of the Vienna Philharmonic Orchestra plays Strauss waltzes every afternoon unless it rains! There is also an outdoor tearoom in the daytime, in front of a large gorgeous classical style building called the Kursalon. Inside the Kursalon, there is waltzing every night, again to the fabulous playing of a smaller group, but all from the Vienna Philharmonic, in other words, the best!

Both in the daytime and in the evenings, peacocks with their brilliant, iridescent colors, parade proudly and freely throughout the park. Several evenings, we have seen peacocks fly up and strut along the balconies on the front of the Kursalon building, which is well-lit at night. The peacocks seem to add an unusually theatrical effect to the music being heard in the park.

The morning after our arrival, we first enjoyed an unbelievable buffet-breakfast in a charming dining room on the second floor, called Cafe am Park, with large windows overlooking an outdoor terrace and the park beyond.

As we had arranged, we then drove the fifty miles, enjoying seeing beautiful hills and landscapes, then farmland as we came to Lotte's house in the country.

It was a small, but pretty house, set among big trees, and just the other side of the drive by the house ran a clear, fresh-water creek. When stopping on a sturdy, new-looking wooden foot-bridge, one could look into the water and see many large, active, healthy trout swimming briskly against the very fast current of the stream.

The water was only about two feet deep, and very clear because it emanated from the adjacent high mountains. One could see those beautiful trout very clearly, and they responded actively to the little morsels of bread I tossed to them! I had no interest in fishing for those trout, although it was legal if one secured a fishing license. I just loved to see those active and seemingly happy fish!

My sister then told me about some friends of theirs who owned the first ski-resort hotel, a picturesque guesthouse chalet, on the road up the big mountain. They had a particularly good restaurant, and Lotte and Hans had made reservations for all of us, including Fred. We drove together through a few beautiful mountain passes with rock-cliffs and trees on one side, and the rushing, bubbling creek on the other, and soon arrived at the quaint and beautiful chalet-hotel.

We were greeted like loved-ones, and served the most delicious Austrian meal with grace and smiles. The dining room was somewhat rustic with pine wood walls, tables and floor. The tablecloths were handwoven with Austrian country designs.

Not far from the Chalet, there was a train station, and one of the trains had tracks with a gear-assembly, which allowed it to go almost straight up the side of the steep mountain to the very top of Schneeberg! It was a clear, sunny day, so my sister suggested that we still had time that afternoon for the two hour ride, and she said that there was a lodge, a giftshop, and a famous little wedding-chapel up on top, and the views alone were worth the trip.

One look at that shiny, black and red, cutest of all trains in this world, and I was sold! I had to ride in it! Marilyn, always a good sport, had her doubts, but came with us, and kept saying later that she was so very glad she did. In fact, she loved it!

The little steam engine's front wheels were smaller than quite large rear wheels, so with two or three passenger cars, it looked comical, like it had it's nose to the ground when on level terrain! Of course, when traveling up steep inclines, it was level, if you were inside!

The train track consisted of two narrow rails with a gear-rail in the center, onto which a gear wheel underneath the little train engine engaged, so as we 'chugged' up the mountain, there was the constant reassuring click, click as the gear wheel would engage and move the train another 'notch' up the mountain. Of course there was also a very heavy-duty set of brakes for use if and when needed. The trip got quite exciting at times when it looked like we were chugging over just air, with rocky cliffs beneath us!

Another pleasant surprise was halfway up the mountain, the train stopped for a safety-check, and to 'rest' the engine for twenty minutes. At the stopping point, there was a coffee shop, and Lotte told us to wait in the train while she ran in and came back with some round loves of freshly-baked 'prune-bread! Why does ambience effect the palate? We were not even hungry, and could eat very little, but it tasted <u>so good</u>!

As Lotte (and Fred) had promised, the views from the top of the mountain were breathtaking. The little stone chapel had 'masterpiece' stained glass windows in rich jewel-tones, and we could understand why couples made the effort to plan what would certainly be an 'unforgettable' wedding on top of Snow Mountain!

The views going down were far more panoramic than on the trip up, because going up, you faced the mountain, and had to turn your head to see the scenery. It was a most enjoyable trip, and at no time did we feel unsafe.

Back at Lotte's house in Sieding, she insisted we have a light snack, then the drive back to Vienna was on broad and smooth freeways, so was easily driven in less than an hour.

The next morning, Lotte came to the Hilton, bright and early, to walk with us through the center (downtown) of Vienna, to see all the fabulous buildings and sights I was longing to see, after fifty years of absence and the destruction of a war.

To my absolute surprise, everything looked exactly as it did before I left! All the fabulous statues were there! The ornate buildings had all been meticulously restored, and yes, there were still the streets made of cobblestones!

The only things that were modernized, did not take-away from the charm of the city, but just provided a little more comfort to existence. For instance, the streetcars were still running, but now were streamlined and practical. A very good and extensive subway system had also been built underneath the entire city, efficiently keeping commuters on the move.

In contrast to when I left Vienna, there were now many, many cars! The main streets around Vienna, The Ring and The Guertel, had been widened, but other streets were too close to the historical buildings, so, as in London, most of them were simply made 'one-way'. Several underground garages had also been built, serving people exceedingly well.

We drove to the center of town, a huge plaza, where we made use of an underground parking structure, and right there in front of us stood the six-hundred-year-old 'Stephansdom' (Saint Stephen's Cathedral) with it's ornate steeple, said to be the tallest in the world, piercing the sky!

The entire church looks like something out of a fairytale, with beautiful ornamented walls, windows, lavish designs everywhere. It is an awesome sight to behold, and because it really cannot be described, I am showing a picture of it in this book. I was able to acquire from a church office, some of the original architect's designs for parts of the elaborate interior.

On the plaza around the church, waiting in line, are the Fiakers, those elegant buggies hitched to beautiful pairs of horses, waiting to take visitors sightseeing around Vienna. I was so elated to see that not only were the magnificent buildings and statues the same, but that many of the customs which added to the charm of Vienna were also maintained!

We all hopped into one of the Fiakers with a characteristic driver and his black derby hat. Then with a clip, clop, the horses stepped us out onto the cobblestone street. It is customary in Vienna, for cars to give a wide berth to the Fiakers, and everyone respects this.

While rolling along The Ring, a broad street circling downtown Vienna, with big, old chestnut trees along each side, we passed many fabulous sights, built several hundred years ago! First we came upon the Vienna Opera House, an impressive building with statues of horses along the roof, ornate columns and massive carved doors.

Further along, we passed several old, but newly renovated hotels, and it seemed as if every building in Vienna had classical statues as part of it's design. Next, we saw two identical, huge buildings, several hundred years old, and elaborately ornamented! One was the Historic Art Museum, and the other the Natural History Museum.

Because it would not do justice to only describe the fascinating sights we encountered on our Fiaker ride, the next few pages will show photographs of some of the most beautiful buildings, statues, fountains, and other points of interest which grace the city of Vienna.

We spent several more days with my sister, driving and walking through different parts of Vienna and visiting famous sights. Vienna is famous for delicious pastries, and we stopped in at the world-famous cafe, called Demel's, where it was hard to choose between the many incredible confectioner's works of art! Vienna coffee was served in small cups with real whipped cream.

There are two streets of note emanating from Stephansplatz (the plaza surrounding Saint Stephen's Cathedral). One is called Karntner Strasse, and the other, The Graben. Both streets, although wide, have been turned into pedestrian malls, with lots of trees and benches, and little tables and chairs for the coffee-houses, in groups along the center.

Both streets have an array of elegant, exquisite shops from the finest jewelry to porcelain, designer fashions to one of the world's most famous

Egon's sister Lotte, husband Hans and 10 year old granddaughter Marilyn at Lotte and Hans' country house in a beautiful little Austrian village near the foot of "Snow Mountain".

Lotte's lovable big tom cat Peterman and Marilyn.

A little creek runs by their house " The fish are this big in it" signals little Marilyn!

A lovely lodge in the mountains where fabulous food is served.

This little engine looks like it's sitting down, but it's designed to conquer steep slopes, up and down the mountain.

The funny little cogwheel train which brings it's passengers up to the top of "Snow Mountain".

Beautiful "Grossglockner" Mountain in the Austrian Alps.

St. Stephen's Cathedral

The Cathedral of St. Stephen. A most beautiful jewel of Gothic art, originally consecrated in the year 1144. A giant door across the facade and a myriad of symbolic decorative motifs were added in 1240. Rising 468 feet above ground level, the overpowering but graceful Gothic steeple was completed approximately 1448. With it's profusions of pinnacle spires and sculpture it is one of the most beautiful and intricate creations ever constructed. During world war II, in 1945, a bomb made a direct hit into the center of the cathedral, but the fabulous steeple remained in tact. "Stephansdome" has now been completely restored to it's original beauty and visitors can again look upon it in awe!

Schoenbrunn Palace

Schoenbrunn - (Beautiful Fountain). Facing the Palace as shown here, is a beautiful monument called the "GLORIETTE", it was built to commemorate the victory of a war at Kolin.

Started by Emperor Leopold I approximately 1683 and completed in the style of Versailles by Empress Maria Theresa between 1744 and 1749. Schoenbrunn is open to the public. Many ornate rooms with gilded furnishings and gorgeous chandeliers provide the visitor with breathtaking sights of beauty.

The Grand Ball Room of Schoenbrunn.

Pictured on left wall is Kaiser Franz Joseph with Prince William, Marilyn's great uncle in foreground.

One of many luxurious sitting rooms of the Palace.

Vienna (City Hall). One of the city's most ornamental buildings, was completed in 1872. The central tower is 325 foot tall and on top stands a 10 foot high figure of a knight in a suit of armor

Vienna's Parliament building is a beautiful example of Greek architecture.

Heldenplatz (Plaza of Heroes). This beautiful facade was erected by Kaiser Franz Joseph as an extension to the Imperial Palace about 1900.

The lovely monumental fountain in front of the building represents the goddess Athena.

The Hofburg is now like the Austrian capitol building with various government offices. It dates back to the 13th century, and was the official residence of the Hofburg family, for seven centuries. The main facade with fabulous statues in it's present glorious beauty was built in 1881.

To the east of the Hofburg is the JOSEFSPLATZ with the equestrian statue of Josef II enclosed on three sides by the Imperial Library.

Karlskirche (church). A unique design, commissioned by Emperor Karl II in 1738.

The STAATSOPER (The State Opera). Beautifully ornamented with statues and arched facades, was officially inaugurated on May 25 1869 with Mozart's "Don Giovanni". The magnificently ornate interior's auditorium can accommodate 2,200 spectators. The huge sound stage is now equipped with all modern amenities to produce many unusual effects, and the Opera's acoustics are excellent.

"Musikverein", the Vienna Philharmonic Concert Hall where the famous New Year's concert is annually broadcast all over the world.

KUNSTHISTORISCHES MUSEUM (Museum of Fine Arts). A most beautiful ornate building in the style of Italian Renaissance. In front, a fabulous statue monument to Austrian Empress, Maria Theresa.

Among many notable masterpieces you will find this beautiful Madonna and child by Duerer.

The interior of the museum is a masterpiece of art itself with beautiful statues, columns and intricate designed floors of marble. High sculptured heavy wooden doors lead to various large galleries.

Detail of the ornate ceilings are masterpieces in their own right.

The RIESENRAD. A world notable attraction in Vienna's amusement park "THE PRATER". This fabulous 200 foot high Ferris Wheel opened in 1879 and has thrilled people with breathtaking views of the city ever since. One can walk around in the full- sized "streetcars" to see the city from various directions, feeling like you are in an airplane when at the top.

(and trusted) art galleries, and there is even a small department store on Karntner Strasse. There are street-musicians entertaining, most of them actually quite good, and they always seem to have quite large, appreciative audiences. These streets contain so many places of interest, one can never tire of walking their length and back, continuously!

One whole day was planned for our visit to Schönbrunn (Beautiful Fountain). It was the Emperor's summer palace, at the edge of the city, and was originally built in 1675, and completed in 1713. The Austrian Empress, Maria Theresia, used it as her primary residence. She had many children, one of whom was Marie Antoinette, Queen of France.

Many movies have used the high-ceilinged, elaborately panelled rooms of Schönbrunn for various royal settings. There is a breathtakingly grand ballroom with a masterpiece-painted ceiling, still being used for elaborate affairs of state. All rooms on the main floor have windows overlooking the most beautiful grounds imaginable, with imposing flower beds along the sides of a promenade leading to a fountain and an unbelievably beautiful monument, called the Gloriette.

The large fountain features, in sculptured marble, larger than life size horses, men and women who are all imaginary "Danube Creatures"! They are somewhat like 'mermaids', but have legs with fins for feet, and other fins on the back of their lower legs and their arms. They are seen on various fountains around Vienna, including a charming one in front of the Historic Art Museum.

Schönbrunn Palace has forty-five rooms, open to the public, and we arranged for a private tour. Every room was a amazing, from painted ceilings to inlaid floors, and panelled walls with masterpiece paintings filling the walls.

There was a moment of rather fun excitement when our lovely lady guide mentioned that in a large painting, a handsome man in a red and white uniform was Germany's Prince William, visiting their last Emperor Franz Joseph. Of course, Marilyn said that Prince William was the uncle of her grandmother, who as a child, had been a companion to his little girl, living in his palace in Berlin! We were able to buy a souvenir book at the shop in the palace with a large color reproduction of the painting. It was really great fun that day!

On Sunday, all shops are closed, and museums have short hours, so my sister wanted us to spend another day at her house in Sieding. We looked forward to the pleasant country atmosphere there, but Lotte had also planned a special surprise for me! She had prepared some of my favorite Viennese specialties, such as Wienerschnitzel and Tzwetchkenknodel!

Wienerschnitzel are breaded veal cutlets, and the 'Unpronounce-ables' are round dumplings made from a potato-and-Ricotta-cheese dough, rolled in crushed poppy seeds and sugar, with a whole Italian plum in the center! Boiling the dumplings keeps all the juices of the plums inside, and it really is a delicious treat! Marilyn says you have to have been brought up on them to like them, but our kids all love them, and I know others who do too!

Incidentally, Lotte also made a sort-of Viennese style 'Boston Cream Pie'. It was a light sponge cake with boiled vanilla custard as the center layer, and fresh fruit in a clear, thick, sweet glaze on top. That was Marilyn's favorite!

My sister was such enjoyable company, and we were always amazed at her fluent command of the English language! Because of this, she and Marilyn got along wonderfully, both loving to converse!

Hans, Lotte's husband was a top executive with a large firm until his retirement, but had no occasions to speak English, but because I am fluent in German, we got along great! We enjoyed going for long walks in the woods nearby, and we talked of many things.

He and Lotte have two sons, the eldest, Herbert, and the other Christian. They are both very intelligent, highly educated, fine and handsome young men. Herbert is an executive with a major Austrian insurance company, and Christian is a university professor. They and their lovely wives speak fluent English, and among a few enjoyable visits with them, was a party Lotte and Hans gave for the whole family, and where we met Aunt Poldi, my mother's only living sister.

The party was at a Weingarten at the edge of Vienna, owned by a couple who were friends of Lotte and Hans. The wife, Annette, was from the United States. She had been on a trip to Germany where she met her husband, who travels all over the world as a pharmaceuticals representative, besides being the son of a family that had owned that beautiful Weingarten for several generations. The atmosphere was charming, and the dinner absolutely authentic Viennese delicious!

Lotte had been Assistant to the President of a large specialty construction company in Vienna, a position she held until her retirement, and she had taken extensive courses in English. It was the company she worked for that built the solid fire 'curtain' for the new Vienna Opera House, and many other specialized building projects in the re-construction of Vienna.

Most of their materials were from the United States, and important manufacturer representatives often visited Vienna. Lotte was wholly responsible for translating all correspondence into English and even writing much of it. When representatives were coming to Vienna, Lotte planned the President's itinerary.

She bought tickets for the opera, and arranged for private sightseeing tours. Actually, our private tour of the Schonbrunn Palace, was arranged through 'connections' from Lotte's past-position with that important company, and she was also able to obtain four tickets to the Vienna Opera! We had arrived in the middle of the opera 'season', and had not planned ahead well on this first visit. The inside of the opera house was even more resplendent than the outside, with magnificent decor of gold, and dark red velvet. Marilyn and I had seen grand opera before, but nothing had ever compared with the stage designs and the magnificent performances of the voices and orchestrations.

Among these amazing days, we reserved another entire day for the Historic Art Museum of Vienna. Before even seeing the unbelievably magnificent paintings, the interior of the building itself leaves one breathless! Marble columns three stories high surround a rotunda with two curved balconies, each high above the other! Inlaid marble floors on all rotunda levels, lead you to tall, shiny, deeply-carved wood doors at the entrances of gallery after gallery of the world's most famous paintings!

All exhibition rooms have frosted glass 'daylight' roofs, to best show the accurate colors of the paintings, but equally amazing are exquisite bass relief sculptures, high around every room, bordering the glass ceilings! There are galleries of paintings representing most of the greatest Renaissance artists! Some of these masterpieces reach ten to fifteen feet in height, by Reubens, Rembrandt, Van Dyke, Titian, Gainsborough, and hundreds of others!

It is very unlikely that buildings such as this museum, with it's intricate decor and massive amounts of marble, would ever be built again! Time moves too fast, that is, people move at a faster pace to finish a job and reap necessary earnings. And after all, these jewel-like buildings are already here, and if we take care of them, they will last forever, and there is really no need for more of the same! In Vienna, there are so many beautiful old ornate historical buildings, the city abounds with them!

Riding around the City of Vienna as a fourteen-year-old youngster, the beauty of all these buildings and parks, although recognized by me, was more of an attitude of acceptance, of being part of my heritage or being.

Fifty years later, as an outsider, a visitor, I am much more in awe of all this beauty and human creation.

I feel akin to all these familiar sights, but not as my home. People have often commented, "You love Vienna! After all, it's your home!" Yes, I do love Vienna and Austria, and have a great compassionate feeling for it as the land of my birth and early development. But I have also come to the realization that while as a youngster, I felt homesick and at times wished to return to live in Vienna, I would feel just as homesick now for my home and family in California! Admittedly, however, it was somewhat of a strange feeling to again be saying goodbye to my sister, and to the familiar sights of Vienna! However, it was a wonderful feeling to be coming home with Marilyn, to our loved ones and the living foundation we had built together here!

As we talked together on the 'plane coming home, we decided that as long as we were able, physically and financially, to make a trip to Vienna, and England too when we could, an annual holiday. We also planned that over the next four years, we would take one of our children and their spouses with us each year!

Traveling west from Europe, by 747 jetplane, keeps the eleven hour flight at only a two hour time difference, from embarkation in London to arrival in Los Angeles. So leaving at noon, London Time, brings us into Los Angeles at two in the afternoon.

We had a smooth and enjoyable flight, interrupted by two movies and several nicely served meals and refreshments. Our son, Egon, Jr. met us in our GMC Motorhome, which was big enough to hold all our luggage! There were not many business transactions to discuss, because during our stay in Europe, I had called him almost every day. He also knew exactly where we were at all times, so could reach me for any emergency, or even if he just had any questions.

Of course, we had a lot to tell him about our adventures!

CHAPTER 21

A Killer Stalked . . .

It gave me a comforting feeling having my son, Egon, Jr. working with me, and as mentioned before, our daughter, Karen, was ordering the materials and keeping inventory. She had also decided to take some accounting courses, and was soon keeping our books in fastidious order.

We were always a very close family, but Karen's husband was originally from Oregon, and they tried living up there. Somehow they had difficulties, were divorced, and Karen returned here with their two little girls, Deanna and Jennifer. She raised them with lots of love and attention, and they have become wonderful young ladies. Eventually, Karen married a fine young man who is well established, and they are very happy and compatible together.

Married for several years, Egon, Jr. had two lovely children, Erin Melissa and Egon Tyler Reich III. He was a faithful husband and never did anything to upset the marriage. Suddenly, his wife left him because she was still infatuated with her old highschool sweetheart. Junior was terribly upset for a long time, but for the children's sake, allowed them to live with their mother, and he supported them financially, and they spent every weekend and holiday with him. Their mother did not neglect the children, and they grew up to be fabulous young people.

The strangest and saddest thing happened to our daughter, Becky's marriage. She and her husband were doing well in his construction business, and raising their two beautiful little girls. They loved to go sailing, and they owned a good-sized sailboat which they kept moored at Dana Point Harbor, about thirty miles south of Newport Beach.

One fateful evening, Randy was down working on their boat, when a young woman came along the dock. Randy knew her and her husband, because they had a boat nearby. She said to Randy that her husband had gone to get some supplies and asked if he would help her with some rigging on their boat, and thinking nothing of it, he went over to their boat with her. He provided the help she had asked, and when he was walking on the way back to his boat, several shots rang out, all hitting Randy in the back and killing him instantly.

As it turned out, the woman's jealous husband, who had been hiding and watching his wife, mistook Randy for a suitor. In a blinding, jealous rage, he shot and killed him! He was apprehended and convicted of murder, but that didn't bring the girl's father back to life!

Becky diligently raised her two girls, Vicky and Melody, and has become a successful executive with a large international firm.

Our eldest daughter, Heidi, married a nice young man when she was nineteen, but somehow they drifted apart and also divorced. Heidi is very artistic (I must say that all of our children show exceptional art talent) and became a licensed beautician, and also a licensed real estate agent, and is doing very well. She has been happily married for many years to a man named Bill, who had several children, some of whom Heidi raised, and she has been a wonderful 'stepmom' to all of them.

Bill is from Lafayette, Indiana, a graduate of Purdue University there, and was an important engineering architect when Heidi met him. He was one of a group of architects who designed the 'single span housing' for the 'Spruce Goose', the world's largest airplane, built by Howard Hughes. It had become a tourist attraction by 'The Queen Mary' ship in Long Beach, California. Bill has also been site-supervisor for many famous buildings, had a pilot's licence since he was young, and flew the company airplanes to out-of-state construction sites, sometimes on a daily basis, when he was working with major building- firms.

This brief synopsis of our 'kids' might lead one to believe that their lives have been somewhat unhappy, even distraught, but we have always taught them that, even in the face of adversity, to be strong and adhere to fine principals.

Our motto is, and always will be, "If circumstances occur, beyond our control, which tend to weaken our spirits and our will, we meet these problems with stronger than ever vigor, to defeat any negative mental conditions which could depress us and thereby obscure the rewards of our ultimate goals."

I am very glad to say that all the children have positive attitudes, and are active 'happy campers' with excellent morals.

Marilyn and I feel greatly rewarded, and we worked hard in our successful food business. Marilyn worked diligently with our accountants, and I still call her 'TG' for 'The Greatest'. If I haven't mentioned it before, this started when we were young and she would type a letter to an advertising client, for the 'secretary's initials' at the end of the letter, she did not want to use her own initials, so she always just made up some like 'IS' (Invisible Secretary)! One day I told her to use 'TG' because it was actually typed by Marilyn - 'The Greatest'!

For one of her birthdays, I got her a car license plate reading, '1 TG'. The plain 'TG' had already been taken, so they suggested putting the '1' in front of it, and I liked that idea! She has had fun with it! Besides being very recognizable from a great distance in a parking lot, several people have come up with clever 'guesses', like, 'One Terrific Gal', and Granddaughter Vicky (Becky's eldest) immediately said, "One Terrific Grandma!" To me it means, "Number One TG, or The Greatest, still!

Marilyn learned accounting to the extent she was the 'Comptroller' of our corporation, producing our Annual Financial Statement, as well as monthly Balance Sheets and Profit-and-Loss Statements. This cut the work of our accounting firm to a minimum, and saved quite a bit of money.

Marilyn and I both owned our own cars, because we both had to drive to various business meetings, and business errands, sometimes to different locations. For business reasons, I mostly leased my car, and was always partial to Cadillacs. That reminds me of a funny story of when our smart and artistic twelve-year-old, Heidi, drew a cute birthday card for me. On the front, it pictured her face with a tear by her eye, saying, "I couldn't afford to buy you a Cadillac, so . . . ", and on the inside, "I got you a little Lincoln!" with a penny pasted below! The idea may not have been original, but the way she drew it was adorable.

Anyway, Marilyn drove a white Chevrolet convertible which she loved, but during the busy days with the business, hardly ever took the time to put the top down anymore. The years flew by, and suddenly that gorgeous 'Chevy' was ready for the 'boneyard', or the 'horsepower glue-factory!' I convinced her to look at Cadillacs, and in the middle of the front showroom window at the dealership, sat the most beautiful car ever seen! It was a white 'Biarritz' with a white leather sports-top and white leather seats with a burgundy-red dash, carpets, and other inside-accents. Absolutely magnificent, it was love at first sight!

It was 1982, and that top-of-the-line Cadillac cost $27,000. The same type car today is $50,000, and whenever Marilyn takes it in for service, they always say that of all the Cadillacs ever sold, that is the only one they call 'The Classic'! The dealer provided an elegant, deeply-engraved metal plaque with her name, Marilyn Reich, on the door of the glove compartment. The car today, 2002, still looks like new with only 43,000 miles driven. Marilyn still loves the car, and you can't even 'talk to her' about buying a new one!

I still have many files consisting of all the past business transactions I had to conclude throughout the years. Just looking at them, can now make me feel tired, but as each one was happening, I never felt there was any problem I couldn't 'take in stride'!

For many of the past years, a most vital and foremost entity to keep the business successful, was keeping the products moving off the shelves! I planned many advertising campaigns, primarily newspaper coupons for the breads, and radio commercials. There seemed to be a constant upheaval in the baking industry, as big National bakeries either merged, sold, or went out of business.

Whenever one of these events occurred, Egon, Jr. and I had to always re-negotiate with the new management, which at times was a major challenge. Somehow, we always endured and for the most part, came out ahead. It took a lot of work, travel, correspondence, and diplomacy.

On several occasions, I have received threats from Franchise-Bread competitors who had a good hold on the bread market. They claimed they could 'put me out of business' if I would not sell-out to them, but they did not want to pay my price, and really 'buy' my company. They wanted to do some kind of 'takeover', which to me was just like 'stealing' my business.

My attitude to them was, "You go your way, I'll go mine!" A good part of my success was the unsurpassed quality and resulting good taste of our products.

Sometimes, there were changes in major bakeries' top management, including CEOs and Presidents, and all transactions going on in their baking-plants came under scrutiny. In order to determine that our business relationship survived, I always tried to keep in close, personal contact with the new top executives. On one such occurrence, a new CEO was appointed at our biggest account. When I called him on the 'phone, I was surprised to find him pleasant and very cordial, saying that he liked our product and would be glad to meet with me to discuss enlarging our distribution!

We planned a meeting in his corporate offices in Kansas City with Egon, Jr., Marilyn, and me. The date we set was three weeks away, which gave us enough time to also visit a bakery in New York. That bakery needed a few one-hundred-pound bags of our bread mixes for test baking. Just at that time, my car was ready to be traded-in for a new model, so we planned that Egon, Jr. would go on ahead in the new Cadillac filled with the bread mixes, and we would fly and meet him in New York. We would then all drive together to Kansas City and back to California.

After our meeting with the New York bakery, we decided to visit Washington, D.C., and were very glad we took the time to see our Capitol City. We were amazed at the Lincoln and Jefferson Memorials, the Capitol Rotunda, the White House, and all the other magnificent historical sights!

The beautiful, pink cherry-blossom trees were in full bloom, and we said to Junior, "See, in Oregon where you were born, this is what the front of our farmhouse looked like this time of year!" It did bring back memories of why we had moved to Oregon, almost entirely because of the incredibly beautiful scenery there! While some eastern and northern scenery might be spectacular, we really were completely, joyously satisfied with views of the ocean and the feeling of 'being home' where we now lived!

But, enjoying our small side-trip, we continued on into Virginia, driving along the Patomac River to George Washington's home, 'Mount Vernon'. Then in the small town of Alexandria, we stopped for lunch at the two-hundred-year-old 'Old Club' Inn, which had been a men's club, and George Washington had been a member. We sat at a table by a huge fireplace, where our waitress, in a cute version of a Dolly Madison costume, said we were sitting right where George Washington used to sit in a big leather chair. The Inn had a giftshop, and Marilyn found several very nice pewter mugs and dishes showing pictures of the 'Old Club', for souvenirs.

Seeing Washington, D.C., and so much of our beautiful country, gave us time to reflect how fortunate we are to be living in this great country, the United States of America!

Arriving in Kansas City, Missouri, we had a wonderful meeting with the CEO, an absolutely fabulous person, and left with expectations of continued success with our breads.

Back at our plant where we made all of our bread mixes, of course everything had to be exceptionally clean and sterile. We prided ourselves on all the good government inspection-reports we received monthly. There were always many bags of various flours, grains, and finished mixes in the large building.

When we arrived from our trip, we were shocked to find the plant flooded, and about a foot of water over the floor of the entire facility! It seems a defective overhead fire-sprinkler turned on, creating a chain reaction, and the rest of them had turned on automatically! Fortunately, there had been no fire, however, the fire department was very helpful in getting the sprinklers turned off, and even pumping all of the standing water out of the plant. They actually did a marvelous job!

We had quite a bit of loss, but fortunately were insured. With some overtime by the plant workers, and Junior and I both helping with the 'clean-up', we were back in production within a couple of days.

All through my business ownership, there never was a time when I could just 'forget about the business'! No, it was a twenty-four-hour-a-day job! I always had a phone by my bed, and when I traveled, I was in touch with the plant daily. I've heard others say that when they leave their office, they leave their business there, but I always felt I had to perform with utmost concentration, and I never minded doing just that!

CHAPTER 22

Why Not?

Anyway, our business was doing well, and just 'off the cuff', I asked Marilyn what she thought of taking another trip to Vienna. Her reply was, "Why not?" So we planned the trip, again for early September.

It had been about two years since Egon, Jr's divorce, and he had met several young women, but had found no real compatibility until recently, he met a pretty young girl on a ski trip. Her name was Lori, and they fell in love, and both felt that marriage was right for them. Lori had never been married, and is about two years younger than Junior. She is a sweet, intelligent girl, and a university graduate in psychology.

They had a nice chapel wedding, and Lori's parents gave them a lovely reception at an exclusive country club in Newport Beach, where they are members. Interestingly, we had met Lori's father and mother before, because they lived across the street from us, and were active, respected members of our community.

This was all happening during the summer, and with our second European trip being planned for the fall, we offered to take them with us for their honeymoon, as another wedding present. Egon and Lori were both excited to be going, and we all started 'counting the days'!

Before leaving, we needed to update our Family Trust and Wills. Our daughter, Becky, was raising her two girls alone, so we helped her purchase a very nice home in the same neighborhood as Egon, Jr.'s house. Their houses were only a couple of blocks apart, and Heidi and Bill had a house nearby also.

Egon, Jr. was handling many important functions at Better Way Foods, so it took some planning for the time the three of us would be away on the trip. Our daughter Karen, was by that time extremely competent in all phases of the operation, and we knew she would manage everything perfectly during our absence.

Besides being meticulous in her bookkeeping, Karen is also a fabulous artist who has won many awards with her paintings. Seeing such talents in our children is like a great treasure to Marilyn and me.

On this trip, we knew exactly where we wanted to stay! Of course, the Vienna Hilton am Stadtpark, and we flew together with Egon and Lori, directly to Vienna with only one transfer in London to Austrian Airlines. Upon arrival in Vienna, we were again met at the airport by my darling sister, Lotte, her arms full of bouquets of flowers, and with her were her husband, Hans, and Cousin Fred.

After getting my rental car, this time a van for all of our luggage, we drove to the Hilton and everyone sat down to a magnificent Viennese dinner in the 'Prince Eugene' restaurant. Egon and Lori both immediately enjoyed the Wienerschnitzel (not to be confused with the 'hot-dog' franchise in the U.S.!), a very special egg-breading of a veal cutlet. It is usually served with Viennese potato salad, made with finely minced onion, a very mild amount of vinegar, oil, salt and pepper, and no sugar nor sweetness. A special cucumber salad is also a usual accompaniment. The taste of these special dishes unfortunately cannot be described, but Vienna is famous for their specialties, and it's worth the trip to Vienna, just for the enjoyment of the food!

Lotte and Hans had an hour's drive home, so did not stay too late, but we made arrangements to come to their home in the country on Saturday. We planned to again have dinner, and show Egon and Lori the gorgeous ski chalet owned by Hans and Lotte's friends. Fred, noticing we were experiencing jet lag, compassionately left early too, with plans to join us the next day.

We had small 'tourist maps' of the city (from the hotel 'Concierge') and we had shown Egon and Lori where they might enjoy just going around 'on their own'. So, being young and active individuals, they were up early the first morning, enjoying the 'courtesy' buffet breakfast, and walking Kaerntner Strasse to Stephanskirche, a short stroll from the Hilton. They also saw part of Stadtpark, and went along a shopping area beside the hotel.

Fred joined us for lunch at the hotel, and we all had room in the van to comfortably enjoy sightseeing, including the place where I had grown up, and the highschool I had attended. Everything looked about as I had left it almost fifty years before! The school building was a classic, ornate design

Famous KAERNTNERSTRASSE in
Vienna, about one mile long, heading
directly to Stephansplatz, is now a
pedestrian mall consisting of shops, cafés,
music and rest areas under beautiful shade
trees. Among other entertainment there
remains the traditional organ grinder, fun
for children and adults.

Newlyweds, on their Honeymoon,
Egon Jr. and wife Lori on
KAERNTNERSTRASSE.

CAFE at the HILTON 1986. Dinner with Egon's wife Marilyn, sister Lotte and "Aunt Poldi".

Here served are Egon's favorites. Wiener Schnitzel (Breaded Veal Cutlet), creamed spinach with egg, and salad.

"A cuisine worth the trip"! Marilyn says this is the real reason Egon goes to Vienna.

Vienna pastries are indescribably delicious! Lots of flavor, natural ingredients, never too sweet, a truly rare taste treat.

with window-boxes with red flowers growing in them, all across the sec-ond-story windows, and huge, deeply-carved wooden doors. Amazingly, it looked shiny clean and refurbished. Marilyn and Lori chose to wait in the car while Egon and I went into the school. I introduced Egon and myself, and we were cordially received. The teachers I remembered had long ago either retired or passed away, but there were fine young men running the school, and I was pleased to see that.

The school is situated in one of the many parks in Vienna, the one where Beethoven and Schubert are buried. Vienna also has several cemeter-ies which rival museums in their number of magnificent marble statues. Their flower-beds and lawns are also always flawless.

As mentioned early in this book, my darling wife, Marilyn, had child-hood rheumatoid arthritis at a very young age, but with nutritional therapy and exercise enjoyed a normal life all the years of raising our children. Now in her sixties, she began noticing pain in her knees, and doctors informed her that the early arthritis had destroyed much of her cartilage. Now, through time and standing, she had 'mechanically worn-away' the remaining 'cush-ion' in her knees, so walking long distances became painful.

One day, it so happened that Marilyn and I were in Fashion Island, a large shopping center in Newport Beach, when I noticed a lady riding a very small 'scooter'. I approached her and asked where she had found such a wonderful tiny vehicle! Mind you, this was enough years ago that such 'wheelchairs' were not commonly seen as they are nowadays.

This one had a comfortable-looking seat, a small platform for one's legs, three tiny, solid rubber wheels, and a post with a steering handle in the front. Only one small battery was needed to power the whole thing! The lady said the name of it was "Amigo", Spanish for "Friend", and she also told us where she bought it. I said to Marilyn that we must immediately get one for her, just for longer walking-times, of course, and it has been of great help ever since!

Because the "Amigo" is small and lightweight, and uses a dry-cell bat-tery, legal for travel on aircraft, we were able to take it along on our trip to Europe. We brought two batteries, and a small battery-charger with us, so we always had the power needed.

The Amigo dis-assembles and fits easily into the trunk of a car, so on some of the sightseeing trips with Egon and Lori, our trusty Amigo went along! To best see some of the inner city of Vienna requires a considerable amount of walking. Egon, Lori, and I did just fine, and Marilyn and her

Amigo were always by our side. With it's tiny wheels, it is very maneuverable, even in small souvenir shops!

We enjoyed re-visiting Kaerntner Strasse with Fred and Egon and Lori, and more than once, on different days, traversed the gorgeous pedestrian promenade, lined on both sides with elegant shops of all kinds. There are large shade trees and benches, and groups of little tables and chairs right in the center for the nearby coffee houses. We enjoyed some of the variety of street musicians, playing classical to folk-music.

Marilyn loves the art gallery which is down the Graben, another pedestrian-only street of exquisite shops which some people call the Beverly Hills of Vienna. The Graben looks similar to Kaerntner Strasse, and there are magnificent fountains and memorial monuments with statues besides. Marilyn kept noticing how 'animated' all the statues look.

Down another side street from the cathedral, we always went into Demel's, the famous confectionery cafe, delighting in their particularly delectable 'Vienna Pastries'!

We had a few days before we were to drive out to Lotte's country home, so we went to Shoenbrunn where Egon, Jr. was excited to see the painting of 'his uncle', and we figured out that he was only 'fourth-removed', which our guide kept saying was definitely close enough to call him his Uncle William.

We also drove up to Kalenberg, a small mountain overlooking the city, and right in the middle of the Vienna Woods. The street up is wide, and made of hand-placed flintstone. I used to ride my bicycle up there, and even remember when they built that gorgeous drive to the top.

The Vienna Woods are full of many varieties of beautiful trees, with the roads lacing through them. There are turnouts at various noteworthy sights. and overlooking quaint villages.

When you get to the top, there's an observation-terrace with telescopes, as part of a charming hotel, and a lovely old church, plus large, new parking areas for tour-busses. The hotel also has dining terraces, with every table enjoying glorious, panoramic views of the City of Vienna and the beautiful Blue Danube River!

We even made it to the Fine Art Museum for a few hours one day, and to the Kaiser's palace. So time passed fast, and on Saturday we drove to Lotte's country house. The drive is along a fabulous super-freeway, through rolling green hills and farmland, past crisp little villages with chalet-style houses. All of the houses had amazing, colorful flowers across the upstairs balcony. Some villages were at a distance, but noticeable by a picturesque church-steeple.

We turned off the freeway onto a well-kept two-lane highway which wound itself through more farmland, and a couple of more villages, then onto my sister's small street, at the end of which is her charming little house in the country. Lotte, Hans, and Fred (who had also driven out to be with us there) all welcomed us, and we were given a tour around the premises.

Lotte's house, itself, is actually located on a large farm. The couple who own it were getting on in years, and no longer wanted to do the work of farming, so they built several attractive cottages to have an income. They still live in a large house in the middle of a nearby meadow, and we enjoyed meeting them. They were very nice and cordial people, saying to make ourselves at home around the place! There were many fruit trees on the farm, so Lotte had all the fruit she could use. We indirectly benefitted, because she used plums and apricots to make my favorite desserts for every-one!

I was anxious to show Egon, Jr. those big, healthy-looking trout in the creek which runs right beside the house, knowing he would love to see that natural wonder! We took some little pieces of bread to throw to them, and the fish gobbled-up the crumbs quickly, before the swift current could carry them away.

In front of Lotte's house is a nice green lawn, and by her front door, sat a beautiful gray and white, gorgeous big cat. The white parts of his fur were as white as new snow, and the shine of the gray patches reflected the cleanest and most beautiful cat I have ever seen! Lotte had two or three cats, but this was her favorite and I could see why! His name was Peterman, and he was a big, but well-behaved gentleman. I picked him up, and it was 'love' imme-diately! I don't think the feeling was quite mutual, however, because he didn't want to be held too long, and soon struggled to get loose, but with-out scratching or biting. As I said, he was a gentleman!

He also had a lot of character, and answered Lotte's call immediately, especially when there was food involved. Often when Hans took long walks in the woods, Peterman was trained to walk along on a leash, which he seemed to eagerly enjoy! Every time we visited my sister, I always immedi-ately looked for Peterman.

As lunchtime neared, we were anxious to see the chalet hotel on the side of the mountain, with it's fabulous restaurant. The actual name of the hotel is Gscheiderhof. Lotte drove her car, and we followed her through beautiful mountain passes and farmland, and when the road began to rise up the mountainside, it came in sight! A most beautifully built, large chalet, surrounded by huge pine trees. The place was operated entirely by one family, including the cooking. They knew Lotte and Hans well, and embraced us all like family, and they all spoke fluent English. Besides two daughters, the father, the proprietor himself, served some of the dishes to our table.

He had a good sense of humor, and came across with several jovial stories and jokes, being a very intelligent and interesting conversationalist. His wife supervised and did some of the preparing of the wonderful, memorable meal. One of their specialties was venison, prepared like a stew in a delightful sauce with large, light and flavorful dumplings. Soups, salads, vegetables, all were prepared to perfection. There was also a bountiful selection of desserts, all created right there in their hotel kitchens. Entertaining conversation, excellent food, and beautiful surroundings left us with wonderful memories of that fabulous place! We certainly wanted to visit there again if time allowed.

There were several other important 'Sehenswuerdigkeiten' (places of note) we wanted Egon and Lori yet to see. The next day, we drove to a lake I remembered spending holidays at as a child. It is called Traunsee, and Marilyn immediately began calling it Swan Lake because of the multitude of white swans living there. A picturesque village on the lake, called Gmunden, is famous for charming folk-art pottery.

I was only six years old when an aunt and uncle took me with them to that lake for their vacation. I remember that it seemed like the most quiet and beautiful place this side of heaven!

We stayed in a little house right on the edge of the lake, with a rowboat and a small boathouse hugging the shore. I recall looking through the clear, shallow water at the edge of the lake, and seeing round pebbles on the bottom, and being fascinated by many little fishes gathering there. It left a lasting impression on me to this day.

Of course, the crystal-clear, blue lake itself with all of the beautiful white swans, provides a memory impossible to forget, along with the high mountains all around, falling steeply into the lake, as well as the little town of Gmunden with it's uniquely designed buildings. The Swan Hotel has large picture-windows surrounding the diningroom, overlooking the lake. The city hall, just across a central plaza, has a large set of Gmunden-ceramic bell-chimes high in the front, with lovely carillon-music coming from them every fifteen minutes, and especially on the hour!

There are several charming excursion boats lined up in the lake, along the edge of the plaza, where there are also rows of stone planters filled with an abundance of colorful flowers. We had an absolutely delicious lunch in the Swan Hotel diningroom, and Egon and Lori, and Marilyn too of course, all loved it there as much as I did.

Sometimes childhood memories seem better than when seen through adult eyes, but this was one place that seemed almost more impressive to me now,

After lunch, we fed some bread to the swans, drove around the lake a ways, taking pictures, and we visited one of the ceramic factories. Marilyn brought home a large blue butterfly whose wings were beautifully painted under the ceramic glaze. What a treasure! Another beautiful day in Austria!

Back in Vienna, my sister, Lotte brought the opera our attention, and the fact that a famous tenor was performing. I believe it was Placido Domingo in La Traviata, and although 'sold out', Lotte, through her former connections in her high position with a famous company, was able to obtain tickets in the sixth row of the orchestra section.

Lori, Lotte and Marilyn all wore long dresses, and with the men in dark suits, we arrived at the famous Vienna Staadtsoper for a very special musical evening! The Vienna Opera is particularly beautiful, inside and out! Originally built many years ago, it has all the amenities of marble halls and staircases, and as one enters the actual huge theater, the seats of dark red velvet, and the rows of ornate little box-seat 'balconies', three stories high along the side walls! The entire inside of the theater was metallic gold and royal red with enormous Austrian crystal chandeliers hanging high above.

Even the stage had been totally rebuilt, with sets of regular curtains, and a new technology 'fire curtain', painted with an opera scene in gold, and other colors. Everything had been refurbished to make the opera a wonderland of opulence and beauty!

The Vienna Opera also boasts one of the finest symphony orchestras, which is actually part of the Vienna Philharmonic. I am fond of many operas, and La Traviata is one of my favorites. Verde and Rossini are my favorite opera composers. We all came away that evening with a feeling of having experienced not only something of great enjoyment, but of having been part of a higher cultural form of art in beautiful music flawlessly performed!

I know it's not possible, but I wish everyone could see such a performance, and I am very thankful we were able to be so fortunate! It's somewhat consoling to reflect that in today's world, video and television can bring

City Hall in picturesque town of Gmunden (two hours drive from Vienna) which rests on the shore of beautiful "Traunsee". We call it Swan Lake because of the many swans that live there.

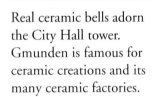

Real ceramic bells adorn the City Hall tower. Gmunden is famous for ceramic creations and its many ceramic factories.

Mountains cascade straight into the lake.

Happy swans and the Boss.

Picture perfect scenery, a reality in Austria.

such performances into many homes. Even though it is not quite the same as being there in person, it's a good alternative.

Recovering from our trance of a night at the opera, we drove back a few blocks along The Ring to the Marriott Hotel where, during the opera season, they have an after-theater buffet, very Continental, but also with some authentic Viennese specialties. It was delightful, and we found their Vienna Pastries particularly luscious!

The Marriott is the newest hotel in Vienna, and the entire top floor is the United States Consulate. We even thought about possibly staying there if we came to Vienna again, which we hoped to keep doing.

The next day, Lotte drove in again, to show us one of the most amazing attractions in Vienna, the Spanish Riding School, featuring the most beautiful and superbly trained white Lipizzaner horses! As a young girl, Lori did competition equestrian riding, and was anxious to see the famous Lipizzaners.

The riders spend a lifetime training and riding, each with their own particular horse, until rider-and-horse become a perfect, almost mechanical unit, performing amazingly difficult tricks and dance-like stepping!

The name, Spanish Riding School, was given in 1572, when the 'school' began training the first horses bred from black Arabian Stallions, and white Spanish Andalusian mares. They were first headquartered in Lipizzaner, a village now in the Karst section of Yugoslavia, but since 1735, have performed in their own show-theater in Vienna.

Built for the training and showing of those amazing horses, there is a special, luminous white interior with two audience-galleries marked by forty-six Corinthian columns. The ceiling is adorned with bass relief decoration, and spectacular Austrian crystal chandeliers. It rivals the look of a huge castle ballroom, with the floor, and a soft, dark brown velvety-looking covering, giving the only clue that it is being used for horses!

As we watched the amazing show, the horses 'danced' in perfect unison, and did many graceful leaps, including their famous 'Airs Above the Ground' when they seem to fly through the air with all four legs tucked high against their body. Lori was particularly appreciative of the show, and all of us both enjoyed it immensely and were greatly impressed!

Salzburg, on the river Salzach (the birthplace of Mozart), is a most beautiful city, situated in a valley bordered by the high Grossglockner alpine range. On a hill in the middle of Salzburg looms an ominous looking castle, dating back to the middle ages, now enjoyed by visitors, even excellent cuisine is served at the castle. Salzburg is also known for its annual International Music Festival, and a fabulous marionette theater. Marionettes act to music and singing of famous operas.

Serene meadows and beautiful chalets abound on the way to Salzburg.

Contented cows are seen grazing in the green pastures.

View of the magnificent high Grossglockner mountain range.

With my daily telephone calls, the business at home was getting along just fine, and sightseeing with Egon and Lori seemed even more enjoyable than when we were by ourselves on our first trip!

Egon and Lori were really enjoying it too. They went some places on their own, and Fred took them one day to meet a young couple who were turning a Baron's two-hundred-year-old Hunting Lodge into a small Inn.

On the days without the kids, Marilyn and I went to the local shops by the hotel, to stock up on toiletries, and also some snacks for the little refrigerator in our room. We also enjoyed going to the coffeehouse in Stadtpark and listening to the afternoon concerts, while Egon and Lori went off on more adventurous pursuits.

But the day soon came that we wanted to leave Vienna, and head toward the Tirolian Alps. After visiting my sister, Lotte, in the country one more time, and saying goodbye to Peterman, we decided to first go to Salzburg, where Mozart was born. It is quite a large town, and became world-famous because of the movie "The Sound of Music", the story about the Von Trapp family and their escape from the Nazi's and Austria.

I have had the privilege and pleasure of having had personal correspondence with Baron Von Trapp's eldest daughter, Maria, who is a very fine and charming person. In the United States they enjoyed a notable career as "The Von Trapp Family Singers" and Maria sent me a CD of their absolutely gorgeous voices singing in perfect harmony! Marilyn and I love listening to it, and treasure it greatly.

CHAPTER 23

"Better Than the Prince"

So the day came when we had to say goodbye to our friends at the Hilton Hotel. When I say, 'friends', I mean all the people working there, from the manager to the doorman, because at that time, the dollar to the Austrian Schilling exchange was very good in our favor. I was, therefore, able to be generous with tips to everyone in the hotel, especially the door-man.

I tipped the doorman every time we all got into the car by the front door of the hotel, and every time we returned. Of course we always had to load and unload Marilyn's small 'scooter', but that was quick, especially with Junior helping.

My nephew, Lotte's son, Christian, once remarked to me, "Your gener-ous tipping fringes on bribery."

I replied, "No, I really don't think about getting special favors. I tip what I can, but mainly because I want to help these poor people who work hard for so little."

At that time, I wasn't sure if he believed me, but another time, he was in my car as we came to a stop at a signal, where I bought a newspaper from a man standing with them in the street, and gave him a tip of fifty schillings (about five U.S. dollars at that time).

Christian was stunned, because there was a man I would never see again, and from whom I certainly could not expect any favors in return. I told Christian that I just wanted to bring that person a minute of happiness. I think he did believe me, and I hope I convinced him that I am not the type of person who would want to take advantage of the poor. I also live my life that way at home, and do my best to help those in need, whenever I can.

One time, in front of the hotel, I noticed an Arab gentleman arrive with an entourage of several Rolls Royce cars, most with veiled ladies inside. I asked the doorman who that was, and he simply said, a prince from an Arab country. I said to him, well he must be very generous with tips; whereupon he remarked, "You are better than the Prince!", meaning I tipped better of course!

I guess that should make me a prince, or maybe it means that it does in the eyes of the doorman and a few others.

As all things eventually come to an end, so did our stay that year at the Hilton, and we headed out toward the fabulous city of Salzburg! The drive takes about three hours.

Salzburg is probably unique to anyplace else in the world. There is a steep hill in the middle of the city, on top of which sits an ancient fortress-type castle, fairy-tale picturesque!

A wide, swift mountain river winds through the very center of the city of Salzburg. Gorgeous hotels and little park-like promenades line one side of the river, and several beautiful bridges bring you over to 'Old Town' on the other side. There one finds narrow, winding cobblestone streets, all leading to a huge central plaza with a large baroque fountain and a monument with a life-size bronze statue of Mozart. Along one edge of the mountain in Old Town, there's a charming street of little fresh-vegetable markets, and small, open giftshops. Many fine shops, art galleries, souvenir shops, restaurants, coffee and pastry shops, line the little streets and surround the plaza, where there are also street-artists, selling their really fine-art originals.

All of Salzburg is like a beautiful jewel, with several magnificently designed cathedrals from the Renaissance period. Some have ornate domes, open, four-sided steeples, and an abundance of carved figures. Inside, the high-domed, sculptured and fine-art painted ceilings and arches give the spacious interiors an ethereal, Godly appearance! Bursts of golden rays, around artistic figures of Mary, adorn the imposing, opulent altars.

To go up the steep-sided mountain to the castle, there is a very long, winding, stone-paved walkway, or a tram on gear-rails which goes straight up! It is quite an experience, riding that tram, but well worth it to see the castle, and the views of the large valley sprinkled with homes and churches.

Surrounding all this, you see the magnificent rocky mountains of the Alps, as far as the Italian Dolomites, looming high into the sky like a master painting!

About ten miles before entering Salzburg, there is a turnoff, onto a road leading up another large mountain, named Gaisberg. Near the very top of that mountain, sits a chalet hotel, called Hotel Kobenzl. We had heard that it was located in a beautiful area, yet only a few minutes' drive from the City.

The first time we drove up that scenic mountain road overlooking velvety meadows with large chalets and beautiful pine forests, we were very impressed. There were healthy-looking brown and white cows, grazing like statues in rolling, green pastures, and an occasional wanderer, wearing 'lederhosen', and carrying a long hiker's staff, strolling along one of the mountain paths that seemed to wend their way everywhere.

Arriving at the Hotel Kobenzl, we were met by an attractive and spirited lady who introduced herself as Mrs. Herzog, the propriator. Each room was like a little individual chalet with panoramic view windows, and a balcony with an abundance of colorful flowers growing in 'window-boxes' along the railing! The view was over green valleys, all of the city of Salzburg, the broad, blue winding river, and the incredible sight of that huge, awe-inspiring fortress! The furnishings throughout were a Tirolian motif, the beds were piled high with featherbeds, down comforters and pillows, and the baths were as large and luxurious as at the Hilton.

There was an elegant restaurant in the main building, with high, view windows of course. Many of the hand-carved wooden chairs had small brass plaques on their high backs with world-famous names on them.. I sat in President Nixon's chair that first evening, as we enjoyed tender medallions of venison and flavorful vegetables for dinner.

In the early morning sunlight, the view of the sparkling snow-capped peaks of the mountains, the high pine-forests, and the tall church steeples, all casting long shadows along the green meadows, and giving a strong three-dimensional quality to the entire City of Salzburg, was absolutely breathtaking!

We drove down the mountain and into Salzburg for a light lunch, because we all agreed we would have dinners at the Kobenzl Hotel. We left our car in a parking area at the edge of Old Town Salzburg, and walked along the little streets and around the main plaza, with Marilyn on her trusty Amigo scooter by our side!

I noticed one curious thing. First of all, I was surprised to see flocks of seagulls! Of course, they were by a river and were very large and very white and healthy-looking, but in the middle of land-locked Austria? Anyway, the river flowed swiftly through Salzburg, and many of the seagulls were simply sitting on the surface of the water, floating rapidly downstream. When they had passed through the town, they took flight upstream, back above the city, then settled themselves again on the river for another rapid ride downstream! It seemed they had found an enjoyable way to spend their days!

Egon, Lori, and I took the tram up the hill to take a tour of the castle. When you get there, it seems even more immense than from a distance! The massive outside wall is six feet thick! We went through rooms built of solid stone, filled with swords, suits of armor, tools of torture, and other oddities used in medieval wars, plus old wooden chests, tables, and ceramic ovens. Walking along inside those turreted stone walls, sort of transported you back to the 'not so good' old days!

Joining Marilyn, we found a small plaza with a special-looking pastry shop or coffee house where they make "Mozart Kugels", a confection, said to have been his favorite. It is a large, round 'bon-bon' type candy, with a center of marzipan, then light chocolate, and an outer coating of dark chocolate, foil wrapped. The weather was warm, and we sat outside, enjoying the same flavorful coffee as in Vienna, and as delightful pastries as ever before!

Salzburg is world famous for it's summer music festival and competition, but that was over when we arrived in late September. Another famous attraction had just returned from it's summer world-tour, the Salzburg Marionettes! Seeing them in Salzburg is the best, because the performances are held in their own exquisite Marionette Theater, which is like a miniature version of the grand opera house in Vienna! Of course, the seats are full-size, luxuriously comfortable, and built so that your view of the stage is unobstructed from every seat.

The marionettes, themselves, are large, two to three feet tall, and are lavishly costumed to suit each performance, which is usually a Mozart opera. The music and the singing is recorded from the finest live operas, so that part of the performance is completely enjoyable!

It's almost impossible to believe that those little 'people' on the stage are not alive, so perfectly are they moved by puppeteers who spend their whole lives mastering the art! The stage settings and lighting are also beyond professional, absolutely inspired!

The entire performance becomes a wonderful enjoyment of fantasy with uncanny realism! Trust me, if you ever have the chance to see the Salzburg Marionettes, do it!

Back on top, at our mountain retreat, the Hotel Kobenzl, after an exciting day in the city of Salzburg, we turned in for a good night's sleep. A bright, sunny morning greeted us upon arising, and at breakfast, Egon asked the proprietor if and when there might be skiing in the area.

He and Lori were both good skiers, but they had not brought their skis because we did not expect snow this early. However, we were told that there is year-round skiing at the 'Gletchers' (glaciers) in Southern Austria, by a place called Kaprun. Egon's ears perked up and we hurried to our rooms where we called and found that ski equipment could be rented, and a room was available at a lodge there.

I made my daily call to Karen, and found that, of course, all was going well at Better Way Foods. Marilyn and I decided to stay in Salzburg and rent a small car, so Egon and Lori could take the van. They were as happy as little kids, first to be going skiing, and then to be taking off for a few days by themselves! After all, this was supposed to be their honeymoon!

Egon and Lori's trip to the Glacier ski area took only the better part of an afternoon. Austria is beautiful, but a small country. Marilyn and I visited some of the churches, but mostly window-shopped around Old Town Salzburg, which has an amazingly Medieval atmosphere.

The second day, intermittently, a light snow began falling. We stayed rather late, and the day was turning to dusk as we returned to our car. We were going along the outside street of vegetable markets under canvas awnings, and little shops with light filling their open side and brightly spilling out onto the darkening walkway. With the snowflakes fluttering down around us, Marilyn remarked, "What an enchanting picture! It looks just like a painting for a Christmas card!"

It was great fun seeing such beautiful sights on a daily basis! Our favorite small plaza in Salzburg had a little 'hobby' shop featuring 'doll-house miniatures', the 'Mozartkugeln' Pastry and Coffee Shop with tables and chairs out in front, and a most unique fine jewelry store. All of the jewelry they carried was local, original, and hand-made of solid gold.

Displayed in their window, I saw a bracelet with delicate handcrafted pink-gold roses all around, and one could see that every rose-petal was separately hand-sculptured! There were tiny, precious rose-leaves between each rose, and it was exquisite! Fortunately, because of the exchange rate being greatly in our favor that year, I was able to buy that fabulous, unusual, one-of-a-kind bracelet for my darling Marilyn! To this day, it is one of our most appreciated treasures!

Egon and Lori arrived back unscathed, and told us of all the fun they had skiing, and about a special, delicious dessert served at the lodge where they stayed. It was called Salzburger Nockerln, and was like a large egg souffle, served with apricot jam.

That very day, we all agreed that because we were about a third of the way to Innsbruck, also a very beautiful and interesting city, we would go there next. We would then drive on through Lichtenstein to Zurich, Switzerland, and from there fly to London to visit our friends and relatives in England, before returning home to Los Angeles.

We all enjoyed one more fabulous venison dinner at Hotel Kobenzl, after which I decided to go for a walk just a little further towards the top of the mountain. It was a very clear night, not too cold, and with a warm jacket, I was comfortable. After a few minutes walk in the dark of the night, I came upon a clearing and stopped to look at the sky. What I saw was our Milky-Way Galaxy in it's brightest glory! The millions of stars were so white, glistening and brilliant, much brighter than millions of crystal diamonds!

They, of course, were millions of suns, giving off their own light, not like our planets, which can also appear bright, but only by virtue of reflection of light from our sun. The sight of that concentration of millions of stars, unobstructed by heavy atmosphere on top of that mountain, was breathtaking!

Interestingly, because of the receding movements of the stars, no matter how bright they appear, they are not blinding, like looking into our sun. So I sat there on a tree stump for about half an hour, enjoying the stars in the stillness, and contemplating what might go on, among all those living objects in our Universe.

A good featherbed night was had by all, and bright and early in the morning, we bid adieu to our friends at the Hotel Kobenzl. Just thinking back about all the beauty of Salzburg, makes one thankful to have had the opportunity to have been there! The drive to Innsbruck took us through picturesque Tirol. There were mountainous green pastures with healthy-looking cows walking along with large low-tone bells around their necks. The cows were a beautiful white and light brown in color, and seemed very calm and content.

The air was clear and fresh as we passed many chalet-type farmhouses with beautifully sculptured roofs and eves, and flowers growing brightly in front of every ornately-framed window and balcony. We particularly noticed how clean and bright everything looked, like picture postcards! It was obvious that the people there did not mind hard work, and were very proud of their homes, farms and livestock.

Our drive to Innsbruck took the better part of the day, because we stopped a few times for refreshments and taking pictures. Arriving in the late afternoon, we found lodging in the Hotel Innsbruck, an amazing place right in the middle of the small city, with new underground parking, a gorgeous, large swimming pool, and a quite elaborate gym and spa..

The hotel was not very big, but nothing in Innsbruck is very big except 'the mountain'! There are some really interesting historical places, one in particular, called 'Das Goldene Dacherl' (The Little Golden Roof). It was constructed by Emperor Maximilian I, in 1498, in memory of his wedding which took place in Innsbruck. It is a small ornate building with a balcony across the third floor, and a curved golden roof-facade, two stories high above, made of solid gold tiles (or so the story goes!) There are questions as to whether sometime in the past, the tiles were replaced with gold-plated ones, but no-one we asked seemed to know or care. It's an exquisitely designed little building and fun to see!

One of the most amazing sights, besides fabulous buildings with Roman columns and statues, is the huge, rocky, snow-capped mountain which looks like it sits right in the middle of the main street in downtown Innsbruck! It's peak reaches into the clouds in the sky, and it actually does more than just look like it's in the middle of Innsbruck, it really is!

You just drive downtown, and at the end of the main boulevard, you suddenly run into a cable-car station. A cable-car takes you half-way up the mountain, where you transfer to another to go all the way to the top. When Egon and Lori saw this, they insisted I take the trip with them. Looking up at the steep rocky cliffs reaching high into the sky, at my age, I was a little leery.

Their prodding finally won out. I was a little apprehensive, but tried to take a 'well, just let things happen' attitude, as we climbed with several other brave souls into a quite secure-looking cable-car. Marilyn had preferred to stay at the hotel, and to browse the many 'wonderful' little shops on the street there.

The trip up the side of the grayish-white rocky cliffs, from inside the cable-car, now seemed quite safe, and actually thrilling! Halfway up, we made the change to the second cable-car which took us up to the top of that amazing 11,000-foot mountain!

The cable-car 'end-of-the-line' was actually still about two hundred feet from the very tippy-top of the mountain, at which point a large cross had been erected. A slightly steep walkway had been carved out of the rock, along which were metal posts with a rope to hold onto, connecting them. We carefully edged our way along the rocky path, and proudly took pictures of each other by the cross.

We were told not to linger too long at the top, because cold winds can come up and make the descent more precarious. As we stood there for a short while, marveling at the view below us, we heard a whooshing sound, and there suddenly appeared right in front of us, not more than ten feet away, a beautiful white sailplane with long slim wings and a partially enclosed cockpit with the pilot in plain sight. He tilted his swiftly-moving plane, and swished by us as we waved!

There were several interesting people with us on the top of that mountain. One man who was visiting from Russia, spoke English and began talking with Egon, Jr. because Egon was wearing one of the loden-green Tirolian hats on which he was collecting the little souvenir pins. The man from Russia said that he had a pin from the recent Olympics held in his country, and because Egon had a few pins (easily replaceable for us) that the Russian liked, they traded. The Russian had more of the Olympics pins, so we did not need to feel guilty when we came home and found that the Olympics pin was quite valuable.

We noticed the temperature dropping suddenly, and a cold wind starting to blow, so we carefully edged our way down the rocky path, holding onto the rope. When we arrived at the cable-car station, there was a car waiting, and we were glad when we arrived safely again at the foot of the mountain, though we reveled in the exhilarating experience we had just enjoyed!

Among the interesting shops near our hotel, was one selling the famous Rouge music boxes, made in St. Croix, Switzerland. We were attracted to an exquisite medium-sized (about fourteen inches long) box with the wood-inlay designs of musical instruments on the lid and all four sides! It was an especially good one, made for a lifetime of enjoyment! It had a heavy brass roller and a multitude of strongly-set 'pins', to create the most elaborately beautiful music-box-type music we had ever heard! Then, the biggest thrill of all was that it played three compositions by Mozart, including the beautiful Glockenspiel from The Magic Flute!

The proprietor of the shop told us that the Rouge Music Box Company creates boxes with appropriate music for each country to which they are shipping. It was late in the season, and the store had marked down the price of those fabulous music boxes, which made it possible for us to acquire another 'treasure'!

Because of the constraint of time, and because our itinerary included visiting more places, we only spent a couple of days in Innsbruck. Our next stop, about half a day's drive through high alps, to the westernmost state of Austria, Vorarlberg. We checked in, for just an overnight stay, at a large, impressive hotel (or ski-lodge), called Arlberg Hospiz. It is located in the village of St. Christoph, which is nestled between several high mountain peaks, and it is where many Austrian ski movies have been made.

The area is a major Austrian ski resort with cable-car-type ski-lifts taking skiers to the tops of the mountains. It is also famous because in the early 'thirties', a world champion skier, Johannes Schneider, made his home there.

When you first walk through the extra-heavy-glass and hand-carved-wood doors of the great Arlberg Hospiz, there is a huge stone fireplace with an inviting, blazing fire! It is surrounded by beautiful sort-of-rustic Tirolian-style, large, comfortable chairs, sofas and tables on thick, soft-looking, hand-woven rugs. There always seemed to be a group of skiers or travelers sitting by the fire, and enjoying the inviting atmosphere of the place!

The rooms were cozy, also with carved wood furnishings, and armoires instead of closets , beautifully painted with flowers and Tirolian designs.

When we arrived, the foothills were still green, and Egon and I took a short walk toward the mountain. Returning, we found we had worked-up an appetite, and all four of us were soon comfortably seated for dinner in the hotel diningroom. The chef had just that day smoked a large salmon, which he wheeled around on a cart, serving slices of it for appetizers. We enjoyed a good and relaxing dinner, and spent a night of relaxing sleep.

I was awakened by the beautiful sound of my wife's voice. She was saying, "Egon, look out of the window!" I jumped out of bed, and what a sight to behold! All of the mountains, the hilly pastures, the trees, the roofs of houses were covered with deep drifts of frosty white snow! The sun had come out, and it was such a pretty sight! A heavy snowfall while we were asleep, had provided us with a glorious morning in a winter wonderland!

After a hearty breakfast, we were off to Zurich, Switzerland. The drive took us through the small Principality of Lichtenstein. As we left Austria, and entered Lichtenstein, there was a border check-station where we showed our passports, and this enabled us to enter Switzerland without stopping again. Lichtenstein uses Swiss currency and postal services, but has it's own government with a Prince as ruler.

A short, scenic drive through Lichtenstein, and a couple of hours through the Swiss countryside, brought us to the picturesque city of Zurich. As we approached the city, we saw the Zurich Hilton right by the big International Airport. It was still early afternoon, so we drove to the hotel to see if we could get reservations for the night. A very nice lady at the desk said she had only one room left, and that she realized we needed two rooms. Being creative in her thinking, she informed us of one possibility. The Presidential Suite on the top floor was available, and she was able to give it to us at a special rate.

The suite consisted of two bedrooms with two baths, separated by a large room with sofas, chairs, tables, and a magnificent large desk. The desk-top was a huge curved piece of heavy-glass, supported by modern pedestals, one with a drawer-section. The place was so spacious and elegant, we were sorry we were not staying longer!

A fast driving-tour that late afternoon and evening was all we had time to see of Zurich. There was a wide river through the city, and marvelous, artistically shaped stone bridges. Again, Marilyn, Egon and Lori, all remarked about how all of Europe has that 'ancient' feeling which one is simply not used to in the United States.

When early morning came, we had much to accomplish, packing and returning my rental car at the airport, for our flight to London.

CHAPTER 24

An Exciting Journey to the Land . . .

. . . With My Initials

There has always been talk about the British Isles being shrouded in fog. Even songs have been written about the London Fog, like "A Foggy Day ♪ in London Town ♪ had me worried and had me down! ♫ I viewed the morning with alarm! The London theater had lost it's charm! How long, I wonder. would this thing last? But the age of miracles hadn't passed, when suddenly I saw you standing right there, and in foggy London Town, ♪ the sun was shining everywhere!" ♪

Sorry, I got a little 'carried away', but my musical nature recalls a song in almost any of my thoughts. Of course, I guess my 'miracle' happened at the Broadway Department Store in Los Angeles!

Getting back to why I was mentioning the fog over Britain, looking out of the window of the 'plane, I could see a cloud-cover over all of the British Isles, following the outline exactly! The channel was bright and clear, not a cloud in the sky! It seemed like an artist had taken his brush and painted gray clouds, just exactly on top of Britain!

I turned to Marilyn and in jest, said, "Typically British!" Marilyn and I really love England, fog and all! Actually, there are many beautiful sunny days!

The great plane landed gracefully at Heathrow Airport in London, and I rented a French station wagon, basically small but ample for the four of us and our luggage. We were going to immediately drive south through the lovely English countryside, to see our friends in Sussex, and again visit our favorite place in England, Arundel Castle! We were anxious to show Egon and Lori the village with it's 'King Arthur type' imaginary atmosphere, but also with lots of historical realism. We had made reservations at the Norfolk Arms, the Medieval inn, where we had stayed before. We again took one of the newer cottages, but Egon and Lori agreed on the 'honeymoon suite' in the 'old tower' for the 'romantic' atmosphere, even though our friends had warned them about ghosts in the more ancient parts of the inn.

In the morning at breakfast, Egon and Lori told the following story. The bed was quaint, but had a nice new queen-size mattress. There was a chest of drawers with a mirror, an armoire for a closet, and a small, but quite new, adjacent bathroom.

As they began getting unpacked, strange things began happening! Lori put some toiletries on the chest of drawers, and soon asked Egon why he had moved them to the other side! Egon insisted he had not touched them, put out his own hairbrush, and was soon accusing Lori of moving it!

They looked at each other, and almost in unison, whispered. "Ghosts?" It remained a mystery as they continued getting ready for bed. Then, when Lori pulled off the flowing bedspread, she immediately said, "Egon, I think I've found the ghost!"

There was a long strip of wood under the legs of the bed on one side. It seemed it made the bed level, because there was a slant to the floor! When they were walking around the room, apparently the floor was slanted just enough to make some objects move that were on the chest of drawers!

We stayed three days in Arundel, because our friends wanted us to see their house, and more of the many attractions in that part of England, and the most incredible of all, that fascinating, Medieval Arundel Castle! A short walk along a tree-lined promenade from the castle, there is an amazing wild bird sanctuary.

There are swans, both black and white. There are all kinds of wild geese, and many of the most beautiful varieties of ducks I have ever seen! There are many other species of birds, large and small, and there are plentiful bird-feeders, always well-filled. Also, along a winding people-path around a lake, there are vending machines which dispense the right kinds of foods for the birds' well-being. We eagerly put coins into the machines, and with our little sacks of food, enjoyed getting acquainted with some of the birds. Some quite large birds charge up to you, but then eat quite calmly out of your hand.

There is also a large building, sort of a bird museum, and an unusually fine gift shop. There are books for sale, and even free pamphlets about the birds, their migrating habits, and the importance of refuge sites like that one.

That amazing bird sanctuary is sponsored by the British Government, and is called "The Wildfowl Trust"; however, it is also dependent on memberships and fund-raisers. It is such a beautiful and well-kept place, it would be worth taking a trip to England just to see it!

Our next stop was Cambridge to visit with my Uncle Josef, and his son, Christopher who is about Egon, Jr.'s age. On our way, I was amazed at how accustomed I had become to driving on the left side of the road. As we neared Cambridge; however, Egon, Jr. chided me for making a slightly wrong turn, so I stopped the car and said, "Here, you drive!".

I knew he was an excellent driver, but he had never driven a car with the steering wheel, and (surprisingly important) the rear-view mirror on the 'wrong' side! He confidently drove a few blocks when we came to a signal crossing where we needed to make a left-hand turn, and Junior found himself turning straight into the oncoming traffic!

Fortunately, it was the edge of town so traffic was light, and there was no mishap! I was very quickly given back the driver's seat for the rest of our travels through England!

We were again enchanted with the ornate gothic-style buildings in all of Cambridge, and were very glad Egon and Lori were seeing it all! My Uncle Josef and his lovely wife, Eva, welcomed us heartily and lovingly! He showed Egon and Lori around the universities, and they were able to see one of the models of his atomic microscope. His original model was already in the London Museum of Science and Industry, with his name on it as the developer.

Josef and Eva have a son, Christopher, who has a darling wife, Susan, and they have two smart, talented and adorable (at-the-time-<u>little</u>) girls, Bryony and Francesca. Christopher and Susan invited Egon and Lori out for an evening with the 'younger crowd' of Cambridge, which they enjoyed immensely!

Christopher cautioned Egon about some boats-for-rent on the river, that you stand in, and push with a long pole. There was something about the poles getting stuck in deep 'muck' at the bottom of the river, and most tourists fall into the water! So the next day, Egon had to try it, and with Lori seated in the boat, he gripped the long pole extra-tightly, and pushed-off from the firm bank of the shoreline. Afterwards he said that he was very grateful for Christopher's warning, because it was even worse than he had thought it would be, but he 'made it' for a nice cruise along the river and back, at least without falling in!

Josef is only about four or five years my senior, and he is constantly pleasant, positive, loving, jovial; and it's always an exhilarating experience to visit with him!

London was our final destination before returning to Los Angeles, and there were many more interesting sights there that all of us wanted to see.

Incidentally, there is a car rental office right as you get to London, where I had learned the year before, to turn-in my rental car. Then, instead of driving those labyrinth streets of London, we took the big black taxis around the city, and even to the airport when leaving.

We stayed at a small 'tour' hotel, called Hospitality Inn, which is very nice, quite reasonable, and the room-rate even includes the usual ample, 'European' hot breakfast in a very pleasant diningroom. The hotel is centrally located, right across from the section of Hyde Park where the Sunday 'art fair' exhibits. Hyde park is surrounded by an elegant, ornate, high black iron fence, outside of which is an extra-wide 'sidewalk' with huge shade-trees all along the parkway.

On Sundays, for about a mile along that fence, hundreds of artists display and sell original paintings, sculptures, and a myriad of various arts and crafts. Amazingly, most are exceptionally good art! Again partially due to the exchange rate being in our favor back then, the prices seemed low, and we bought several very nice sketches and paintings.

One of the first things we did in London was take Egon and Lori to Madam Touseaud's Wax Museum, where they were as impressed as we had been with the realistic replicas of the royal family in all their regal attire! The many other famous notables were also absolutely amazing!

The famous 'London Theater' was a 'must see', and thanks to our hotel concierge, we all particularly enjoyed Andrew Lloyd Weber's "Starlight Express" in it's original theater with trains swirling around over our heads!

In my opinion, among all of the impressive sights, the most shocking and astounding is the Tower of London! It stands majestically beside the beautifully decorative Tower Bridge, which crosses the Thames River. The Thames is a large river which snakes it's way through the city of London.

The Tower of London has been kept like it was in the fourteenth century. The ominous spiral stone stairway inside a small tower leads to a room

A VISIT TO
UNCLE JOSEF
IN
CAMBRIDGE

Enjoying dinner. From left; uncle Josef, Marilyn, Josef's wife Eva, Josef's son, Christopher's wife Susan, with their baby girl Bryony, Christopher and Egon (standing).

View of a Cambridge Collage with Cathedral in background.

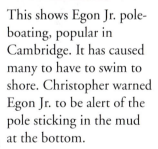

This shows Egon Jr. pole-boating, popular in Cambridge. It has caused many to have to swim to shore. Christopher warned Egon Jr. to be alert of the pole sticking in the mud at the bottom.

Nuclear Scientist, Uncle Josef, in Cambridge. Builder of the first F.I.M. Atomic Microscope.

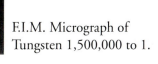

Prototype of part of the first F.I.M. Microscope in process of being built.

F.I.M. Micrograph of Tungsten 1,500,000 to 1.

where Sir Walter Raleigh was imprisoned most of his life until he was finally beheaded by Henry VIII. Another area where Anne Boleyn, one of Henry VIII's wives, and others were beheaded, is there, complete with chopping block!

Then there are the Tower of London guards, called "Beefeaters", wearing unique and outstandingly handsome red, black and gold uniforms. Some of the Beefeaters serve as tour guides, detailing many of the dark and occasionally pompous royal activities.

We found that the most beautiful and fascinating sight in the Tower was the collection of the Crown Jewels. To see them, one must walk under the square central building, down several flights of well-guarded stairs, until you arrive at a room which itself is like a large vault protected by several guards in uniform. In the center of this vault, in a circle are large, brightly-lit individual display cases, which contain all the fabulous crowns, encrusted with diamonds, rubies, and many other gems. There's a solid gold scepter, with deep designs, then the "Star of India" diamond mounted on top, which is the largest cut and polished, single clear diamond in the world!

Visitors may get a closer look into each thick, heavy-glass, clear protected case, but must keep moving. You may move quite slowly, but are not allowed to stop. There is, however, a circular wooden catwalk with a waist-high railing, all at just about a four-foot distance from the jewel cases, where you are allowed to stop and gaze and admire those beautifully-crafted marvels of gold and jewels. I stood there in awe for some time, contemplating the intense reality of that huge, rare natural diamond in the scepter.

And then there were the Ravens! They are big, beautiful black birds, meticulously cared for by the staff, strutting around the lawns and grounds of the 'Tower'. Their wings are clipped so they cannot fly away, because legend has it that if the Ravens ever disappear from the Tower of London, the British Empire will collapse! (So, as long as the Ravens remain {and they have a few atomic bombs in their arsenal} Britain has nothing to worry about!)

I really love England, and so does all my family! We took a tour around London, and spent a day browsing Harrod's Department Store.

Now the time had come to board our flight from London to Los Angeles, about eleven hours, non-stop. It was a 747 Super TWA plane, and we passed the time with two movies, and plenty of meals and refreshments, pleasantly served. We left London at noon, London time, and would arrive about two in the afternoon, the same day.

That is because the earth turns the same direction that we were flying. Only the earth rotates at approximately 660 miles per hour, while our 'plane was going 550 miles per hour, so the earth gained about two hours on us.

Should our 'plane go 660 miles per hour, our arrival time would be the same as our London-departure time. Another interesting fact is that our earth travels around our sun at 66,000 miles per hour. No wonder we get old so quickly! Many scientists contemplate about what time is, or how to describe time. It has been called a 'fourth dimension', and other mysterious names. I simply call time, "The measurement between two or more events." A 'fourth dimension' may refer to a sphere or a globe, but not time.

Anyway, our flight took us over Greenland (a misnomer if ever there was one!). On that sunny, clear day, looking out the 'plane's window, we could see millions of square miles of white snow and ice, with thousands of mountain peaks, barely showing above the snow-drifts. Fabulous huge icebergs edged the ocean shores, and mile-long sheets of thick ice floated on the water. It is a breathtaking sight of pure wonderment to see such vast natural creation!

The feeling is impossible to describe, and to get the real and total impression of that natural wonder of our planet, can best be experienced from 30,000 feet above the earth! Photographs cannot do it justice, because you lose the vastness!

We arrived safely in Los Angeles, with our lists of foreign purchases for the 'Customs' inspectors. They never paid much attention to Marilyn's list of a teddy bear, a few porcelain figurines, and even the music box. We heard they were looking for people bringing in large amounts of 'duty-free' alcoholic beverages, and maybe even valuable Swiss watches, but not our typical 'family souvenirs'!

It's great to travel, but there is no more wonderful feeling than arriving back at home!

Our daughter, Karen had kept the business running smoothly, and of course I kept in touch by 'phone throughout our trip. To keep any business running smoothly takes full attention to all details, and I found there were a few problems waiting for me to resolve. Some could even be considered urgent, and therefore stressful, but I always kept on top of, or ahead of potential trouble. Foremost, I always tried to meet the needs and requirements of my clients.

To do something for pure pleasure, is the best way to relax, so I acquired some very good tape-recording equipment, microphone, and a turntable with an assortment of song-orchestrations. Every night after work, for several years, I spent three or four hours singing. Sometimes I would fill a two-hour sound-reel with one song until I thought it was perfect, or at least OK. It was fun to sing to orchestrations, although they were not arrangements made to accompany a singer. It was a challenge to make the music and my rendition of the song compatible, and the full orchestrations did make impressive backgrounds for my voice! In time I accumulated a multitude of large tape-reels, which were the accepted form of recording back then. CDs had not yet become popular.

During the years of 1984 through 1987 several interesting and important occurrences took place. Because the money exchange rate stayed in our favor, and the European trips were within a reasonable budget, we decided to take along our three daughters and their husbands, one couple each year. We felt it would widen their horizons, and of course, it would really make the trips a lot more fun for us! We basically planned the same itinerary, but different little adventures seemed to happen on each trip!

Our eldest daughter, Heidi, and her husband, Bill, made the next trip with us, and we enjoyed a humorous little event while we were in southern England. We decided to visit the little town of Crowborough, Sussex, where as a young boy, as previously written in this book, I had stayed in the residence of Sir Arthur Conan Doyle. I had opened a savings account in the small local branch of Lloyd's Bank, with the amount of one British 'pound'. Now, almost fifty years later, I asked Heidi and Bill to go with me into the bank to see if the 'one pound' I had deposited in 1939 was still there.

As I introduced myself to the very nice bank manager, and gave her my name, she smiled and said, "We've always wondered what ever happened to you! Your one pound is now forty pounds!"

Well, I replied that I might as well take the money, and close the account, which seemed to make the people in the bank happy that they not have to carry the account any longer. A funny thing happened as I took my withdrawal. An elderly gentleman standing behind me, commented that now he was the longest steady depositor in that branch of Lloyd's Bank.

I should have asked them how long they carry an inactive account, because here in the United States, such accounts are eventually dissolved.

$ \qquad $ \qquad $

During our yearly trips, I often solved business problems by 'phone from Europe, and basically we managed very well. Egon, Jr. and I were taking steps to increase our national distribution, and when the bakery in Chicago was sold to Anheuser Busch, the beer company, they in turn sold it to another large national bakery. All that meant additional negotiations, and money spent by us on advertising and promotions. Somehow, we always managed to survive, I guess partially because of the quality of our product, and in good part because of the work Egon, Jr. and I did to keep the breads selling. We had even added Miami, Florida to our distribution.

An interesting time was experienced by everyone, when suddenly in the middle eighties, inflation went berserk! Raw materials jumped six-to-eight-fold, and of course like all of the bakeries, and the retailers, we had to raise our prices several times within a few years. We were, however, able to keep our profit margin constant.

Real estate prices went sky high, and interest rates were raised to astronomical heights. To ward off further inflation, I remember when the Bank of America offered me 17% on a straight savings account. I accepted their offer of course, but inflation eventually leveled off, which was good.

Marilyn and I were living alone at 'Baycliff Manor' the gorgeous, three-acre estate on Upper Newport Bay, and seriously gave thought to selling the property and buying a smaller home in the lovely neighborhood where our children lived. I felt we should be able to sell for several million, which did not seem excessive for that kind of a property.

However, just at that time, the Orange County Airport was being enlarged, with construction of a new main terminal and a proposed large increase of daily flights. Our property was not really near the airport, nor were we under the flight paths. Nevertheless, because of the unknown, or what impact so many flights would have, even on properties five miles away from the airport, as much as people liked our property, there was this, "Let's wait and see!" attitude. I didn't know myself, what it would be like when the airport was finished, and how much impact the whole area would experience.

In 1987, I still had the property on the market, when one day a realtor approached me, saying that he had a buyer for Baycliff! It came as rather a surprise, because we still did not know what the results would be from the finished airport, and thought that it was not possible to find a buyer at that time.

However, Marilyn and I discussed the various aspects of selling, and the fact that we were getting on in years, and decided that it would really be more convenient living closer to both the children and our business.

The Realtor offer was quite a bit lower than our originally anticipated selling price. We told him that for a reasonable seven-digit amount, and cash-out only, we would sell. In a few days, we opened a thirty-day escrow, which did not give us much time to find our new home.

Good fortune was with us as usual. Marilyn kept saying that one of the things she was going to miss the most at Baycliff was a big, old Liquid Amber tree, so when she saw a gorgeous one by a house we looked at, and the entire place seemed like a 'find' for our other requirements, we were actually able to move in thirty days.

The 'new' house was within blocks of all of our adult children's homes, and was a nicely-shaped two-story with a large add-on 'conservatory'. We use that lovely, bright, glass-walled room for our six-foot, parlor-sized Steinway grand piano, and there is still enough space for both my recording equipment, and even my large wooden easel and oil-paints.

My darling wife, Marilyn used her professional interior and exterior expertise to change the facade of an ordinary brown house, into a white-with-red-brick Colonial charmer!

On each side of the three-car garage, a boring, six-inch strip of plaster became a wide red-brick panel with a large brass lantern, and a conical-topiary of Blue-Juniper with colorful pink and white Impatiens planted at the base.

Basically, Marilyn had immediately seen that the house had certain good features like deep eves to allow for the brick facades, and a wide, pointed-roof gable with clapboard siding over the front of the garage. There was a wonderfully deep roof over the front entrance area, which was being wasted on a muddy atrium for dead ferns!

Out came every plant in the entire yard, and I panicked as the cement-layers came in and 'worked their magic'. I pictured a bare, cement-front house, but Marilyn had designed a mirror-image pathway on the right side of the garage, matching one that already existed on the other side. She did cement all along the right side of the garage, which I soon realized could not be seen from the front, and was wonderfully practical!

The house is at the end of a cul-de-sac, with a little grass-and-big-trees 'park' on the right-hand side. Marilyn also designed a new white-wood fence, gate, and arbor to 'finish' the wider right-side of the house. She also planned a large red brick circle-planter, and another along the length of the garage on the left side.

Her 'front porch' is the 'pie'ce de resistance' of her entire house re-do! She wanted the railing-posts a certain distance apart, and a wide top-rail for sitting! She wanted a 'porch box' covering an outside water-faucet, but made a certain way she remembered from childhood!

I helped a lot with some of the finalizing of the designs, the exact sizes of the planters, and other things. We had also found a fabulous cabinet-maker who was even willing to do things like the arbor-gate, and Marilyn's special 'porch box'. He really did the final designs of the porch-posts, and the wood paneling around the windows - so gorgeous!

Marilyn finished new plantings with pink Hibiscus along the 'park' wall, a lemon tree and pink variegate, 'Martha Washington' Ivy-Leaf Geraniums in the circle planter, then large grafted Gardenias with Impatiens puffing around them in the long planter, and along the front-porch railing. So simple, but very, very effective, and looking the same year-round!

A lady, who was buying another house in the neighborhood, rang our doorbell to ask about the unusual design of our new front doorway, and said that ours was the prettiest house in the entire neighborhood!

It's a two-story house, and when we first moved in, we had a wrought-iron banister replaced with a pretty Colonial-style. It has a dark wood handrail, and white turned posts with a large post at the end. At Christmastime, Marilyn hangs a holly-swag on the bannister with a large red Gucci-ribbon bow on the white end-post. We have had a stair-elevator-chair installed because of Marilyn's painful knees.

The livingroom is lovely with a white brick fireplace without a mantle. It needed a large, vertical painting, and the first time we looked, we found one picturing a pretty lake with a mother and her little girl standing beside it. We always seem to find exactly what we go looking for, even if we don't know what it is when we start out!

There's a front corner window, just perfect for the old Spanish table,

Egon and Marilyn's present home, attractive, comfortable and most of all it's "A HAPPY HOME".

Their Christmas décor reflects Marilyn's talent and good taste!

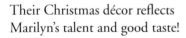

With Christmas dolls, Santas and Rocking Horses (even one the grandchildren can ride). The spirit of Christmas at the Reich's is always a joyous time!

which is high enough for a small Christmas tree! There were even white, wide wooden shutters already in the house, and when we close the lower ones at Christmastime, it looks like we have a tall tree in the window!

We had a nice pair of chairs which fit perfectly on each side of the high table making a perfect corner-window arrangement. To the right of the front door, sits a pretty Magnavox stereo we had bought when we were first married, and the music box from Innsbruck is on top. Hanging above it is a pretty gold-framed mirror that came with the Linda Isle house.

Somehow, whenever we move, Marilyn takes the things we have, and makes the new house look like she went out and bought exactly what the new house needed! I know she studied decorating, but she definitely has talent besides!

The diningroom looks out onto a walled backyard with a green lawn and such big trees all around, it looks more like a 'city park' than any house we've ever owned! The china cabinet is the only piece we kept that is a little too big for the dining room, but the table and chairs are 'normal' size, and the colorful, old German dishes do look so home-like and elegant on display!

Then, this wonderful house has one more charming room downstairs, with glass doors opening out to a pretty side-garden, quite large, again because of the cul-de-sac giving us extra property. We needed to use that room for a 'study' or home-office, and so decided to buy two new desks, lovely mahogany ones! So we were soon 'functioning' well with our Mac computer, a Xerox copier and a fax machine.

The house came with central air conditioning, a super furnace, and an extra large capacity water heater. We found we were immediately as completely comfortable in our new, actually quite spacious home to 'retire' in as we had ever been anywhere, and it was so great living right by the kids, and seeing them all, almost every day!

Egon and Lori soon blessed us all with a baby girl named Marilyn June Reich. June is Lori's mother's middle name, and my Marilyn was thrilled to have a 'namesake' granddaughter! She is such a pretty child, and I still call her Princess Marilyn!

About a year later, Jack Edward Reich was born. 'Jack' for Lori's father, and 'Edward' for Egon's Grandpa Edward, Marilyn's dad whom we all loved and still miss greatly to this day! We were so proud of Egon and Lori for using family names with such memorable qualities! When Jack was little, we called him Jackie, but at about age ten, he would only answer to 'Jack'!

No sissy name for him! He looks just like Lori, almost too handsome for a boy!

Both Marilyn and Jack started taking ice skating lessons when they were about two and three. After a few years, Jack tried Ice Hockey for awhile, but began finding other sports more enjoyable. Marilyn, on the other hand put heart and soul into figure skating for years. When she was still just little, she would set her own alarm clock, get up early and make her own eggs for breakfast, then wake her mother who would drive her to the ice rink a few blocks from their house. Lori would go home and back to bed, while Marilyn would get in a lesson and three hours of practice before school every weekday morning for years and years. She won many competitions, and their house is filled with trophies!

When our 'Princess' Marilyn was nine, something came up that required my taking a trip to Vienna on business. It was to be just a few days' trip, and too 'short notice' for my wife, so Egon and Lori let me take the 'Princess' with me! In Vienna, I knew of a well-known skating coach, I wanted 'little' Marilyn to meet. We had a wonderful, fun flight, and Marilyn was adorable!

It was January and mid-winter in Europe with snow everywhere. For me, it was an unusual sight, because we had always visited there in early September when the weather was mostly still warm.

'Little' Marilyn and I bundled up in warm clothes, and enjoyed the snow as something beautiful and decorative. When we checked in at the Vienna Hilton, I was impressed how Marilyn, still such a little girl, took all of her clothes from her suitcase and arranged everything neatly in the drawers of one of the chests. I even snapped a picture of one drawer, it looked so nice.

On a previous visit, I had discovered Vienna's fabulous, huge indoor skating rink, and I had arranged my business schedule so that early the first morning, I could take Marilyn there to skate. To our surprise, it was closed! A guard informed us that during January through March, it is cold enough in Vienna that they use two outdoor rinks. This saves the expense of freezing the artificial ice in the big rink.

We went over to one of the outdoor rinks, and Marilyn began skating quite well when a sudden wind came up. It was so cold, my hands froze right through my fur-lined gloves, and although Marilyn kept trying to skate, I didn't want to have a little 'frozen' Princess, so we quit for the day.

We tried again the next morning with Marilyn wearing her ski-outfit,

but she soon found that skiing and figure-skating require different clothing, and we went back to the hotel to change into something comfortable.

I tried showing her the Fine Art Museum, but she did not seem too
interested, so we walked across to the Museum of Natural History which
completely fascinated her! She had seen dinosaur skeletons before, but the
displays were outstanding, and there were actually some animal-reproduc-
tions that were not familiar to her at all! She took many pictures with her
own little camera she had brought along, so we had a great day!

While I kept my business appointment the next day, Lotte drove in and
took Marilyn shopping. Marilyn chose a large Austrian costume-doll, and a
life-size furry stuffed cat, that looked amazingly like Lotte's favorite real cat,
'Peterman'. After I completed my business with a bakery, the three of us
took a short drive through the Vienna Woods. Most of the trees were bare
of their leaves, and all were covered with ice and snow, creating a winter
wonderland!

The day before our departure, we drove out to the country, to visit
Lotte in her charming cottage. We first went to lunch at Lotte and Hans'
friends' chalet-inn at the foot of 'Snow Mountain', and when we returned
to Lotte's, Marilyn went outside onto the little wooden bridge over the
creek. She turned toward me, holding her hands about twelve inches apart,
meaning that she was seeing trout that big in the stream. She was fascinated
that there were so many, so big, and actually so silvery beautiful!

We said goodbye to 'Auntie Lotte' and 'Uncle Hans', and thanked them
for everything, and we enjoyed another dinner and breakfast at the Hilton
before taking our flight back home. It was really a pleasure traveling with
that darling 'Princess' Marilyn, and showing her the 'sights' of Vienna!

Still enthusiastically ice skating, at the age of fourteen, Marilyn was able
to accomplish triple jumps, and she took her "Freestyle 10" test. This test
demands the highest requirements of jumps, spins and moves. It is the pre-
cursor test for becoming eligible for the actual Olympic tryouts.

Marilyn passed every part of the test with flying colors, and received the
highest possible award, called "The Double Gold".

At the age of fifteen, Marilyn had grown to about five-foot-ten-inches
tall, and while she looked like a long-legged gorgeous 'Barbie Doll' out on
the ice, whenever she fell, it was a long way down! One day she noticed a

Grandson Jack, getting his first freestyle Ice Skating award at nine years of age.

Granddaughter Marilyn, winning one of many First Place awards in Freestyle Ice-skating.

Jack Reich – ready for HOLLYWOOD!

Pretty is as Pretty does. If the shoe fits - wear it!

Marilyn at age fourteen…

During her Freestyle 10 Contest, where she received her "Double Gold" award!

pain in her lower back, and it was discovered that she had a hairline fracture in one of her vertebra.

By the time it healed, Marilyn had been excelling in track and field in school, and is now also enjoying water polo, and has a Scwinn Bicycle sponsorship for Triathlons, including a very selective two-week training camp in Florida this summer. She is now sixteen, a fabulous athlete and seems to become more beautiful every day. She is also a very sweet, considerate person whom the whole family adores!

Jack has a clever sort of mind. At the age of three, he could put-together the most intricate adult-jigsaw-puzzles. By age five, he would work with his dad building computers, and could install the softwear in a new computer all by himself. He is now fifteen, can build computers, is talented in art, and is still very handsome!.

CHAPTER 25

Looking For the Stars . . .

Our son, Egon, Jr., for some reason, even before junior-highschool age, has been something of an electronic genius. He could always figure-out and fix anything, whether it was the furnace, the clothes dryer, or the telephone. He had a whole collection of meters and gadgets which would assist him in finding the trouble. When home-computers began appearing on the market, he totally loved and engrossed himself in that technology. I have watched him read a two-inch-thick technical book through so fast I couldn't believe it, and he retains every word!

He also became intensely interested in the science of Astronomy. We kept purchasing bigger and bigger telescopes, until he finally had one that required it's own trailer which looked like a miniature observatory, with an actual dome-top that section-opened for viewing.

He had joined a large Astronomy Club which had 'Star Parties' out in the desert, but finding viewing sites without city 'light pollution' was becoming increasingly difficult.

Of course, just a few miles south of us, is the Mount Palomar Observatory, housing in it's dome the famous two-hundred-inch reflector telescope, which was the biggest in the world at that time.

All lighting is restricted for miles around the area. Even street-lights have large black hoods, which lets the light be seen downward, but allows no light to escape toward the sky.

Palomar Mountain has a peak to the side, and slightly above the one where they built the observatory, so one day, Egon and I approached a realtor in that area to inquire about purchasing some land up there. As luck would have it, the ten acres which formed the entire top of that highest peak of Mount Palomar, was for sale! There were many questions besides the normal 'Title Search' that we felt we needed to know.

Because we wanted it for the same type of use as the already-existing observatory, we could not imagine any problems with Egon's planned 'Star Parties' which were for no other purpose than astral viewing.

We did ask, however, about the legality of cutting-down a section of huge old trees at the very top to clear a viewing site. The terrain was not level, and besides clearing the area, we needed to terrace a long slope of land into large, flat 'viewing pads'. There was only a dirt road up to the property, which was badly in need of grading.

In discussing all of these projects, the realtor assured us that we would have no problems. It would be our property, and we could do whatever we wanted on it, within the bounds of zoning ordinances. It was zoned for single residency, and we were not going to build a hotel, nor for that matter, any permanent structure.

As for the tree-removal and the grading, he insisted that we could cut all of the trees that we wanted to, on our property. Everything went smoothly through escrow, and, very shortly, we were excited to be the owners of the mountain-top right next to Palomar Observatory!

We hired a local contractor who was recommended by the realtor, and soon the stillness of the mountain was shattered by the roaring engines of tractors, and chain-saws. The contractor and six men worked for thirty days, and we were at last able to proudly survey the most perfect 'Star Party' site, anyone could ever imagine!

We were there, admiring our new property, when a Forest Ranger with three Deputies appeared and accused us of criminally breaking the law by clearing that large an area without a permit. Furthermore, they claimed that a permit to cut that many trees would have not been issued anyway!

The Ranger continued with horrifying statements about our likely being fined $10,000.00, and possibly going to jail as well! They asked who owned the property, and because we said that it was in Junior's name, they 'read him his rights', as if they were going to arrest him right then and there!

However, they then asked for a $500.00 'deposit against future fines'. I don't know if this was even legal, but it did not seem like we were in any position to argue. We tried to tell him that the realtor who sold us the property had assured us we had every legal right to clear the area, and they just replied that we had been mis-informed.

We left the place quite distressed, and immediately sought the help of an attorney. Again, my life-long good fortune held true! The group of attorneys who took care of my corporate matters, had in their offices, one who specialized in property and real estate law. After hearing our plight, he delved deeply into all of the ordinances, rules and laws pertaining to exactly that location, and found that within the exact boundaries of our property, we were totally legal in what we did. He arranged with the U.S. Forestry Department to have a meeting up at our property, with some of their officials, and the Rangers who had confronted us. The Rangers were very surprised to find they were in error. All actions against us were dropped, and our $500.00 was refunded with an apology.

We are forever thankful to that extremely diligent and hard-working, brilliant young attorney, Donald McIntire. Don is also a fine family man, and he and Egon, Jr. became better acquainted, with Don even bringing his children to 'Star Parties' on the property.

A few people living on the mountain were slightly less than friendly, because they liked the animals, and wanted to keep the area in it's completely 'natural' state. However, the local fire department people are greatly respected by everyone there, and they were trying to raise money for new fire-fighting equipment. We talked with the fire department, and arranged a plan.

Most of the trees from our property had already been cut into 'firewood' logs, and we had the cutting finished, so that the wood had a value of several thousand dollars. We donated it all to the fire department, and found the 'neighbors' much more friendly after that.

Egon continued to have a fence built around the entire ten acres, with a heavy gate across the road. He had a large house-trailer placed at the top of the level sites, and of course had his own little observatory-trailer up there too.

In order to subsidize the continued road-grading (sometimes even just after a heavy rain), and the many expenses of the 'Star Parties', such as rental toilets, etc., Egon had to organize his own 'non-profit club'. This worked out very well, and many amateur astronomers became steady members. On viewing nights, it was quite a sight to see so many telescopes pointing at the stars.

Egon had become good friends with some of the management people at the Meade Telescope company, and was becoming more and more involved with astronomical computer imaging. He was also designing and building computers for telescopes.

Although Egon was very helpful with Better Way Foods, I felt it was important for him to make greater use of his talents with electronics, astronomy, and most of all, computers.

There was a large office not being used at the time, in the front of the Better Way Foods plant, and another closed-off room just behind it for the computer manufacturing. And so Egon, Jr. opened Compu-$ave, a computer manufacturing and developing firm.

With only a small amount of advertising, he immediately found a need for custom-built computers for businesses. It soon became known how knowledgeable he was, and he became very successful, doing business with many major companies, even world wide.

His recognition as an important computer developer and astronomer, has been recently substantiated by his receiving a Doctorate in Computer Science, Magna cum Laude (With Highest Honors). He passed all of his final examinations with 100%, and also received 100% on his Thesis, the subject of which was a new development improving a certain feature of the computers used in deep space travel. His recent scholastic achievements have been partially due to a Microsoft scholarship program, eligibility for which includes extremely high qualifications.

Needless to say, our whole family is very proud of such a conscientious, talented, and self-motivated person (besides being tall and very handsome!).

CHAPTER 26

Retirement . . .
With a Look Toward New Achievements

Two days after Christmas, and a day after my birthday, in the year 1993, Marilyn and I flew to Austria, fulfilling my dream of once more seeing Vienna decorated for the Holidays, and covered white with snow!

Being after Christmas Day, the Hilton Hotel in the lobby, was already featuring New Year's Celebrations, and several large signs in English, read, "New Year's Eve in Vienna will give you the Luckiest Year of Your Life!"

'Good Fortune' symbols were everywhere, from horseshoes to small figures of elves finding tiny red 'lucky' mushrooms, to amazing table-centerpieces in the diningroom, real growing clover plants, having all four-leaf leaves! Marilyn still carries one of those 'four-leaf clovers' in her wallet.

We spent the early part of New Year's Eve in Demel's famous pastry shop, comparing travel stories with a lovely couple from San Francisco, who just happened to be sitting at the tiny table next to ours.

We had fortunately found street-parking just around the corner from Demel's, and had enjoyed window shopping with the Christmas ornaments all still on display! The cold snow on the ground made it chilly outside, but we were cozy and warm in Demel's, however, we had been warned that the crowd could get a bit rowdy toward midnight, and the popping of fireworks seemed to be getting closer when we drove back to the Hilton. Our large balcony-window overlooked the skyline of beautiful old Vienna, and the night was filled with gorgeous elaborate bursts of fireworks until after two in the morning. It was as exciting a New Year's Eve as we had ever spent, and we flew home with anticipation of good things to come!

Early in the new year (1994) I was developing plans of expansion for Better Way Foods' bread franchising, when the CEO of Interstate Brands

Corporation (the biggest baking company in the United States), whom we had recently met with concerning distribution, contacted me. He almost casually mentioned that they were interested in purchasing my company!

Better Way breads had good distribution in major cities throughout the Nation, and in the greater Chicago area, had large, valuable shelfspace in almost every supermarket. Recent contacts were making increased distribution very hopeful.

However, I was now seventy-one years old and after due consideration, established a selling-price. Being a franchise, our fixed assets were comparatively small, actually just a few mixing and packing machines, but our distribution and profit margin were considerable.

Thinking entirely from my standpoint, I sat down with our accounting firm, and determined what I needed to pay all creditors, and what I would need in cash to be able to sustain us in retirement after taxes.

About five years earlier, a corporation-realtor had wanted to sell our business, and Marilyn had learned how to do a company-evaluation based on profits rather than assets, so she was able to do all of the presentation papers for the CEO to take to his Board of Directors. The purchase of our company was accepted at our price, and it was concluded with a total cash transfer.

They even added a generous fee for my availability as a consultant for the next three years, which I was more than glad to accept.

I paid all of our debts and mortgages, and after paying high Capital Gains taxes, even with the most conservative investments, have been able to remain financially stable. We have enough income to live, perhaps not extravagantly, but certainly comfortably for the rest of our lives.

At the time that I am now writing this book, it has been over thirty years since I established Better Way Foods, and I am proud to say that the taste and quality of my breads has certainly played a major role in the endurance of the products which I am still buying every week from the supermarket.

Life in retirement certainly became different, but by no means inactive or boring. During the three years of my continued association as a Consultant with Better Way, I spent time at our plant every day, making certain that production was running flawlessly.

I had always been fortunate in having good employees. A few months before I sold my company, I had hired a new Plant Manager, a young man, Jose Mathus. He and his lovely wife, Sondra, and two children, a very nice, handsome boy named Pablo, and a pretty girl named Rosalba had immigrated from El Salvador. It turned out that Jose was an extremely intelligent and well-educated man with full Certified Public Accountant credentials in his own country. He was willing to take a job requiring physical exertion because, while he understood everything told him in English, his pronunciation needed vast improving at that Time. He was taking night-courses in English, so in only a short time, he was conversing fluently.

Jose was amazing at both production and organizing. Under his management, production was always current, the plant orderly, in fact, spotless. He even developed and kept a fabulous inventory system, so we knew at any minute of any day, the status of our hundreds of ingredients.

He apparently liked working for me, and I certainly was grateful to have someone as conscientious working for me. Jose, to me, was like one in a million, maybe a billion!

When Interstate Brands bought my company, they very soon saw Jose's potential, and I believe he is now Assistant Comptroller of a large Interstate Brands subsidiary company. Anyone having Jose associated with their company is indeed fortunate.

Jose's competence at Better Way, gave me the peace of mind, to enjoy beginning some oil painting in the evenings, and I still enjoyed singing to records, and making tapes of my voice.

As the years went by, our daughter, Becky also continued her singing, recently as Lead Alto with the California Master Choral. Her concerts areamong the highlights of our lives!

Becky's girls, Vicky and Melody, blessed us with four great-grandchildren. Vicky's first was a lovely little girl, named Jessica, and later a darling boy named Kelly after his father.

Melody has two very smart and handsome boys, Matthew and David. We hear from them, and about them often, but they live in Minnesota, and of course we are in California. Becky visits them twice a year, spending a week or so, spoiling the boys! They think she is the greatest grandma ever, because while she is there, she buys them 'a toy a day'. This was something that started on a visit when they were very little, and somehow became a tradition!

Becky really is a fabulous 'grandma', spending a great deal of time with the two that live near here, and doing a lot for all of her grandchildren. Fortunately, Becky at the age of fifty, is a well-paid executive in a large International corporation.

Marilyn and I of course, love all of our grandchildren and great-grandchildren. We often get to see Vicky and her husband Kelly, and their especially adorable Jessica and Little Kelly, because they live only about an hour's drive away. We talk daily with Becky who lives just blocks from us, and we enthusiastically follow the grandchildren's activities.

Jessica learned to play the saxophone when she was quite young, and has become proficient at it. Also, she started playing Soccer at the age of six, and I used to drive out where they live on a Saturday morning. It was delightful to watch those little girls in their uniforms taking the game so seriously, especially with parents shouting helpful hints from the sidelines! When Little Kelly became old enough, he also became an ardent Soccer player.

Now, both twelve-year-old Jessica and her brother, Kelly, are very involved in 'off-road-track' bicycle racing, and proudly bring home many trophies. We love them all, and look forward to their visits.

Earlier in this book, we have told things about our daughters, Heidi and Karen, who are at this time successful and happy in their lives. All of our grandchildren are amazing, with Egon Tyler Reich III still in Russia as a missionary, and also still working at the U.S. Embassy as a Russian translator. His sister, Erin, with her gorgeous red hair (exactly like my mother's) and her beautiful singing voice, still lives with her mother, an hour's drive away, but we get to keep in touch at family parties.

Karen's younger daughter, Jenny, just graduated from College, but is continuing in a University in the fall. Her eldest, Deanna, is married to Douts Thiaw from Senegal, Africa, a Pre-Med student at Irvine University. Deanna just graduated from Fullerton State University, and the very weekend of this writing, had an absolutely gorgeous baby boy, named Malik Taylor.

What a joyous life we are having, with every one of our four children

Retired but not Retiring!

Marilyn and Egon pictured here at retirement age attending a "Beach Party" (in Huntington Beach) given by their daughter Heidi and husband Bill. They are enthusiastically looking forward to new challenges and creative projects. Most of all they enjoy their wonderful family and each other!

and their spouses living nearby, all eight grandchildren doing well, and now five great-grandchildren to enjoy!

Before I reach the close of this book, there are a few more people I want to say a few words about, who have been an important part of our lives. Two special friends, Ray and Judi McKenzie and their two wonderful children, Scott and Sheri spent every Christmas and most other holidays with our family for many, many years while their children were younger.

They were close friends of Bill, our Heidi's husband, and Ray had been Bill's flying instructor in Lafayette, Indiana They lived in Africa for awhile, then when Ray became a pilot for a cargo-transport airline, they had to move near Los Angeles. Heidi and Judi became 'best friends', and there is nothing I enjoy more than listening to Ray's flying and traveling adventures.

Judi, besides being 'movie star' pretty, is certainly one of the world's best gourmet cooks, and recent dinners at their house have been memorably delicious! Both Ray and Judy are very congenial people and we feel privileged to be among their friends!

One more mention of certain important people in our lives. Besides the association with the excellent real estate attorney previously mentioned, we greatly appreciate our financial advisor, and Family Trust expert, Michael Harms. Every time Marilyn and I would work on our Trust with a previous attorney, Marilyn would come away with a list of questions for our CPA that the attorney could not answer. Michael Harms is both an attorney and a CPA, so it was a real pleasure working with him and his bright and efficient co-workers on our Trust.

We also want to thank our CPA, Bradford Benton for his excellent and expert service to our company and for our personal taxes as well. And many, many thanks to our wonderful Family Doctor, John Gordon Miller, M.D., whose conscientious attention to our well-being through many years, has helped us live a better and healthier life!

CHAPTER 27

A Heartwarming
Fiftieth Wedding Anniversary

The years kept rolling by, and suddenly November 27, 1998, our fiftieth wedding anniversary had almost arrived! The old adage "Time flies!" certainly applies here!

Our son and daughters and their spouses planned an anniversary party of grandiose proportions! It was held in one of their houses that had a large open entryway and lovely back garden, and they used caterers famous for their grilled-on-the-premises steaks and chicken, and particularly gorgeous buffet table on the terrace. We were overwhelmed by the many generous gifts from family and dear friends, and then came the highlight of the party!

Egon, Jr. entertained us with a concert, Jack playing piano, Egon playing a beautiful elaborate electric guitar, Erin singing, and more; but then our amazing son presented us (and every guest) with professional-looking Compact Disks (CDs) made from tapes of my singing!

They were in plastic boxes, looking just like they came from a store, and the labels on the disks were printed with a picture of Marilyn and one of me, and reading, "Christmas Songs by Egon Reich I". They were printed in colorful green and white with a little Christmas tree design, and also said in smaller print, "Dedicated to Marilyn and Egon Reich on their Fiftieth Wedding Anniversary!"

The guests seemed as shocked and thrilled as Marilyn and I were, and although we loved and appreciated all of our gorgeous gifts, the CD that Egon, Jr. presented us with brought tears to our eyes, and we are forever thankful and grateful for having such a thoughtful and wonderful son.

For the entire Anniversary Party, from the white and gold balloons by the sign-in table with the white feather pen, to the Viennese pastry desserts, to lovely live piano music during dinner, and on and on and on, we give our most heartfelt thanks to our fabulous, thoughtful daughters and son and their spouses. It was absolutely perfect and completely wonderful!

That CD from Egon, Jr. really started something! He had worked for many months, spending his evenings after work, and while I was out playing Badminton at a gym, searching through hundreds of my large reels of sound-tapes to find the songs he wanted.

My tape-reels were not organized, and were all mixed up, with dozens of different types of songs on every reel. He had his own CD pressing equipment, and even digitally mastered each song.

I was surprised and amazed to learn how all this could be done to create a perfect, completely professional sounding Compact Disk record! Of course, this immediately gave me the idea of going through all of my recorded tapes, accumulated over thirty years, and put all of the good ones onto CDs!

I really did not realize when I started, what a job it was going to be, to pick out the best version of each song from so many taped reels. I spent over three months, virtually ten hours a day, seven days a week, before I had a planned set of four disks, all numbered, arranged, and organized. The original recordings were all made on good equipment, although sung to records at my home. I love both popular music and classical, so the first set of disks have both, and I tried to select ones which were best-suited to my voice.

The next step was to take the tapes to a professional 'sound studio' to have them digitized, restored, edited, and burned into original reproduction-disks.

At this point, I also prepared artwork for the labels. We looked at CDs being sold in the stores, and the 'albums' of four CDs usually had a little booklet inside. We gave this some thought, and I wrote a short autobiography, and designed a booklet to enclose.

Although my tapes originally lacked studio-recording control, the digitizing eliminated background noise (even a baby crying in one!), and they all came out sounding surprisingly wonderful, or so my 'fans' tell me!

Now I am nearing the end of my story. I will be seventy-nine this December, and Marilyn is seventy-seven, and except for a few minor 'aches and pains', we are very happy, as much in love as always, and extremely active.

Egon Jr. and Lori jubilant over getting his Doctorate Degree.

The first CD of Egon Sr's. Songs, made by their son Egon jr. and given to Marilyn and Egon on their 50th Wedding Anniversary

Egon Sr. made these subsequent CD's.

1.

2.

3.

4.

5.

6.

Our Children and Grandchildren who made our 50th Wedding Anniversary a memorable one.

1. Left to right, daughter in law Lori, daughters Karen, Heidi, and Becky.
2. Daughter Heidi with husband Bill.
3. Daughter Karen with husband Miles and her daughter Deanna with husband Douta and their new baby boy Malik in oval.
4. Becky's daughter Melody by one of Egon's paintings, and Becky's other daughter Vicky.
5. Egon II with wife Lori and his four children, Egon Tyler Reich III, Erin, Marilyn, and Jack.
6. Karen's younger daughter Jenny.

For instance, this book had no 'ghost writers', but was first all hand-written by me writing many hours daily, and incidentally I wore-out sixteen pens doing it! Then it was edited and typed into the computer in correct manuscript form by my 'TG' (The Greatest) exceptionally smart, beautiful, and darling beloved wife, Marilyn.

So, health permitting, and God willing, Marilyn and I both look forward to many more active and creative years. I've been writing and it's getting late in the evening, so with loving thoughts, I wish you all a good night, and happy days ahead!

Journey Through Life

In the long journey I took through life
      I saw beauty, but also experienced strife.
I tasted good food, heard many a kind and reassuring word,
        Great joy was known, and beautiful music was heard!

Then there were the evil orators, the liars, the cheats,
        And hoards of terrorists boasting of their feats!
I also saw the disregard some gave to body and soul,
        With immorality, abuse of drugs and alcohol.

I listened to teachers who took time to study the unknown,
        Mostly unappreciated, and often alone.
Those who have disdain for the poor, and wallow in greed,
        Take advantage of the workers in menial jobs of need.

There are also the real unsung heroes of our days,
        Continuing to lead humanity in essential ways.
The scientist, the artist, and the workers on the streets,
        All those who protect us, performing difficult feats!

I believe that good will always over evil prevail,
        And we will ultimately cast the 'Devils' - 'in jail'!
Yes, it's a world of good and bad,
        But it's a great life that I've had!

I've eluded many obstacles, coming through mostly unscathed.
        Could it be because I was mostly well-behaved?
I learned to give, not just to take,
        Bringing rewards for me and for my family's sake!

And when it comes my time to leave this world behind,
        This ardent wish will occupy my mind,
That wherever or whatever spirit I might be,
        That my darling wife, Marilyn, be forever with me!

And those we touched, and those we bore,
        Will remain with us in loving spirit forevermore!
God's spirit has guided me along these many ways,
        And I thank all those who helped me through these
                                                    wonderful days!